RESEARCH

&

Writing

A Complete Guide & Handbook

Shah Mahmoud

BETTERWAY PUBLICATIONS, INC.
WHITE HALL, VIRGINIA

Published by Betterway Publications, Inc.
P.O. Box 219
Crozet, VA 22932
(804) 823-5661

Cover design by Rick Britton
Cover photograph by Tim Lingo, Newlight Studio
Typography by Blackhawk Typesetting

Library of Congress Cataloging-in-Publication Data

Mahmoud, Shah
  Research and writing : a comprehensive guide and handbook / Shah Mahmoud.
    p. cm.
    Includes index.
ISBN 1-55870-244-X : $29.95. — ISBN 1-55870-243-1 (pbk.) : $18.95
    1. Report writing. 2. Research. I. Title.
LB2369.M33 1992
808'.02—dc20

MAH

91-43216
CIP

Printed in the United States of America
0 9 8 7 6 5 4 3 2 1

This book is dedicated to the memory of my Parents: With Deepest Appreciation and Gratitude for giving me life and character,

And my Grandparents: Who taught me to laugh, enjoy, cry, and achieve.

To my sisters and brothers in everlasting memory of our fun-loving but brief times together.

Also in memory of Ahmad Shah, Ghazi, and Habibia Schools in Khandahar and Kabul, in Afghanistan, where I spent the happiest days of my life. To the memory of so many caring teachers who taught so well, in unheated classrooms where, due to lack of facilities, floors and sticks were used as blackboards. The dedication, concern, and guidance of these early teachers became my model. To the many good Mullahs in the village of Showheen Arghandab who enlightened me about human compassion, empathy, and behavior.

To the memory of the thousands of children who were systematically mutilated and slaughtered in Afghanistan. These innocent children perished by the toy bombs, dread, horror, and depravation that were brought upon them by a war without justification.

Thanks to Toledo University in Ohio, Columbia University in New York, and Rutgers — The State University in New Brunswick, New Jersey to which I owe my scholarly debts. Toledo, a distinguished learning institution, aroused the quest and virtue of knowledge in me. Columbia, a citadel of learning, gave me skills in scholarship, intellectual reasoning, and the academic pursuit. Rutgers, where I started my teaching profession, was a creative and challenging academe that influenced my collegial behavior and the methods and joys of teaching.

Lastly, to the many teachers who taught me and to the many whom I taught.

And thanks to the many students for whom I wrote this volume and those who read, used, critiqued, and enhanced my content and writing style.

Contents

Introduction

All too frequently students and professionals write reports, term papers, and lengthy manuscripts without proper guidelines. Some instructors take for granted that students are familiar with proper methods and techniques of research. Through many years of teaching, the author's practice has been to provide students with condensed guidelines for the preparation of assigned papers. These guides have proven to be very effective instructional tools for students at both the graduate and the undergraduate levels. Students using these guidelines have shown increased productivity and motivation for engaging in research and writing.

This book is written for those seriously interested in learning how to conduct research and how to write with greater expression. Of course, there are many books already on the market devoted to the techniques of research; however, this book is unique. This work gives particular attention to library cataloging systems and includes a thorough discussion of how to use the computerized online systems frequently found in major libraries. Most books devoted to research techniques spend too little time discussing the Dewey Decimal and Library of Congress cataloging systems. These systems are the basis of computerized systems and are used extensively by smaller libraries throughout the country. This book corrects those oversights. The thorough discussion of computerized research sources makes this book more up-to-date than many of the books that are currently on the market. Another unique quality is the use of illustrations and examples, allowing this book to be easily read and understood.

Among those who would benefit from using this book are executives preparing reports or presentations, freelance writers interested in researching a new topic, and anyone who wishes to produce a carefully contemplated book, manuscript, or report.

The information in this book is presented in a practical manner. It begins with the selection of a topic, then guides the reader from the beginning research to the final written product. The design and accomplishment of research and writing are highlighted, rather than the analysis of data. The chapters of this book feature:

- Library information arrangements
- The scope of material in the library
- Methods of gaining familiarity with computer facilities
- Using computerized database and online systems
- Ways to gather information in the library efficiently
- Procedures for efficient reading and for putting information together
- A presentation of conventional writing formats

Chapter 1 focuses on necessary planning steps in research and writing. Chapter 2 presents discussions on the arrangement of information in the library. Chapter 3 presents information on library resources and discusses preparing bibliographical information. Chapter 4 introduces computer-based technologies suitable for research and writing. Chapter 5 gives an overview of plagiarism and details copyright regulations. The purpose and the different kinds of reading necessary to undertake and launch a successful research project are discussed.

Chapter 6 focuses on a systematic method of noting and recording important information. Chapter 7 shows the necessary steps in writing a first draft: revising, documenting, editing, proofreading, and typing a paper are presented in order to show the author the steps to the final draft of the manuscript. Chapter 8 is an overview of punctuation and spelling, including some grammatical terms. Chapter 9 presents critical details for the process of documentation. Acceptable formats, such as those recommended by the Modern Language Association (MLA), The American Psychological Association (APA), the *Chicago Manual of Style*, and the Council of Biology Editors (CBE) are presented. Chapter 10 is a review of the basic mechanics of presenting the final manuscript in a conventional form. Chapter 11 overviews business and employment-related correspondence. The last part of the book features useful appendices for quick reference and review.

Read, consult, and add this book to your library. It will assist you in reading, writing, and locating information throughout your academic and professional life.

Getting the Most from Your Research

1

INTRODUCTION

Research and writing are probably the most complex and difficult of all creative activities. They can be great sources for intellectual challenge, joy, and pride, or they can induce anxiety, discontent, and frustration, leading many to abandon a project. Aspiring authors, unfamiliar with the mechanics of research, often lose patience and momentum. They become discouraged, and writing becomes a burden.

The human mind is filled with multiple and fragmented thoughts. If these thoughts become a final copy without a plan, the result may be disorganized, incoherent, and meaningless. Writing skills will lead the author to the accomplishment and presentation of a well-balanced paper. Effective writing skills demand knowledge, discipline, effort, and organization.

To write effectively, one must choose a method that is orderly and logical. Writing should progress from topic selection, to research, to composition, and finally, to the completion of the work. An overview of research and its applications appears throughout this book, with the purpose of making research and writing a productive activity. In addition, this book guides the reader through the writing process — from selecting a topic to constructing the final paper. There are various sources of information, most giving similar sequences for preparing and writing research papers. Those who have not written formal research papers will find this information particularly useful.

STEPS TO WRITING A RESEARCH PAPER

People write to communicate ideas. The subject of any particular writing focuses on a theme. The explanation of the theme becomes the goal of the writer, who must prepare for this by stating an objective. This objective may be the desire to see one's name in print, to voice an opinion, to share information with others, to complete an assignment, or to experience the sheer joy of writing.

The writer should select an interesting topic. Such a topic may be general or concentrated in one's field of expertise. Writing should then proceed in a conscientious but flexible fashion from topic selection to the finished work. The selection of a suitable writing style is important for clear presentation. Following these steps will result in an organized and well-documented paper aimed at a specific audience. The following steps will be explored as an aid to aspiring writers:

* Selecting a topic
* Locating appropriate source materials
* Preparing a working bibliography
* Narrowing the topic
* Writing a proper thesis statement and developing an outline

- Writing the rough draft
- Documenting the paper
- Writing the final draft

SELECTING A TOPIC

Important considerations in the selection of a topic include one's interests, experience, knowledge, and goals, but they are not limited to these alone. Other criteria to be considered may include timeliness, length and depth of the subject, research method, and required effort. It is reasonable to expect that a social scientist would write about social science, which reflects his interest and knowledge. Similarly, a biologist would choose to write about biology. The topic must be interesting enough to sustain the writing and research effort. In addition, a paper with a well-chosen topic will be seen as worthwhile by the author's intended audience. Following are some guidelines to keep in mind when selecting a topic:

1. Find a subject that interests you.
2. Information on the subject must be accessible.
3. The research and writing must be worth the effort.
4. The subject should be of interest to its intended audience.
5. The final work must add to existing knowledge.

LOCATING APPROPRIATE SOURCE MATERIAL

After one selects a general topic and becomes acquainted with the subject, a survey of available material on the chosen topic should be conducted. This survey determines the accessibility of information on hand and in local and area libraries, original data collection, and other aspects. Material can be located with the use of computer facilities or the card catalog available in the library. In locating the appropriate material a researcher should identify the audience for whom the work will be written. It is also important for the researcher to evaluate the amount of time and effort required for completing the project.

PREPARING A WORKING BIBLIOGRAPHY

The sources of information will become the basis for the working bibliography (a compilation of books, magazine articles, encyclopedia articles, directories, interviews, etc.) that the author may wish to use. To begin research, one must know where to locate information pertaining to a topic. Information relating to the chosen topic can be classified as primary or secondary information.

Primary information can be gathered from sources such as interviews, questionnaires, letters, wills, and other first-person documents. *Secondary information* is obtained from materials such as books, magazines, and reports. It is a fitting practice to use a combination of primary and secondary sources. This leads to writing a well-researched and authoritative paper. A working bibliography is a list of the sources of the researched information, which includes authors, titles, and call numbers. Working bibliographies also contain other significant data, such as publication details, lists of tables, lists of illustrations, and the nature of the included information. The working bibliography will save time for later referrals and will help during the preparation of the footnotes and bibliography (if you choose to use these in your paper). Since a writer constantly discards irrelevant information and collects additional desired materials upon discovery, the working bibliography changes throughout the research process.

There are many ways to prepare a working bibliography. The most useful tools for preparation are the more recent computerized search systems and the traditional card catalog. (The popular LS/2000 computerized system is discussed in Chapter 4.) Computers are competing with and replacing traditional card catalogs. It is still important to understand the traditional cataloging system because older materials are sometimes not included in the computerized system. The Library of Congress system is the basis for most computerized systems. Some libraries, especially smaller ones, still may not have these computerized systems. Therefore, time is well spent learning about traditional, though less efficient, cataloging systems.

NARROWING THE TOPIC

Begin by skimming through the gathered information and other resource material. Focus on finding an interesting topic. In selecting a topic, consider one's own personal qualifications and abilities for writing on the subject. Other considerations include: Is the topic interesting and worthwhile to write about? Can writing be objective, especially on controversial topics? Is the topic manageable in terms of availability of information and the constraints of time? Examine whether the scope of the topic is too limited or too broad for the intended purpose. To avoid tediousness, abstain from taking any notes at this stage. The following is an example of this topic-narrowing process:

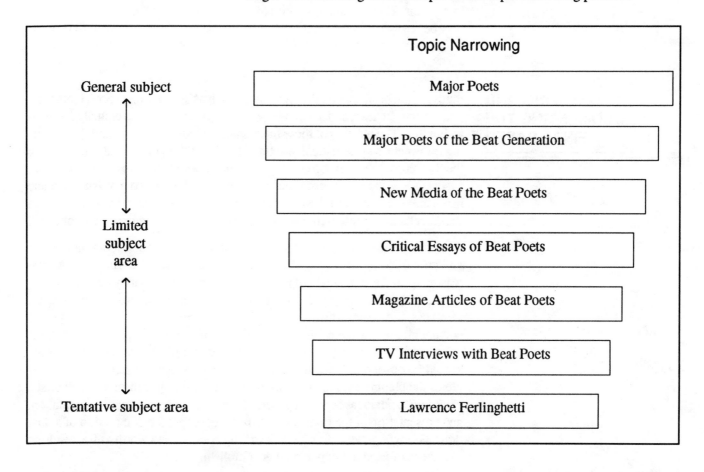

Topic Narrowing

General subject — Major Poets

Limited subject area

- Major Poets of the Beat Generation
- New Media of the Beat Poets
- Critical Essays of Beat Poets
- Magazine Articles of Beat Poets
- TV Interviews with Beat Poets

Tentative subject area — Lawrence Ferlinghetti

Narrow a general subject sufficiently so that it will focus on a limited subject. Next, select a tentative topic; this topic must fit the assignment and be appropriate for the application of time and effort. Avoid broad, uninteresting, or trivial topics. For example, the History of Writing is too broad a topic. The topic Importance of Pencils in Writing is trivial. The History of the Pencil might prove to be a challenging and manageable topic. When the topic is narrowed satisfactorily, one is ready to begin developing a thesis statement.

DEVELOPING A THESIS STATEMENT AND AN OUTLINE

To ensure focused and well-organized writing, it is important to develop a thesis and a preliminary sketch in the form of an outline. This outline will indicate the principal features, structures, concepts, and purposes of the material to be written. Writing without a thesis and an outline leads to disorganization, impatience, postponement, and even desertion of the writing project. Popular outline formats, with their associated numbering styles and their use in various writing efforts, will be presented under a later heading in this book. Understanding and using correct outline formats reduces writing difficulties, contributing greatly to the joy of the accomplishment. The thesis statement will formulate and chart a focal point, giving a sense of purpose to the written material. Also, this statement will help in the selection of an appropriate title for the research paper. The thesis statement should become the basis of confidence and motivation for the author.

The purpose of a thesis statement is to lead to a hypothetical proposition requiring evidence for its support or rejection. The content of the paper should include analysis of concepts and research arguments that affirm or negate the hypothesis. Through manipulation of ideas and research findings, conclusions may be reached and substantiated. If formed correctly, the thesis will provide a focal point that serves as a guide to justified conclusions.

WRITING AND DOCUMENTING THE FINAL PAPER

Studying the basic mechanics of writing, such as note-taking, correct punctuation, copyright laws, and the avoidance of plagiarism, is a prerequisite for good authorship. The mastery of these mechanics includes gathering and documenting information systematically and lawfully, writing a first draft, and editing the final copy. A writer is a conceptual thinker who associates knowledge and experience with new information to formulate an integrated new truth. On one hand, the researcher is a steward of the knowledge presented by others; yet on the other hand, the researcher is both an inventor and a creator of new concepts.

A guarding function must be observed through the avoidance of plagiarism and violation of copyright laws. The synthesis of one's style, harmony of words, reasoning, and arrangement of newly discovered thoughts may be an improvement over previously expressed statements. If it is necessary to use the work of others, the writer must "give credit where credit is due" through proper documentation and acknowledgment of the work's origin. Special conventions provided for the use of quotations, footnotes, comments, and bibliographies should be observed. Once the writer understands these techniques and completes the planning stage of gathering and assembling information, he or she can begin to put ideas down on paper. Major revisions, editing, documentation, and presentation of the final copy are in order before the completion of a final draft. Following these steps makes writing creative and worthwhile, resulting in a sense of productive personal accomplishment.

The Library, the Card Catalog, and the Classification of Books

2

The library is an important part of the system of learning and research. It is a warehouse of accumulated knowledge and information containing immense, varied, and accurate testimonial records of experts in the form of published works. The library is where an individual can become educated and find extensive information on almost any subject of the present or past.

One cannot expect to become educated by browsing through various stacks of books in the library; specific research skills are necessary to locate information efficiently. It is essential to be well acquainted with the contents, resources, and physical layout of the library. An individual should start with a leisurely tour of the library or ask for assistance from the specialists on duty. Items to look for may include special brochures, tapes, tours, programs, computer resource facilities, and other available materials. The library staff is there to help with problems, and these skilled professionals are usually more than happy to give their assistance. In addition, most libraries have special guides and handouts for users.

It is rewarding to become familiar with the location and contents of the reference room, open and closed stacks, special collections, periodical room, audio/visual department, photocopying and microfilm rooms, computers, newspapers and magazines, study room, reserve section, and information desk. As stated above, many libraries offer general and special tours for individuals or groups interested in learning about the use of the facility. The wealth of information should be appreciated when undertaking orderly research on a topic. Knowledge of the library and its classification system helps one research more efficiently. Attempting to find what one needs without full knowledge of library resources can lead to inefficiency, frustration, and wasted time.

The key to success in the library is becoming familiar with the circulation desk, card catalogs, computer facilities, periodical indexes, reference works, encyclopedias, and special collections. Library holdings are classified as either *reference* or *circulating materials*. The reference collection includes indexes, abstracting services, encyclopedias, bound periodicals, and other materials. These are located in special areas and cannot be checked out of most libraries. The required material may also be obtained by the use of available computers and other retrieval and copying equipment. The circulating collection contains materials such as books, periodicals, and pamphlets, which are in open stacks and may be checked out.

Many regional libraries, particularly those in state university systems, are "inter-connected." This means the combined holdings of all connected libraries are "online" and available for use by patrons. The term "online" means the information and other source material may be located elsewhere, but the user has access to this stored information through the computer terminal at the library. Connected libraries lend their holdings to each other; thus, if a book or other material is not available in one library, arrangements can be made to borrow it from another library. Also, one may wish to use software programs such as word processing, graphics programs, graph-making programs, spreadsheets, and many other educational computer services available in these libraries.

THE CARD CATALOG ARRANGEMENT

The card catalog is a master key to quick and efficient use of a library. The arrangement of the card catalog is very similar to that of a telephone directory or dictionary. The card catalog is a collection of alphabetically arranged, 3-inch by 5-inch cards. Each card represents a book, manuscript, or film. The card catalog also covers a vast array of other material including periodicals, encyclopedias, government publications, and microfilms. These cards are arranged in trays within drawers and stored in large cabinets.

The card catalog includes a series of these cabinets (Figure 2-1), which are usually located in a central area near the main entrance. Labeling and numbering drawers help to indicate the location for a subject heading, an author, or a title. The numbers indicate which slots the drawers came from so they can be returned properly after use. Each drawer contains several hundred cards. Special raised cards with tabs on them, called "Guide Cards," separate the cards

Figure 2-1

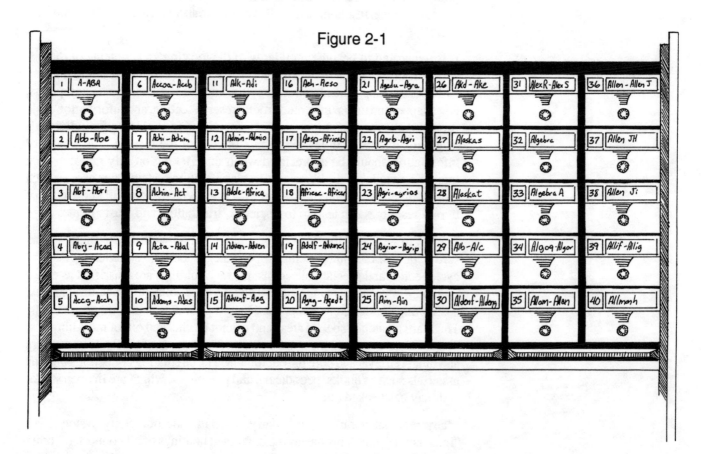

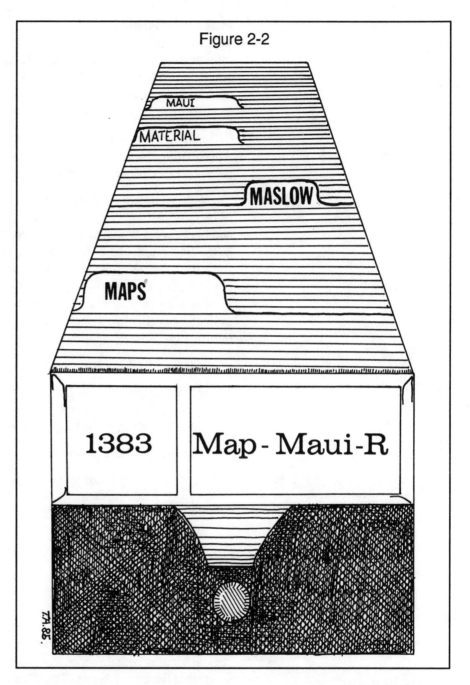

Figure 2-2

into sections (Figure 2-2). The typed words or phrases on guide cards indicate where cards for specified headings can be found. This is a convenient method for finding the location of a desired card. Alphabetically arranged files store these cards under three headings: author cards, subject cards, and title cards. The author card is the main card for a book and is filed in alphabetical order by the author's last name. It lists the most complete information about the work and which libraries in the system have this specific book. The subject card is kept in order by the subject heading, which is often typed in red ink at the top of the card. These cards help the researcher to locate other books that cover the subject area. Subject cards also help in finding a book whose title or author is vaguely familiar. The title card is filed according to the title. If one knows the exact title, particularly when the same author has many published books, time can be saved by looking directly for the specific reference under this card. (For an example of these cards and information included on them, see Figures 2-3 and 2-4.) Each of the three cards identifies the same work and carries the same call number, located in the upper lefthand corner of the card. Some libraries organize all cards alphabetically in catalogs called *dictionary catalogs*. Other libraries divide cards into two alphabetical arrangements, one for subject cards and one for author and title cards.

Call numbers are used to arrange books on the library shelves (Figure 2-5). After finding the assigned number of a specific book in the card catalog, the researcher can locate the book in the library or ask for it at the circulation desk.

These cards contain other useful information as well. For example, one can tell if the information is current from the publication date on the card. The page numbers reveal how much there is to read. In addition, the card details illustrations, maps, and charts available. The title and subject headings, which show the contents of the book, are located near the bottom of the card. When bibliographical notations are present, they may direct a reader to other sources. With some practice, one can quickly learn to select or reject a book by evaluating available details in the card catalog. The following is a list of the information included on a typical subject card:

1. Subject: Tells what the book is about

2. Call Number: Key to finding where the book is located in the library, printed on upper lefthand corner of the card. Books are arranged on the library shelves according to call numbers (Figure 2-5).

3. Author's and coauthors' names

4. Title and facts about publications: publisher, date, and edition

5. Number of pages, volumes, illustrations, and height of the book

6. Special information: for example, if the book contains a bibliography

7. Other subheadings

8. Facts for the librarian

In addition to regular catalog cards, there are two other major kinds of reference cards. One is the *See Cross Reference* card that guides the researcher to related topics that may contain other relevant information. These cards are similar to indexes at the end of books. The other is the *See Also* card, which guides the researcher from one heading to another. The following are examples of referrals on these cards:

SEE CROSS REFERENCE
Heroin   see Narcotics
Scuba   see Aqualung

SEE ALSO REFERENCE

Advertising
    see also
       Retail trade

Climatology
    see also
       Statistical weather forecasting

Figure 2-3

Subject card

```
HF              Management
5548.8
.M374    Maslow, Abraham Harold.
           Eupsychian management: a journal,
         by Abraham H. Maslow. Homewood, Ill.,
         R.D. Irwin, 1965.

           xvi, 277 p. 23cm. (The Irwin-
         Dorsey series in Behavioral
         science)
         Bibliography:p. 267-277.


NcBoA        bn 8/13/75   NJ BBnT    65-27843
```

Title Card

```
HF              Eupsychian management
5548.8
.M374    Maslow, Abraham Harold.
           Eupsychian management: a journal,
         by Abraham H. Maslow. Homewood, Ill.,
         R.D. Irwin, 1965.

           xvi, 277 p. 23cm. (The Irwin-
         Dorsey series in Behavioral
         science)
         Bibliography:p. 267-277.


NcBoA        bn 8/13/75   NJ BBnT    65-27843
```

Author Card

```
HF
5548.8
.M374    Maslow, Abraham Harold.
           Eupsychian management: a journal,
         by Abraham H. Maslow. Homewood, Ill.,
         R.D. Irwin, 1965.

           xvi, 277 p. 23cm. (The Irwin-
         Dorsey series in Behavioral
         science)
         Bibliography:p. 267-277.


NcBoA        bn 8/13/75   NJ BBnT    65-27843
```

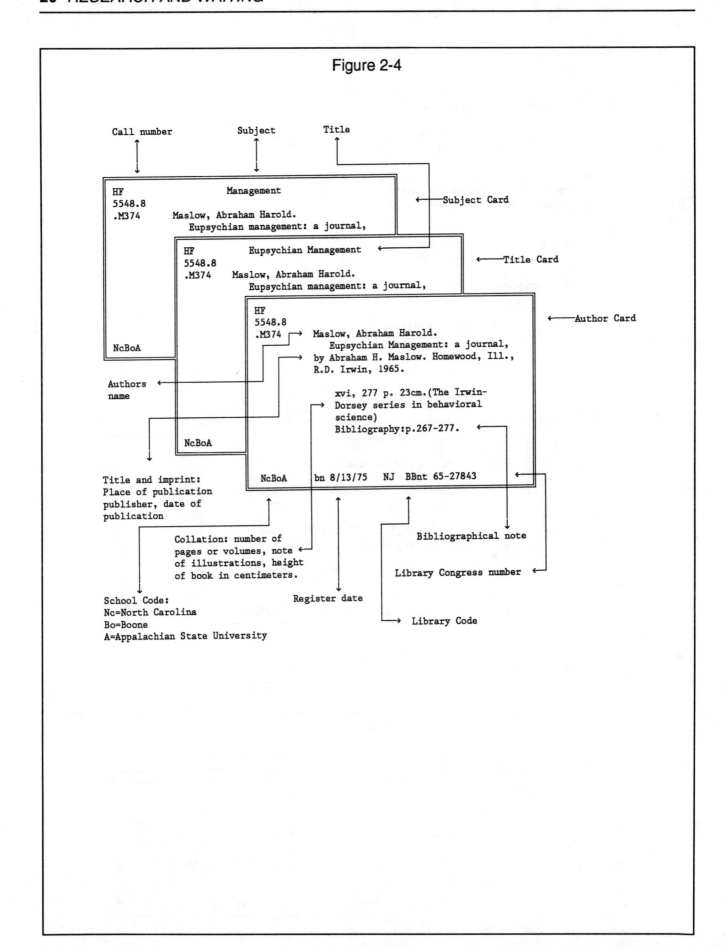

Figure 2-4

Another kind of card found in the card catalog is the *analytic card*. This card refers you to a specific part of a book, such as a certain play, story, or poem, or a chapter dealing with a particular subject. Smaller libraries sometimes use these cards for classifying essays, plays, short stories, and biographies. In addition, cards are often filed under agencies, editors, coauthors, illustrators, and translators. Familiarity with a library's card arrangement is essential, as the arrangement of books and other materials on shelves depends on these call cards and their assigned numbers.

SPECIAL ARRANGEMENTS

Biography Arrangements

The practice of classification, location, and arrangement of special collections, maps, atlases, rare books, local history books, new books, fiction books, biographies, children's books, popular magazines, and newspapers varies for each library. Some libraries classify and arrange their collections of biographies by disciplines or professions. For example, biographies of all U.S. presidents would be classified under history, then assigned an appropriate call number according to the Dewey Decimal or Library of Congress system. Other libraries list all biographies alphabetically by the subject's last name. Biography titles are printed at the top of the book's spine with the author's last name indicated underneath. Grouping biographies by subject gives the researcher an opportunity to compare and utilize several works on the same subject. Regardless of the arrangement used, the researcher must become familiar with the library's method of organization.

Fiction Arrangements

Most libraries arrange works of fiction in a different manner than nonfiction books because of their popularity and use by patrons. They may be located in a separate section on special shelves. Some libraries may group fiction publications by category, such as mysteries, westerns, romances, and adventures, while other libraries may list fiction books alphabetically by the author's last name. These libraries will shelve the fiction material according to the intended readership, such as juveniles, young adults, or adults. The letter "F" (Fiction) or "JF" (Juvenile Fiction) may be assigned to these publications.

Within each group, fiction publications are arranged alphabetically by the author's last name. At the top of the spine of the volume, one will find the title of the book followed by the author's last name. At the bottom on the spine are two letter representations: the top letter may be either "JF" or "F", and the bottom letter is the first letter of the author's last name.

Nonfiction Shelves

It is important to remember that assigned call numbers are the keys to finding books in the library, just as names are the keys to locating numbers in a telephone directory. Call numbers are assigned carefully according to a classification system and are exhibited clearly on the spine of the book and also in the upper lefthand corner of the corresponding call card. If it were not for the call number arrangement, locating a specific book among thousands in the library would be difficult. Books may be arranged according to these numbers on multi-leveled shelves called *stacks*. Some libraries restrict the use of stacks. In a *closed stack* system, one must ask the attendant at the circulation desk to get a book. In an *open stack* system, one is free to find the book on the library shelves. The open stack method decreases labor costs for the library, while increasing the accessibility and enjoyment of browsing for the researcher. Libraries may use a combination of open and closed stacks or restrict only rare and special collections to closed stacks. Located at both ends of each stack are stack numbers that indicate the call numbers of books on the individual stacks. Books within each section are arranged on these shelves in ascending order, from left to right, and from top to bottom.

Figure 2-5
The Arrangement of Learning Materials in the Library

THE COMPUTER CARD CATALOG

Library Computer Terminals

The proliferation and use of computers have prompted many libraries to supplement or replace traditional card catalog arrangements with computerized location systems. Using computer terminals, library patrons can obtain information about books, periodicals, pamphlets, and other materials. These computer terminals are easy to use and have access to databases that are frequently updated. A database is a collection of specialized information (in this case, information about books and other materials in the library or elsewhere) arranged in a manner such that a user has access to them. Arrangement of information in the library databases is similar to that of the traditional card catalog, in that it is listed by subject, author, and title. This arrangement allows users both inside and outside the library to have access to bibliographic and other information contained in the databases. Databases are placed in the *online* system, meaning a user has immediate access to this information through a connected computer terminal. The usefulness and efficiency of searching a database become clear only after one has used the system to search for a project.

Computer Use   Library computers are "user-friendly" and include simple on-screen instructions for their use. Let us suppose one wants to locate the call number and other information on the book *Eupsychian Management*, by Abraham Maslow. When a typical library computer is turned on, the following information will appear on the screen, allowing one to specify the type of search desired (Figure 2-6):

FIGURE 2-6
MAIN MENU

```
PUBLIC CATALOG                    Searching: APPALACHIAN STATE UNIVERSITY


   Enter the NUMBER of search you wish to perform

             1 - By AUTHOR
             2 - By TITLE
             3 - By MAIN SUBJECT HEADING
             4 - By PERSONAL NAME AS SUBJECT
             5 - By FACULTY/COURSE RESERVES
             6 - For OTHER Searches

                  OR

   Enter a KEY WORD to see possible matches

CHOICE:

   Enter ? for GENERAL INSTRUCTION.  To ENTER, type number then press RETURN.
```

Typing the number (2) on the keyboard and depressing Return will produce the following message on the screen:

Enter author's full or partial name in this format: Last, First

Type in "Maslow, Abraham" and depress the Return key. The computer screen will show the following information (Figure 2-7):

FIGURE 2-7

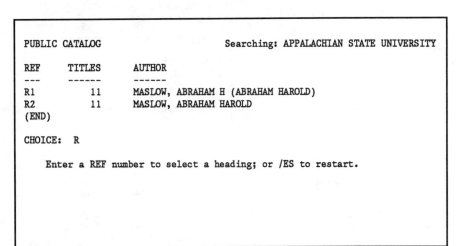

```
PUBLIC CATALOG                        Searching: APPALACHIAN STATE UNIVERSITY

REF      TITLES      AUTHOR
---      ------      ------
R1         11        MASLOW, ABRAHAM H (ABRAHAM HAROLD)
R2         11        MASLOW, ABRAHAM HAROLD
(END)

CHOICE:  R

   Enter a REF number to select a heading; or /ES to restart.
```

Select "REF 1" by typing the number (1), and depress the Return key. The first page of the information will present the following ten titles (Figure 2-8):

FIGURE 2-8

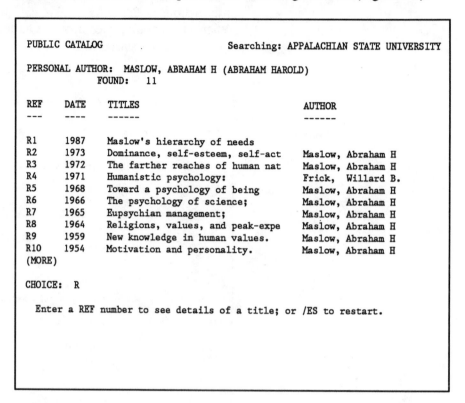

```
PUBLIC CATALOG                      Searching: APPALACHIAN STATE UNIVERSITY

PERSONAL AUTHOR:  MASLOW, ABRAHAM H (ABRAHAM HAROLD)
                  FOUND:   11

REF     DATE    TITLES                              AUTHOR
---     ----    ------                              ------

R1      1987    Maslow's hierarchy of needs
R2      1973    Dominance, self-esteem, self-act    Maslow, Abraham H
R3      1972    The farther reaches of human nat    Maslow, Abraham H
R4      1971    Humanistic psychology:              Frick,  Willard B.
R5      1968    Toward a psychology of being        Maslow, Abraham H
R6      1966    The psychology of science;          Maslow, Abraham H
R7      1965    Eupsychian management;              Maslow, Abraham H
R8      1964    Religions, values, and peak-expe    Maslow, Abraham H
R9      1959    New knowledge in human values.      Maslow, Abraham H
R10     1954    Motivation and personality.         Maslow, Abraham H
(MORE)

CHOICE:  R

  Enter a REF number to see details of a title; or /ES to restart.
```

Select "REF 7," by typing the number (7), and depress the Return key. The following information will be presented with the availability of the material in the library (Figure 2-9):

FIGURE 2-9

```
PUBLIC CATALOG                      Searching: APPALACHIAN STATE UNIVERSITY

  Maslow, Abraham H
    Eupsychian management; a journal, by Abraham H. Maslow.
  Homewood, Ill., R. D. Irwin, 1965.
  xvi, 277 p. 23 cm.
  The Irwin-Dorsey series in behavioral science
  Bibliography: p. 267-277.
  Psychology, Industrial

LOCATION          CALL#/VOL/NO/COPY           STATUS

ASU/BLK/STK       HF5548.8   .M374 c.1        Available
ASU/BLK/STK       HF5548.8   .M374 c.2        Available
ASU/BLK/STK       HF5548.8   .M374 c.3        Available

(END)  Press RETURN to continue or /ES to start a new search:
```

Whenever the number (5) is selected from the main menu, any materials placed on reserve by the faculty are identified. Entering the number (6) from the main menu will provide for additional information as indicated in the following example (Figure 2-10):

FIGURE 2-10

```
PUBLIC CATALOG                          Searching: APPALACHIAN STATE UNIVERSITY


    Enter the NUMBER of search you wish to perform

            1 - By SUBJECT
            2 - By SERIES
            3 - By CALL NUMBER
            4 - By AUTHOR/TITLE KEY
            5 - By SUBJECT - JUVENILE LITERATURE
            6 - By MATERIAL TYPE
            7 - by GOVERNMENT DOCUMENT NUMBER
            8 - by ISBN
           (END)

CHOICE:
```

Conclusion

Using the computer terminals in the library, even with a limited amount of information about a book or an article, one can quickly locate the call number and bibliographic information for that work. In addition, most computer systems offer access to other national or regional library collections. This allows patrons to obtain information on the subject from other libraries throughout the region.

Many libraries have placed the collection of their card catalogs (author, subject, title) on microfilm. This means all the information contained within a card catalog is available to many users at the same time on a microfilm reader. The machines used to read these films are very simple to operate. Microfilms simplify the logistics of maintaining large card catalogs. They are easily updated and many users can get access to the entire card catalog simultaneously. A more detailed discussion of computer-aided research in the library is presented in Chapter 4. Familiarity with the traditional arrangement of books in the card catalog system will greatly assist researchers in the use of computer-based systems. Libraries use two classification systems of call numbers — the Dewey Decimal system and the Library of Congress system.

CLASSIFICATION OF MATERIALS IN THE LIBRARY

The Library of Congress System

The Library of Congress or LC System, developed by the Library of Congress, is used to index the library's massive collection of books and other informational materials. Widely copied, this system is used by larger academic and research libraries. Many libraries use a combination of the Library of Congress and Dewey Decimal systems. Today, most libraries are attempting to convert to the Library of Congress System and computer-based inquiry systems. As a result of the rapid increase in the use of computer systems, changes have taken place in the codes for cross-referencing Library of Congress subject headings. These changes will be discussed later under the topic of computer searches.

The Library of Congress System (LC) uses the alphabet to start each call number on every book. This makes the system efficient and flexible in accommodating large numbers of possible divisions and subdivisions. Twenty-one major divisions (A-H, J-N, P-V, and Z) make up the LC system. These divisions include almost all types of information. Currently, the letters W, X, and Y are reserved for possible future expansion in fields of knowledge yet to be discovered. The letters I and O are not used in order to avoid confusion with Arabic numerals one and zero. The major listings of the categories or fields of discipline in the LC system follow:

Major Categories in the Library of Congress System

A. General Works
B. Philosophy, Psychology, and Religion
C. Auxiliary Science of History
D. History and Topography (except America)
E. America (general)
F. United States (local)
G. Geography — Anthropology
H. Social Sciences (general)
I. Not used
J. Political Science
K. Law
L. Education
M. Music

N. Fine Arts
O. Not used
P. Languages and Literature
Q. Science
R. Medicine and Related Subjects
S. Agriculture — Plants and Animals, Industry
T. Technology
U. Military Science
V. Naval Science (general)
W. Reserved for future
X. Reserved for future
Y. Reserved for future
Z. Bibliography and Library Science

The major classifications listed above are further divided into smaller but more specific groupings, resulting in 676 subdivisions. The addition of a second letter to the base letter creates these subdivisions. Following is an outline of major listings and sub-listings of the classifications of the Library of Congress:

Outline of the Library of Congress Classification

A   General works
AC   Collections. Series. Collected small works
AE   Encyclopedias (General)
AG   Dictionaries and other general reference books
AI   Indexes (General)
AM   Museums (General). Collectors and collecting (General)
AN   Newspapers
AP   Periodicals (General)
AS   Academies and learned societies (General)
AY   Yearbooks. Almanacs. Directories
AZ   History of learning. The humanities (General)
B   Philosophy

BC   Logic
BD   Speculative philosophy
BF   Psychology
BH   Aesthetics
BJ   Ethics. Social usages. Etiquette
BL   Religions. Mythology. Rationalism
BM   Judaism
BP   Islam. Bahaism. Theosophy, etc.
BQ   Buddhism
BR   Christianity
BS   The Bible
BT   Doctrinal theology
BV   Practical theology
BX   Christian denominations
C   Auxiliary sciences of history (General)

CB	History of civilization	HD	Economic history and conditions
CC	Archeology (General)	HE	Transportation and communication
CD	Diplomatics. Archives. Seals	HF	Commerce
CE	Technical chronology. Calendar	HG	Finance
CJ	Numismatics	HJ	Public finance
CN	Inscriptions. Epigraphy	HM	Sociology (General and theoretical)
CR	Heraldry	HN	Social history. Social problems. Social reform
CS	Genealogy	HQ	The family. Marriage. Woman
CT	Biography	HS	Societies: Secret, benevolent, etc. Clubs
D	History (General)	HT	Communities. Classes. Races
DA	Great Britain	HV	Social pathology. Social and public welfare. Criminology
DB	Austria	HX	Socialism. Communism. Anarchism
DC	France	J	General legislative and executive papers
DD	Germany	JA	Collections and general works
DE	The Mediterranean Region. The Greco-Roman World	JC	Political theory. Theory of the state
DF	Greece	JF	General works. Comparative works
DG	Italy	JK	United States
DH	Netherlands (Low Countries)	JL	British America. Latin America
DJ	Netherlands (Holland)	JN	Europe
DK	Soviet Union	JQ	Asia. Africa. Australia. Oceania
DL	Northern Europe. Scandinavia	JS	Local government
DP	Spain	JV	Colonies and colonization. Emigration and immigration
DQ	Switzerland	JX	International law. International relations
DR	Balkan Peninsula	K	Law (General)
DS	Asia	L	Education (General)
DT	Africa	LA	History of education
DU	Oceania (South Seas)	LB	Theory and practice of education
DX	Gypsies	LC	Special aspects of education
E	America (General)	LD	United States
F	United States local history	LE	America, except United States
G	Geography. Atlases. Maps	LF	Europe
GA	Mathematical geography. Cartography	LG	Asia. Africa. Oceania
GB	Physical geography	LH	College and school magazines and papers
GC	Oceanography	LJ	Student fraternities and societies, United States
GF	Human ecology. Anthropogeography	LT	Textbooks
GN	Anthropology	M	Music
GR	Folklore	ML	Literature of music
GT	Manners and customs (General)	MT	Musical instruction and study
GV	Recreation. Leisure	N	Visual arts (General)
H	Social sciences (General)	NA	Architecture
HA	Statistics		
HB	Economic theory. Demography		
HC	Economic history and conditions		

NB	Sculpture	R	Medicine (General)
NC	Drawing. Design. Illustration	RA	Public aspects of medicine
ND	Painting	RB	Pathology
NE	Print media	RC	Internal medicine. Practice of medicine
NK	Decorative arts. Applied arts. Decoration and ornament	RD	Surgery
NX	Arts in general	RE	Ophthalmology
		RF	Otorhinolaryngology
P	Philology and linguistics (General)	RG	Gynecology and obstetrics
PA	Classical languages and literature	RJ	Pediatrics
	Modern European languages	RK	Dentistry
PB	General works	RL	Dermatology
PC	Romance languages	RM	Therapeutics. Pharmacology
PD	Germanic languages	RS	Pharmacy and materia medica
PE	English	RT	Nursing
PF	West Germanic	RV	Botanic, Thomsonian, and eclectic medicine
PG	Slavic. Baltic, Albanian languages and literature	RX	Homeopathy
PH	Finno-Ugrian, Basque languages and literatures	RZ	Other systems of medicine
	Oriental Languages and Literatures	S	Agriculture (General)
PJ	General works	SB	Plant culture
PK	Indo-Iranian	SD	Forestry
PL	Languages and literatures of Eastern Asia, Africa, and Oceania	SF	Animal culture
PM	Hyperborean, Indian, artificial languages	SH	Aquaculture. Fisheries. Angling
	Literature	SK	Hunting
PN	Literary history and collections (General)	T	Technology (General)
PQ	Romance literatures	TA	Engineering (General). Civil engineering (General)
PR	English literature	TC	Hydraulic engineering
PS	American literature	TD	Environmental technology. Sanitary engineering
PT	Germanic literatures	TE	Highway engineering
PZ	Juvenile belles lettres	TF	Railroad engineering and operation
Q	Science (General)	TG	Bridge engineering
QA	Mathematics	TH	Building construction
QB	Astronomy	TJ	Mechanical engineering and machinery
QC	Physics	TK	Electrical engineering. Electronics. Nuclear engineering
QD	Chemistry	TL	Motor Vehicles. Aeronautics. Astronautics
QE	Geology	TN	Mining engineering
QH	Natural history (General). Biology (General)	TP	Chemical technology
QK	Botany	TR	Photography
QL	Zoology	TS	Manufactures
QM	Human anatomy	TT	Handicrafts. Arts and crafts
QP	Physiology	TX	Home economics
QR	Microbiology	U	Military science (General)

UA Armies: Organization, description, facilities, etc.	VB Naval administration
UB Military administration	VC Naval maintenance
UC Maintenance and transportation	VD Naval seamen
UD Infantry	VE Marines
UE Cavalry. Armored and mechanized cavalry	VF Naval ordnance
UF Artillery	VG Minor services of navies
UG Military engineering. Air forces. Air warfare	VK Navigation. Merchant marine
UH Other services	VM Naval architecture. Shipbuilding. Marine engineering
V Naval science (General)	Z Books in general
VA Navies: Organization, description, facilities, etc.	

To further narrow the divisions in a discipline, the LC system takes the initial base division of letters and adds Arabic numerals sequentially from 1-9999. Observe below the skeletal expansion of "HF" under Commerce, where *Eupsychian Management*, by Abraham Harold Maslow, has the call number HF5548.8/.m374. The letter "H" indicates that the book is categorized under Social Sciences. The addition of the second letter "F" designates the book as a Commerce classification. The assigned Arabic number 5548.8 distinguishes it further under General Works in Business. The lower case "m" stands for the author's initial, while the numbers "374" represent the author's differential number. The business subdivision runs from 5001 to 6201. Under the Business classification, disciplines narrow again. For example, 5601-5689 represents Accounting/Bookkeeping, and 5721-5733 represents Business Correspondence.

BREAKDOWN EXPLANATION OF THE CALL NUMBER (HF5548.8/.m374)

H	Social Sciences (general)
HF	Commerce
5000	Business
5500	Personnel, Executives, and Clerks
5548	Office Organization and Management
5548.8	General Works
m	First letter of author's last name
374	Author's cutter number

The LC system allows for simplicity, flexibility, and precision in assigning designations to a specific work. For expansion of unknown future fields and disciplines, HK, HL, and HW, for example, are reserved under H for Social Science additions. This flexibility may be illustrated by comparing the DD system to the LC system. Under the DD system, Law, General Technologies, Organizations, Collection, Patents, Political Science, and Education are assigned the number 600, while under the LC system each has its own designated letter.

Figure 2-11

HOW TO USE LIBRARY OF CONGRESS SUBJECT HEADINGS

1. Make a list of topics from the Library of Congress Subject Headings. Select the topics that are the most promising. A list of topics from the example above might include:

```
Main Heading             ⟶    Management-General Work
A "see also" Heading     ⟶    Management-Literature
An "xx" heading          ⟶    Management Bibliography
Subdivision of           ⟶    Managing Your Boss
Main Heading
```

2. Look up topics on your list in the card catalog in order of importance. There may be problems looking up your topic such as:
    a. Not enough books
    b. Books are checked out
    c. Books do not have information you need

    That is how alternate topics ("sa", " xx", "dash") can be of great assistance.

3. Here is how your subject headings will look in the card catalogue:

```
              MANAGEMENT -- LITERATURE

   HF      Porter, Lee David
   5635        Developing Control Concepts in the
   .P28        20th Century/ Lee D. Porter.--New
   1986    York: Gorland, 1986.
               1X, 324 p.: ill.; 24 cm--
               (Accounting thought and Practice
               through the years)
               Bibliography: p. 286-324.
               ISBN 0 -8240-7854-3 (alt. paper)
```

```
              MANAGING YOUR BOSS

   HD      Kotter, John P., 1947 -
   38.2        Power and Influence/John P. Kotter
   .K68    --New York: Free Press, c1985.
   1985        IX, 218 p. :ill.; 25cm.
               Bibliography: p. 207-212.
               Includes index
               ISBN 0-02-918330-8
```

```
              MANAGEMENT - BIBLIOGRAPHY

   REF     BAKEWELL, K.G.B.
    z          MANAGEMENT PRINCIPLES AND PRACTICES
   T164     A GUIDE TO INFORMATION SOURCES/
   .07         (Edited by) K.G.B. Bakewell.--
   B25     Detroit: Gale Research Co., c.1977.
               xix, 519 p.; 23cm.-- (Management
               Information Guide; 32)
               Includes Indexes
```

There are some refinements within the LC system. For example, one letter does not show each major category, as in the case of Philosophy B, which includes Psychology and Religion. Some have assigned pairs of letters, as in the case of Economics HB through HJ. In cases where the disciplines are too general to be classified under any one category, they have been assigned simple letters, as in the case of World History. For additional explanation of how to use the Library of Congress subject headings, see Figures 2-11 and 2-12. The codes for cross-referencing subject headings are explained in Figure 2-13.

Additional refinements have taken place in the method by which subject headings are cross listed. These changes first appeared in the *Library of Congress Subject Headings Manual*, 12th edition. Some of the changes are shown in Figure 2-13.

Figure 2-12

TO USE LIBRARY OF CONGRESS SUBJECT HEADING

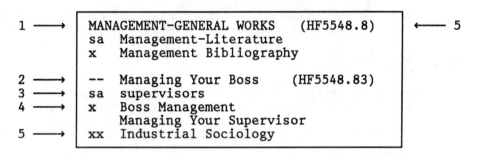

```
1 ───▶    MANAGEMENT-GENERAL WORKS    (HF5548.8)      ◀─── 5
          sa  Management-Literature
          x   Management Bibliography

2 ───▶    --  Managing Your Boss      (HF5548.83)
3 ───▶    sa  supervisors
4 ───▶    x   Boss Management
              Managing Your Supervisor
5 ───▶    xx  Industrial Sociology
```

1. MAIN SUBJECT HEADING - The main subject heading is in bold print. The main subject heading should be used before looking at the "dash", "see also", and "xx" terms. (Do not use the "x" terms.) These terms assist after using the main subject heading.

2. DASH - The dash identifies subdivisions of the main subject heading. These subdivisions may help you narrow your topic, or your precise subject may be presented here. They may also have their own broader topics.

3. SEE ALSO - The "see also" is used for topics related to your main subject. This should not be a substitute for the main subject heading, rather to assist with the main subject heading.

4. NOT APPLICABLE - The "x" identifies subject headings not used by the Library of Congress. Do not try to look up these headings. They will not be found in the Library of Congress.

5. BROADER TERMS - The "xx" identifies subject headings that may be related to your topic. This is not to be a substitute for the main subject heading. It should assist with the main subject heading.

6. CLASSIFICATION NUMBER - The Library of Congress gives some, but not all call numbers for certain subjects. Do not rely on just this technique to find books. The Library of Congress does not give classification numbers for all main subject headings.

Figure 2-13

<u>TO USE LIBRARY OF CONGRESS SUBJECT HEADING</u>

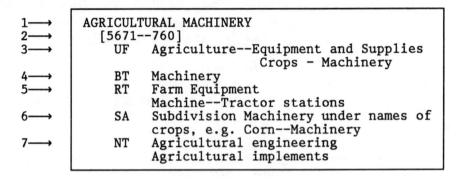

```
1→      AGRICULTURAL MACHINERY
2→      [5671--760]
3→          UF    Agriculture--Equipment and Supplies
                  Crops - Machinery
4→          BT    Machinery
5→          RT    Farm Equipment
                  Machine--Tractor stations
6→          SA    Subdivision Machinery under names of
                  crops, e.g. Corn--Machinery
7→          NT    Agricultural engineering
                  Agricultural implements
```

1. MAIN SUBJECT HEADING -- The main subject heading is typed in bold print.

2. CLASSIFICATION NUMBER -- The Library of Congress gives some, but not all call numbers for certain subjects.

3. UF (USED FOR) -- The UF identifies uses of the subheading and means "see from."

4. BT (BROADER TERM) -- The BT identifies broader, more general subheadings, and can be translated as "see also from."

5. RT (RELATED TERM) -- The RT identifies related terms, and can also be translated as "see also from" and lists closely related terms.

6. SA (SEE ALSO) -- The "see also" is used for topics related to the main subject heading. This listing is similar in use to the "see also" in illustration 9.

7. NT (NARROWER TERM) -- The NT identifies narrower but related subjects.

Note: Alterations in the style of cross reference cards for card catalogs is not required by these changes in cross reference codes. For additional information see <u>Library of Congress Subject Headings</u>, 12th edition Volume II, Cataloging Distribution Service, Library of Congress, Washington D.C., 1989.

The Dewey Decimal System

The Dewey Decimal System (DD) is an older system that many libraries, particularly smaller ones, still use. This system is named for Melvil Dewey, who as a student at Amherst College devised the system and wrote a paper on the subject in 1867. The DD system, unlike the LC system, assigns numbers to subject areas and uses letters with combinations of other numbers to stand for the author's name and title. Dewey divided all known knowledge into ten broad groupings and assigned each group a set of numbers from 000 to 999. The system uses numbers in sets of tens and hundreds, based on the decimal system. The general subject area takes an entire "hundred," and divides into "tens," which are more specific. The system is further expanded by the use of a decimal. The assigned combination of numbers and letters in the call number is found on the spine of the book and on the upper lefthand corner of each corresponding card in the card catalog. These numbers are the keys to finding books in the library.

In the past, libraries that did not have very extensive holdings preferred the DD system because of ease of use and simplicity. In smaller libraries, the DD system improves accessibility to assigned material. Every library may choose which system to use based on preferences and resources. Some libraries use both systems.

The Dewey system assigns 000's to Generalities. The 100's deal with man's thoughts and experiences and the phenomena of Nature-Philosophy. The 200's deal with man's deities and gods, which are under Religion, while the 300's concern man's relations with man, and are under Education and Society. Communication and Languages, along with related areas, denote the 400 numbers. The 500 numbers pertain to abstract phenomena — Natural Law and Science. The 600's deal with the manipulation and application of knowledge by man. The Arts are in the 700's, while 800 numbers deal with man's interpretation and the expression of nature through Literature. Mankind's accumulated knowledge, experience, discovery, and the earth are under general geography and history, the 900 category. The ten major groupings of the DD system are organized as follows:

THE TEN MAIN CLASSES OF THE DEWEY DECIMAL CLASSIFICATION SYSTEM

000-099	General Works (books about books, magazines, newspapers)
100-199	Philosophy and Psychology (human behavior, excludes psychiatry)
200-299	Religion (history, law, mythology)
300-399	Social Sciences (economics, education, occupations)
400-499	Languages and Communication (linguistics, grammar, dictionaries)
500-599	Pure Sciences (botany, chemistry, physics)
600-699	Technology, Applied Sciences (business, farming, medicine, psychiatry)
700-799	Fine Arts and Recreation (music, sports)
800-899	Literature (plays, poetry, speeches)
900-999	History (biography, geography, and travel books)

Within each of the above broad categories, ten additional divisions have been created. An outline of the ten general classifications and the one hundred subdivision groups is presented below.

The Divisions and Subdivisions of the Ten Main Classes of the Dewey Decimal System

000	GENERAL WORKS	390	Customs and Folklore
010	Bibliographies and Catalogs	400	LANGUAGES AND COMMUNICATION
020	Library Science	410	Linguistics and Nonverbal Language
030	General Encyclopedias	420	English and Anglo-Saxon
040	General Collected Essays	430	Germanic Languages
050	General Periodicals	440	French, Provincial, Catalan
060	General Organizations	450	Italian, Romanian, etc.
070	Newspapers and Journalism	460	Spanish and Portuguese
080	General Collections	470	Italic Languages
090	Manuscripts and Book Rarities	480	Classical and Greek
100	PHILOSOPHY AND PSYCHOLOGY	490	Other languages
110	Ontology and Methodology	500	PURE SCIENCES
120	Knowledge, Cause, Purpose, Man	510	Mathematics
130	Pseudo- and Parapsychology	520	Astronomy and Allied Sciences
140	Specific Philosophic Viewpoints	530	Physics
150	Psychology	540	Chemistry and Allied Sciences
160	Logic	550	Earth Sciences
170	Ethics (Moral Philosophy)	560	Paleontology
180	Ancient, Medieval, and Oriental Philosophy	570	Anthropology and Biological Sciences
190	Modern Western Philosophy	580	Botanical Sciences
200	RELIGION	590	Zoological Sciences
210	Natural Religion	600	TECHNOLOGY, APPLIED SCIENCES
220	Bible	610	Medical Sciences
230	Christian Doctrinal Theology	620	Engineering and Allied Operations
240	Christ, Moral and Devotional Theology	630	Agriculture and Agricultural Industries
250	Christ, Pastoral, Parochial	640	Domestic Arts and Sciences
260	Christ, Social and Ecclesiastic Theology	650	Business and Related Enterprises
270	History and Geology of Christ Church	660	Chemical Technology, etc.
280	Christ, Denominations and Sects	670	Manufacturers Processible
290	Other Religions and Comparative Religions	680	Assembled and Final Products
300	SOCIAL SCIENCES	690	Buildings
310	Statistical Method and Statistics	700	FINE ARTS AND RECREATION
320	Political Science	710	Civic and Landscape Art
330	Economics	720	Architecture
340	Law	730	Sculpture and the Plastic Arts
350	Public Administration	740	Drawing and Decorating Arts
360	Welfare and Association	750	Painting and Paintings
370	Education	760	Photography and Photographs
380	Commerce	780	Music

790	Recreation (Recreational Arts)	900	HISTORY
800	LITERATURE	910	General Geography
810	American Literature in English	920	General Biography, Genealogy, etc.
820	English and Anglo-Saxon Literature	930	General History of Ancient World
830	Germanic Languages Literature	940	General History of Modern Europe
840	French, Provincial, Catalan Literature	950	General History of Modern Asia
850	Italian, Romanian, etc., Literature	960	General History of Modern Africa
860	Spanish and Portuguese Literature	970	General History of North America
870	Italic Languages Literature	980	General History of South America
880	Classical and Greek Literature	990	General History of Rest of the World
890	Literature of Other Languages		

These one hundred groups are divided, as stated before, into ten subgroups. If one wanted a book on Management, it would be listed in the 600's under Technology (Applied Sciences). Management is under the number 650, which accompanies business and related enterprises. The subject "Management" is under "General Management" with a corresponding number 658. As illustrated below, 650 expands into ten subdivisional areas with assigned numbers for each area.

650   Business and Related Enterprise

651   Office Services

652   Processes of Written Communication

653   Shorthand

654   (unassigned)

655   Printing and Related Activities

656   (unassigned)

657   Accounting

658   General Management (General Administration)

659   Advertising

Additional classifications may be created by further division of topics into precise areas. This is demonstrated by the use of a decimal point and the addition of more numbers to the topic. It is possible to have numbers up to ten digits. This makes the system very flexible in describing and locating a specific book. For example:

323.4   Civil Rights (General Rights)

323.44   Freedom and Liberty (Specific Rights)

323.6   Citizenship

If a book on the subject of Economics is needed, it would be located in the 300's. It is assigned the number 330 under Social Science. The discipline of "Physics" is under Pure Sciences (500-590), with the corresponding number 530. As the classification number becomes longer, the assigned subject becomes more precise and specific.

CUTTER AUTHOR NUMBERS OF THE
DEWEY DECIMAL SYSTEM

Besides using major divisional and subdivisional or class area classifications, a book or author number may distinguish one work from another. These numbers consist of alphabet letters and Arabic numerals called Cutter Author Numbers, named after C.A. Cutter, who devised this refinement. In a call number such as 608/B961i, the number 6 stands for major classification, Technology (Applied Sciences), while the number 08 subclassifies it as general work. Next is the "B," which stands for the initial of the author, with 961 being the book number. Finally, the lower case "i" stands for a key word from the title of the book. It serves to distinguish between books on the same subject written by the same author. For example, 780.3/B368d is *Dictionary of Music* by Beard, while 780.3/B368c is *Concise Dictionary of Music* by the same author. Another example is 330.9/H36m *The Making of Economic Society* by Heilbroner, Robert L., while 330.973/H36l is *The Limits of American Capitalism* by the same author.

Sources of Information in the Library

3

There are two major objectives in the presentation of the material in this section: (1) to acquaint the reader with the variety and characteristics of reference materials available in the library, and (2) to provide the reader with an understanding of how to locate appropriate references through the use of bibliographic sources. The intermingling of reference and bibliographic materials is initially confusing when sorting through the extensive information in the library. In light of these concerns, and in keeping with the focus of this book, this material is presented in a framework of two dimensions: timeliness and the level of specificity involved in the variety of resources. These dimensions, however, cannot be adhered to strictly. This presentation attempts to move from a "starting point" through the dimensions of time and specificity to current sources such as newspapers. Because public and government documents span these dimensions, they are treated separately.

Dimensions also exist within the presentation of each of the reference types (Figure 3-1).

An encyclopedia can be defined as an alphabetically organized, descriptive summary of general and/or specific areas of knowledge. Such dimensional characteristics of reference works help to clarify and contribute to the overall framework presented. The order of the presentation follows a somewhat general to specific path that allows for a natural flow throughout (i.e., from discussing general non-current reference works to specific indexes and governmental sources). As such, this book attempts to parallel the presentation of the reference works with the presentation of various bibliographic sources. It is also helpful to observe the needed information in light of content, timeliness, organization, and sources (Figure 3-2).

Libraries contain vast collections of information sources that are of significant merit not only to a writer and researcher, but to everyone who values knowledge. Libraries are at the service of anyone wishing to make use of the holdings they contain. When familiarity with the arrangement of library materials is achieved, one is ready to begin the search for specific knowledge. A productive search will begin with the study of unabridged dictionaries, almanacs, atlases, encyclopedias, yearbooks, concordances, gazetteers, books, computer databanks, and microfilms. The inquiry for knowledge can be further expanded to include periodicals, indexes, bibliographies, biographies, computer databases, and government publications and documents. Figure 3-3 explains this search process.

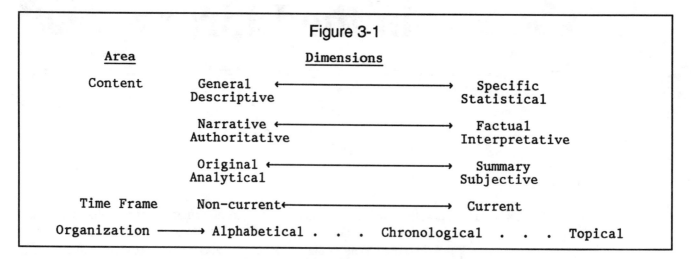

Figure 3-1

Area	Dimensions	
Content	General Descriptive ←——————→	Specific Statistical
	Narrative Authoritative ←——————→	Factual Interpretative
	Original Analytical ←——————→	Summary Subjective
Time Frame	Non-current ←——————→	Current
Organization ——→	Alphabetical . . . Chronological . . . Topical	

Figure 3-2

Reference material	Content	Timeliness	Arrangement	Bibliographic
Dictionaries	General	Non-current	Alphabetical	Guide to Reference Books
Encyclopedias	General Specific	Non-current	Alphabetical	Guide to Reference Books
Newspapers	Specific	Current Non-current	Topical	Indexes Databases
Periodicals Magazines	General	Current Non-current	Topical	Indexes Database

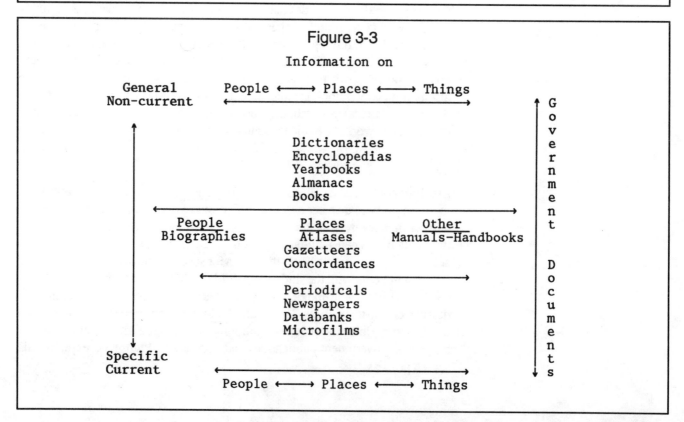

Figure 3-3

Information on

REFERENCE WORKS: GENERAL, NON-CURRENT

Dictionaries

A dictionary is an alphabetical listing of the definitions of words, including information on them. The dictionary is also a familiar and indispensable tool for research work. Spelling, abbreviations, meanings, proper names, antonyms, synonyms, idioms, pronunciation, foreign words, grammar, and other data can be found in these valuable books. They contain more useful details than we are able to use. Often, in haste to check on a spelling or meaning, people overlook the fact that dictionaries also provide illustrations, plates, names, places, events, and bibliographies. When properly used, a dictionary is a helpful initial source of exploratory information. The clarity, conciseness, and alphabetical arrangement of a dictionary provide a path to knowledge, along with fresh material for many thoughts, poems, and essays.

Dictionaries have been important to people for many years. Archaeologists have uncovered primitive dictionaries that were inscribed on clay tablets centuries ago; they predate the first systematic dictionary developed later in Germany. The Grimm Brothers, known for their collection of fairy tales, produced the first dictionary for public use, *Deutsche Grammatik*, in 1819. In 1721, Nathan Bailey published the first comprehensive dictionary, and Dr. Samuel Johnson is credited with the compilation of the first English dictionary in 1755. Seventy-three years later, in 1828, Noah Webster published the first comprehensive English dictionary in the United States.

Several different kinds of English dictionaries exist. It is best to consult a knowledgeable librarian about which dictionary to use. The dictionary format is an arrangement and listing of information in alphabetical sequence. A variety of dictionaries exist for synonyms, antonyms, acronyms, slang, history, economics, politics, foreign languages, and letters. Some dictionaries provide encyclopedic information about a variety of subjects. Their main advantage is linguistic information, which is not found in encyclopedias. To be able to use a dictionary productively, it is important to understand the manner in which material is arranged and presented. It is important to become familiar with the preface, introduction, table of contents, and other keys to the dictionary's use.

There are three dictionary classifications. The first is the specialized dictionary, which is concerned with a specific subject, such as the *Dictionary of the Bible* or *Dictionary of Education*. The second is for dictionaries that deal with special aspects of words, such as synonyms, antonyms, or slang, such as the *New Roget's Thesaurus of the English Language*. The final category includes dictionaries that deal with many aspects of all the words in a language — the common, "everyday" dictionary. These classifications may be further broken down into three types: abridged, unabridged, and general purpose.

The abridged dictionary is typically a single desk volume or college-type dictionary. Some of the most popular and commonly recommended abridged dictionaries include:

American Heritage Dictionary of the English Language. New York: American Heritage Pub. Co., 1982.

Funk and Wagnall's Standard College Dictionary. New Updated ed., New York: Funk and Wagnall's, 1984.

Oxford American Dictionary. New York: Oxford University Press, 1982.

The Random House College Dictionary. Rev. ed. New York: Random House, Inc., 1983.

The Shorter Oxford English Dictionary on Historical Principles. 34th ed. Oxford: Clarendon Press, 1973.

Webster's New Collegiate Dictionary. 2nd College ed. New York: Simon and Schuster, 1980.

World Book Dictionary. 1987 ed. Chicago: World Book, Inc., 1987.

The second type is the unabridged dictionary. This is a large, comprehensive, encyclopedic dictionary composed of over half a million entries in several thousand pages. These massive dictionaries are usually located on a special desk or pedestal in the library. The most authoritative unabridged dictionaries include the following:

Funk and Wagnall's Standard College Dictionary of the English Language. New York: Funk and Wagnall's, 1987.

The Random House Dictionary of the English Language. 2nd unabridged ed. New York: Random House, Inc., 1987.

Webster's New International Dictionary of English Language. Springfield, MA: G & C Merriam Company, 1959.

Webster's New Universal Unabridged Dictionary. 2nd ed. New York: Dorset & Baber, 1983.

Webster's Third New International Dictionary of English Language. 2nd ed. Springfield, MA: G & C Merriam Company, 1981.

The third type of dictionary is the general-purpose dictionary, which deals with a limited selection of words in a particular language. Examples include English language and foreign language dictionaries.

Dictionary of American Regional English. Cambridge, MA: Belknap Press of Harvard University Press, 1985.

The Oxford Guide to the English Language. Oxford, England: Oxford University Press, 1986.

Encyclopedias

An encyclopedia is an alphabetically listed collection of information that covers general or specific areas of knowledge, in one or more volumes. It is a one-stop information source offering a condensed overview of many topics. Encyclopedias are a good starting point for preliminary research for several reasons: they provide a quick overview of a topic, define terms, and help locate references to sources of information on the subject. Encyclopedias also provide brief information on the history, statistics, organization, and other important aspects of a topic. Some encyclopedias also include short and relevant bibliographies for further study. The articles in encyclopedias are written by specialists and experts, which makes any reference cited from them authoritative.

Encyclopedias may be general or specialized and targeted in their content. To determine content coverage, it is necessary for one to become familiar with the indexing, organization, and coverage of the material in an encyclopedia. A topic may be covered under several other subject entries. Information on recent happenings and discoveries is not included in these publications, because it takes time for publishers to update encyclopedias. Updating is done through the issuance of supplements or yearbooks, or by printing new editions. The following are representative of general and specific encyclopedias.

AMERICAN

Afro-American Encyclopedia. North Miami, FL: Educational Book Pub., 1974.

AREA STUDIES

Australian Encyclopedia. 4th ed. Sydney, Australia: Grolier Society of Australia, 1989.

Encyclopedia of Latin America. New York: McGraw-Hill, 1974.

Kodansha Encyclopedia of Japan. Tokyo, New York: Kodansha Publishing Company, 1983.

EDUCATION

American Educators Encyclopedia. Westport, CT: Greenwood Press, 1982.

Encyclopedia of Education. New York: Macmillan, 1971.

Encyclopedia of Educational Research. New York: Pergamon Press, 1987.

GENERAL REFERENCE

Chamber's Encyclopedia. New rev. ed. London: International Learning System Corporation, 1973.

Colliers Encyclopedia. New York: Macmillan, 1990.

Encyclopedia Americana. Westport, CT: Grolier Inc., 1990.

Encyclopedia Britannica. Chicago: Encyclopedia Britannica Inc., 1990.

The New Columbia Encyclopedia. New York: Columbia University Press, 1975.

HEALTH/MEDICINE/NUTRITION

Encyclopedia of Bioethics. New York: Free Press, 1978.

Foods and Nutrition Encyclopedia. Clovis, CA: Pegus Press, 1983.

McGraw-Hill Encyclopedia of Food, Agriculture and Nutrition. New York: McGraw-Hill, 1977.

Parents' Encyclopedia of Infancy, Childhood and Adolescence. New York: Crowell Publishing Company, 1973.

World Encyclopedia of Food. New York: Facts on File, 1982.

HISTORY

Encyclopedia of Military History. New York: Harper and Row, 1986.

Encyclopedia of Southern History. Baton Rouge: Louisiana State University Press, 1979.

Simon and Schuster Encyclopedia of World War II. New York: Simon and Schuster Pub., 1978.

LAW/CRIMINAL JUSTICE

Encyclopedia of American Crime. New York: Facts on File, 1982.

Encyclopedia of Crime and Justice. New York: Free Press, 1983.

Encyclopedia of Legal Information Sources. Detroit: Gale Research Company, 1988.

PHILOSOPHY

Encyclopedia of Philosophy. New York: Macmillan, 1972.

PSYCHOLOGY/PSYCHIATRY

Baker Encyclopedia of Psychology. Grand Rapids, MI: Baker Book House, 1986.

Encyclopedia of Psychology. New York: Wiley, 1984.

International Encyclopedia of Psychiatry, Psychology, Psychoanalysis and Neurology. New York: Van Nostrand Reinhold Company, 1983.

RELIGION/MYTHOLOGY/OCCULT

Encyclopedia of Islam. New York: Macmillan, 1983.

Encyclopedia of Occultism and Parapsychology. Detroit: Gale Research Company, 1984.

Encyclopedia of Religion. New York: Macmillan, 1987.

Encyclopedia of Religion in the South. Macon, GA: Mercer, 1984.

New Catholic Encyclopedia. New York: McGraw-Hill, 1979.

SCIENCE/TECHNOLOGY/ENVIRONMENT

Encyclopedia of American Forest and Conservation History. New York: Macmillan, 1983.

Encyclopedia of UFO's. Garden City, NY: Doubleday, 1980.

How It Works: The Illustrated Encyclopedia of Science and Technology. New York: Marshall Cavendish, 1978.

Illustrated Encyclopedia of Aviation and Space. Los Angeles, A.F.E. Press, 1971.

McGraw-Hill Encyclopedia of Environmental Sciences. New York: McGraw-Hill, 1980.

McGraw-Hill Encyclopedia of Science and Technology. New York: McGraw-Hill, 1988.

SOCIAL SCIENCE

Encyclopedia of Social Work. New York: National Association of Social Workers, 1983.

International Encyclopedia of Social Sciences. New York: Macmillan, 1979.

Social Science Encyclopedia. Boston: Routledge and Kegan Paul Publishing Company, 1989.

WOMEN

Encyclopedia of Feminism. New York: Facts on File, 1986.

Yearbooks A yearbook illustrates a year's events through articles, charts, narratives, statistics, and tables. It contains facts, data, and events that occurred during the year chronicled. Yearbooks are compilations of general, specialized, and statistical information for the previous year, presented in brief and concise format. If up-to-date information about current events is needed, one should search current newspapers and magazines. In order to find such information for the immediate past year, one must use yearbooks. A great deal of important information and statistical data, including that from governmental organizations and scientific and educational societies, is included in yearbooks.

The *Statistical Abstract of the United States,* currently in its 109th edition and subtitled "National Data Book and Guide to Sources," is an example of a yearbook. It contains close to two thousand charts, tables, illustrations, and other information on many social, political, and economic subjects. Its esoteric detail covers a variety of data, such as the percentage of Americans who wear seat belts or the percentage of births by Caesarean section. Since government publications cannot be copyrighted, the abstract is often quoted and reproduced.

Yearbooks also include very specialized annuals such as auto repair manuals, gun catalogs, stamp catalogs, commodity yearbooks, and yearbooks of churches and organizations. Publishers of encyclopedias often print yearly supplements to update the book's information. One should become acquainted with yearbooks in one's field of research and interest.

Most public, private, national, and international organizations issue yearbooks and annual reports that cover important events, developments, trends, data, and relevant statistics for the period. Yearbooks constitute an important, up-to-date summary of political, social, economic, and other events and subjects. Examples of some notable yearbooks include the following:

The Annual Register: World Events. London: Longings, Green and Co., 1958-date.

Facts on File Visual Dictionary. New York: Facts on File, 1941-date.

McGraw-Hill Yearbook of Science and Technology. New York: McGraw-Hill, 1961-date.

Municipal Yearbook. Washington: International City Management Association, 1934-date.

The Statesmen's Yearbook: Statistical and Historical Annual of the States of the World. Ed. John Paxton. New York: St. Martin's, 1982-date.

Statistical Yearbook/Annuaire Statistique. New York: United Nations, 1948-date.

The Year Book of World Affairs. London: Stevens Publishing Co. Inc., 1947-date.

Yearbook of Agriculture. Washington: Government Printing Office, 1984-date.

Yearbook of the United Nations. Lake Success, NY: United Nations, 1947-date.

Some yearbooks are collections of articles and papers delivered at yearly meetings by members of academic and professional societies. These books are referred to as "Annual Proceedings." The included material in the proceedings is mostly theoretical and academic in orientation. They contain current research on topics of interest to the academic community. Most of the included articles are well reasoned and documented. There are regional, national, and international proceedings. Review of these books is integral to research and writing good theses and dissertations. Some examples are:

Proceedings of the American Management Association

Proceedings of the American Marketing Association

Proceedings of the American Psychological Association

To use a yearbook productively, the researcher must know which book is designed to provide the kind of information needed. It is obvious that the *Statistical Abstract of the United States* has a greater variety of information than the *Proceedings of the American Marketing Association*. To use yearbooks efficiently, one should: (1) become knowledgeable about the yearbooks that exist in the field of interest, (2) learn how these yearbooks are organized, and (3) note the kind of information presented as well as the time period covered.

Almanacs   An almanac is a book or pamphlet published once a year. It contains a multitude of facts, statistics, and other information in a compact format. The almanac offers an interesting "grab bag" of knowledge and is a welcome addition to any personal library. A general almanac may include information on famous people, associations, sporting events, zip codes, tax deadlines, astronomical calculations, climatology, economics, and technology. Since a general almanac is broad in coverage, its index is very helpful in obtaining information. Frequent revision of almanacs helps to convey accurate and current information. The following are among the most useful general-purpose almanacs:

CBS News Almanac. Maplewood, NJ: Hammond Almanac, Inc., 1979.

The Dow Jones-Irwin Business and Investment Almanac. Ed. Sumner N. Levine. Homewood, IL: Dow Jones-Irwin, 1989.

Information Please Almanac, Atlas and Yearbook. Ed. Theodore B. Dolmatch. 37th ed. New York: Simon and Schuster, 1983.

Official Associated Press Almanac. Maplewood, NJ: Hammond Almanac, Inc., 1976.

Reader's Digest Almanac and Yearbook. Ed. David C. Whitney. Pleasantville, NY: The Reader's Digest Association, Inc., 1987.

The World Almanac and Book of Facts. New York: Newspaper Enterprise Association, 1968-date.

Specialized almanacs, such as the *Almanac of Politics*, exist, listing biographies and other significant information about presidents, congressmen, senators, and other noted people in public life. It is worthwhile to become familiar with specialized almanacs in one's field of interest.

CATEGORICAL REFERENCE WORKS

Biographies are accounts of people's lives — their accomplishments, attitudes, character, philosophy, and any significant history. They also highlight major events that occurred during the subject's lifetime. Biographies are second only to fiction in popularity among readers. These books are written to pay tribute

Biographies   to people who have made unusual and outstanding contributions (both good and bad). History places these humans with noted achievements on a permanent honor/dishonor roll. These heroes/villains reveal much about their times, people, and culture. Subjects of these biographies may be contemporary, famous, or infamous. A researcher should read about the accomplishments made by people in his or her field of specialty and research.

Researchers frequently need detailed information about individuals of historical significance. Biographies are ideal starting points for those interested in a panoramic view of a person's life, events, and actions, or for simple facts such as birth dates and addresses. Most library books that deal with the subject are classified under biography, autobiography, and biographical information. Biographical material may be limited in scope to people of a particular nation and/or profession. Biographies may also be specialized to the living or the deceased. Some examples are *Artists-Biography, United States Currency-Biography*, and *Football-Biography*. Some may list brief sketches, such as the *Who's Who*, while others may present articles several pages long exemplified by the *Dictionary of American Biography*.

Autobiographies are diaries, details, and narrations written by authors on themselves. These books reveal much about their accomplishments, aspirations, and lives. An outstanding example is the autobiography, *Memoirs of The Second World War*, by the late British Prime Minister, Sir Winston Churchill.

When seeking information about a number of notable individuals in the same field, collective biographies should be consulted. These books allow the reader to review and compare many biographies of individuals and their contemporaries in the same field. Collective biographies are written in a concise and brief format. In a library organized under the Dewey Decimal System, this material is assigned the number 920. Individual biographies are on stacks arranged by number and then alphabetically by the subject's last name.

Although biographical information can be found elsewhere in the library (such as in encyclopedias, annuals, dictionaries, magazines, and newspapers), reference sources used for this purpose include biographical indexes, essay-type sources, and biographical dictionaries.

Biographical Indexes. Biographical indexes are special books that list cumulative biographical material on noted individuals, celebrities, and famous people. They include people of all professions, occupations, and countries. The included indexes are arranged by last name as well as by profession. The following are some well-known biographical index books:

Biography and Genealogy Master Index. 2nd ed. Detroit: Gale Research Company, 1980.

Biography Index. 42 vols. New York: H.W. Wilson, 1988.

The New York Times Biographical Service. New York: Arno Press, 1974.

Essay-Type Sources. Essay sources are classified by country, time period, and living or deceased persons. These essays include people of all occupations and professions. Several pages or a few paragraphs may be written on individuals. These books highlight important events, dates, pictures, and sketches of people. Essays inform the reader about other significant material that may exist elsewhere on the subject. Important sources include:

Current Biography. New York: H.W. Wilson, 1940.

Current World Leaders. Santa Barbara, CA: International Academy, 1970-monthly.

Encyclopedia of World Biography. New York: McGraw-Hill, 1973.

Biographical Dictionaries. Biographical dictionaries contain biographical information on prominent and national figures. These dictionaries include information concerning affiliation, education, interests, publications, background, positions, birthplace, and current residence for individuals. There are many types of localized and specialized *Who's Who* publications available. The number and variety of these books are legendary. These books are classified by professions, geographical regions, and living and deceased persons. The following is a representative sample:

Appleton's Annual Encyclopedia of American Biography. Rev. ed. New York: D. Appleton, 1968.

Dictionary of American Biography. New York: Collier Macmillan, Inc., 1946.

Encyclopedia of World Biography. New York: McGraw-Hill, 1973.

International Who's Who. Europa Publications, Ltd., 1935.

Webster's Biographical Dictionary. Springfield, MA: Merriam Publishing Company, 1980.

Who's Who in Advertising

Who's Who in American Education

Who's Who in American Government

Who's Who in Des Moines

Who's Who in the East

Who's Who in India

Who's Who in the Movies

In selecting which biography to use, it is helpful to become familiar with the arrangement and organization of the material. It is also important to read the preliminary pages concerning the arrangement, abbreviations, and efficient use of these books.

Atlases

The word "atlas" historically meant a volume of maps, tables, or illustrations bound together, indicating the systematic development of a geographical subject. The name is derived from Greek mythology (a Titan named Atlas was condemned to separate the heavens and the earth by supporting the sky on his shoulders). Generally, people associate atlases with sources of geographical and/or travel information. For example, the common bound volumes of maps that the American Automobile Association and most oil companies provide are considered travel guides as well as atlases.

The material contained within an atlas serves as an excellent source for finding specialized information quickly. Geographical atlases may be general, regional, national, topical, or topographical. A topical atlas illustrates a particular subject. It may be quantitative, indicating annual average precipitation, or qualitative, indicating the distribution of climate in a certain area. A topographical atlas presents the configuration of a surface, including its relief, as well as the locations of streams, lakes, roads, cities, and capitals. This atlas can be of large scale, which is detailed for highly developed cities and rural areas; medium scale, most commonly used for rural areas; or small scale, covering a few square miles and used for purposes such as regional planning. An example of a topical atlas is *Rand McNally's Cosmopolitan World Atlas* and an example of a topographical atlas is *Rand McNally's Commercial Atlas and Marketing Guide.*

Atlases are an important source of knowledge for the study of social sciences, history, geography, and anthropology. In addition to geographical atlases, there is a variety of atlases in other fields. The *Agriculture Atlas of Nebraska,* for example, provides details on soil, water, climate, and plants in that region. It also contains other information, such as different types of livestock and their average costs, as well as profitable strategies for marketing.

The *Bible Atlas* is a specialized work devoted to the geographical elucidation of the Bible. This atlas contains maps and other matters of historical interest. Charts and brief explanatory paragraphs are used, along with quotes and drawings to trace significant stories from the Bible. Events such as Jesus's travels or Moses's exodus from Egypt are examples of topics presented in the *Bible Atlas* through the use of maps, charts, and illustrations.

Economic atlases present detailed information and data concerning imports, exports, business comparisons, and economic growth. Such information is presented in tables, graphs, and charts and is easily used by individuals who require specific business and economic information. Such information is useful for starting or relocating a business, developing a marketing plan, and many other projects that require economic data.

The descriptive materials contained in atlases of different fields make excellent resources. In the library, atlases and maps are usually placed in portfolios or specially designed cases that are arranged on the shelves horizontally. Examples of some atlases are:

Agricultural Atlas of the United States. Maps and Charts. Chicago: Rand McNally, 1982.

The Macmillan Bible Atlas. Maps. New York: Macmillan, 1968.

The National Atlas of the United States of America. Maps. Chicago: Rand McNally, 1983.

National Geographic Atlas of the World. Maps. Washington: National Geographic, Inc., 1981.

The New York Times Atlas of the World. Rev. ed. In collaboration with the *Times* of London. New York: Times Books, 1981.

Oxford Economic Atlas of the World. Maps and Charts. London: Oxford University Press, 1972.

Gazetteers   Gazetteers are geographical dictionaries that list (in alphabetical order) names, terms, places, and other geographical information. These books describe features of the cities, continents, countries, counties, lakes, bays, mountains, oceans, seas, and villages. In a geographical gazetteer, detailed statistical information is provided for thousands of places. A complete gazetteer includes variant spellings, pronunciations, population statistics, altitudes, locations, and data on trade, industries, cultural institutions, monuments, and other relevant information about an area. Depending on significance, the layout of articles may include headings, alternative titles or variants, derivations, locations, descriptions, populations, and historical value.

Some specialized uses for the gazetteer include population statistics, number of schools in a city, lengths of rivers, economic data, cultural data, and social data about a geographic location. The gazetteer is a good reference source for specific geographical information. Gazetteers are listed in the card catalog under Geography. They have subject subdivisions under the name of the country or state, such as California-Gazetteers. It is important to note the date of publication in order to determine how current the information is in the issue. Some popular gazetteers are:

The Columbia-Lippincott Gazetteer of the World. Ed. Leon T. Seltzer. New York: Columbia University Press, 1962.

Dictionary of Mountaineering. Peter Crew. Harrisburg, PA: Stackpole Books, 1969.

Encyclopedia of World Travel. Eds. Nelson Doubleday and C. Earl Cooley. Garden City, NY: Guide Books, 1979.

Macmillan World Gazetteer and Geographical Dictionary. Eds. T.C. Collocott and J.O. Thorne. New York: Macmillan, 1961.

The Statesman's Year Book World Gazetteer. John Paton. New York: St. Martin's, 1986.

World Facts and Figures. Victor Showers. New York: Wiley, 1989.

Other Categorical Reference Works

Manuals and Handbooks. Manuals and handbooks are excellent sources for brief and specific information. Manuals give quick information on how something is used, built, repaired, or put together. Two good examples of manuals are *Chilton's Automobile and Lawnmower Repair Manuals* and *Robert's Rules of Order*. Handbooks include digests, guides, manuals, and many other small books that detail broad subjects in brief detail. Some of these books may be "do it yourself" instruction books (manuals), while others may offer summaries (digests). A variety of manuals and handbooks exists. It is beneficial to become familiar with those applicable to one's field of interest. Examples of some popular manuals and handbooks are:

A Manual of Copyright Practice. 2nd ed. New York: Oxford University Press, 1956.

The Chicago Manual of Style. 12th ed. Chicago: University of Chicago Press, 1982.

The Negro Handbook. Chicago: Johnson Publishing Company, 1974.

Robert's Rules of Order. New rev. ed. Sarah Corbin Robert. Glenview, IL: Scott Foresman Company, 1981.

Webster's New World Secretarial Handbook. New rev. ed. New York: Simon and Schuster, 1989.

Brochures, Bulletins, Reports, and Pamphlets. These documents contain information that is specific to particular fields of interest. Government agencies, trade organizations, businesses, foundations, and academic institutions produce a variety of these publications. The existence of a comprehensive index to cover all of them would not be practical. The Vertical File Index in the library is a good source to consult in locating some of these publications.

Through familiarity with associations in the field of one's interest, an individual will know about the originator of some publications. This familiarity will make one knowledgeable about these sources; for example, in education (the Carnegie Foundation) or in small business (the Small Business Administration). In the field of investments, the New York Stock Exchange will guide one in locating some of these documents. The *Gebbie Information Sources* and the *Business Pamphlets Information Sources* are good references in looking for brochures, bulletins, pamphlets, and reports.

SPECIFIC/CURRENT REFERENCE WORKS

Periodicals

Periodicals (journals, magazines, newspapers, newsletters, serials) contain recent information on events, issues, and topics that is not found in published books. Periodicals also include compilations of academic and professional articles. These publications are issued at such intervals as daily, weekly, biweekly, monthly, bimonthly, quarterly, semi-annually, or annually. Periodicals are intended to be continued indefinitely; issues may be gathered and bound together in hard covers and placed in open or closed stacks, or they may be on film known as *microfiche*. These films are usually located in a separate room or area in the library called the Microfiche Center. Periodicals are also kept on computerized database systems.

Using periodicals in any research activity in the library is indispensable. Articles contained in periodicals present information that is usually brief and more current than material contained in books. Their inclusion in research lends authoritativeness and timeliness to written material. Some important advantages of periodical sources include:

- They contain the most recent information on subjects and issues too contemporary to be found in books.

- Periodical articles are often short and easy to read, although some may be quite technical and long, depending on the discipline and the magazine. For example, there is quite a difference in the style and content that may appear on an industrial chemical accident in *Business Week* and *Life* magazines, contrasted with the *American Medical Journal* and the *American Chemical Journal.*

- Subjects that are limited and not of sufficient importance to receive book treatment can be covered extensively in journal articles.

- Several articles give quick, comprehensive, and varied points of view, unlike the typical one-sided treatment in a long book.

- There is a time lag before books are published, particularly in the scientific, technological, and medical areas, during which research and its results are first described in periodicals.

The arrangement of serials or periodicals varies at every library. In most cases, the main collection is arranged in open stacks, while popularly used publications are placed in closed stacks behind the public services desk. This is to facilitate and control usage.

As a general rule, periodicals are grouped in alphabetical order by title with certain exceptions to this arrangement. The first exception is that many periodicals are organized alphabetically by the name of the particular association, society, or institution that published them. For example, publications of the *American Management Association* are found under American Management Association. The second exception deals with titles that are abbreviated. These publications are arranged at the beginning in alphabetical sequence. For example, the *ABA* (American Banking Association) *Banking Journal* is found at the beginning of the "A's" rather than with the "Ab's." Also, *ESQ*, which stands for *Emerson Society Quarterly*, is found at the beginning of the "E's" rather than in the "Esq's."

Newspapers   Newspapers are publications that appear regularly, daily or weekly, containing news events, opinions, advertisements, and other items of general interest. The origin of modern newspapers is traced to ancient Rome. According to the following information from *Collier's 1990 Encyclopedia*, in 449 B.C., the *Acta diurna* ("daily acts") chronicled the political and social events of the empire. Julius Caesar in 60 B.C. decreed that a daily recording of news be posted. The first known newspaper called *Ti Chau* (The Peking Gazette) was published in China during the eighth century. The first English-language news sheets were printed in Amsterdam in 1620. With the invention of the Gutenberg press, newspapers become popular in Europe in the 15th century. The biweekly *London Gazette* (1665), still published in London, reporting official records, was the first newspaper in a modern sense. In the United States, newspapers originated in Boston with the publication of the *Public Occurrences Both Foreign and Domestick* in 1690. The influential *New York Times* appeared in 1851.

Newspapers are an important source of current and past information that includes specific contemporary knowledge, which is frequently too narrow in scope to be published in books. Newspaper coverage of local, regional, national, and international events is exhaustive. Newspapers may contain news events, illustrations, book reviews, photographs, biographical features, and articles from all fields of knowledge. For a panoramic view of any given period, newspapers furnish a contemporary perspective on developments, facts, and opinions of the times.

Newspaper editorials, articles, letters, pictures, and illustrations present an overview of the attitudes, opinions, and standards of the society at any specific time, on issues, people, places, and events. They exert a powerful influence on public opinion and scholars, providing clues as to when and where to find additional information. The coverage of specific names, dates, statistics, and other details may be difficult to find elsewhere. If one wanted the total reaction of the people of the United States toward the assassination of Dr. Martin Luther King, Jr., newspapers would be informative sources. Numerous indexes to newspapers exist. For example, if one were to implement an index search for newspaper articles on earthquakes in the *National Newspaper Index*, the information presented in Figure 3-4 would be produced on the screen.

To discover information for localized research purposes, one should look for and study information in local newspapers. Local libraries keep vertical files for local newspapers. These files contain important articles and other information about the area. This material is arranged in alphabetical order by subject and kept in special folders. Newspapers published regionally, nationally, and internationally are designated by their respective areas of coverage and should be researched in this manner.

PUBLIC AND GOVERNMENT DOCUMENTS

Public documents constitute a good source of authoritative, statistical, and practical information. People interested in the business, economic, social, and political life of the American people will find these publications, in all their diversity, an excellent source of reliable information. These publications are printed at the local, state, regional, and national levels.

Government-published documents are comprehensive in diversity and content and are published in many forms and formats. A government document is any manuscript that is published by an organized government department. These documents are printed by the government at its own expense. The variety of publications includes maps, charts, leaflets, newspapers, filmstrips, periodicals, bibliographies, laws, court cases, congressional hearings, treaties, presidential messages, posters, and other materials. Popular examples of these publications include: *Congressional Record, Congressional Directory, Statistical Abstract of the United States*, practical "how to" manuals, and various annual reports issued by different agencies of the government.

Figure 3-4

Topic: Earthquakes

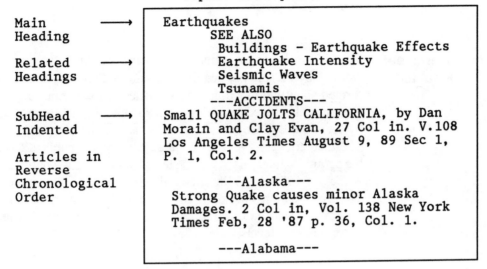

Main
Heading

Related
Headings

SubHead
Indented

Articles in
Reverse
Chronological
Order

```
Earthquakes
     SEE ALSO
     Buildings - Earthquake Effects
     Earthquake Intensity
     Seismic Waves
     Tsunamis
     ---ACCIDENTS---
Small QUAKE JOLTS CALIFORNIA, by Dan
Morain and Clay Evan, 27 Col in. V.108
Los Angeles Times August 9, 89 Sec 1,
P. 1, Col. 2.

     ---Alaska---
Strong Quake causes minor Alaska
Damages. 2 Col in, Vol. 138 New York
Times Feb, 28 '87 p. 36, Col. 1.

     ---Alabama---
```

Index: National Newspaper Index

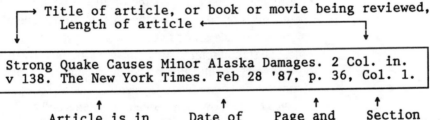

Title of article, or book or movie being reviewed,
     Length of article

```
Strong Quake Causes Minor Alaska Damages. 2 Col. in.
v 138. The New York Times. Feb 28 '87, p. 36, Col. 1.
```

Article is in   Date of   Page and   Section
New York Times   paper   numbers   in newspaper

Familiarity with the nature of information contained in public documents should be an important part of the learning and research effort. Some public information documents include practical knowledge and are easy to read. They can be used as guides or for statistical references. Two examples include the publications of the Small Business Administration and the *Statistical Abstract of the United States.*

Purpose of Government Documents

The United States government is perhaps the single largest publisher in the world. Government publications are intended not only to keep the public informed about the functions and activities of the various departments of the government but to educate the public. For this purpose, the federal government, by act of the U.S. Congress, has designated some libraries as "depositories." These libraries receive free of charge government publications for the use of the public. A library must have at least 15,000 titles to qualify as a depository. A majority of college libraries are depositories of government documents. These publications are classified in many different ways, such as by content or agency of publication. The approach discussed here is classification by federal, state, and local levels.

Classification by Federal, State, and Local Levels

Federal Documents. At the federal level, the United States Government Printing Office (GPO), an independent part of the legislative branch of the government, is the chief source of all publications. The Superintendent of Documents is responsible for their distribution. Generally, government publications are not classified in card catalog systems. In order to locate a desired topic, one should refer to an index or a bibliography that is entirely dedicated to government publications. Special databases are prepared for government documents on computerized systems. Federal, state, and local documents are arranged by their own classification systems and are kept in separate sections in most libraries. A librarian can give information showing where government publications are stacked. The following three reference books are very helpful in locating older government documents containing historical information.

CIS/Index to Publications of the United States Congress (1970—). Washington: James Adler.

Poor, B. Perley. *The Descriptive Catalogue of Government Publications of the United States 1774-1881.* Washington: GPO. 1885. 1,392 pages.

United States Department of the Interior, Division of Documents. *The Comprehensive Index to the Publications of the United States, 1881-1894.* 1905.

Since 1895, the *Monthly Catalog of Government Publications* has been the most inclusive source for federal documents. It provides information on documents produced by the three branches of the government. The *Monthly Catalog* includes introductory guides, descriptions, and illustrations of how to use, locate, and evaluate an entry. Each volume is separately indexed. Cumulative indexes are published annually, or every five and ten years. The *Monthly Catalog's* indexing and listing methods are similar to those of the *Periodical Index*. This indexing is based on Library of Congress subject headings. The included index is arranged by author, title, subject, series, stock number, and title keyword. Once familiar with the *Monthly Catalog*, one should look in it for the desired subject under the title and related subject headings. The *Monthly*

Catalog uses a system that has combinations of letters and numbers assigned by the Superintendent of Documents to be used in locating each document. The system is composed of symbols, letters, and Arabic numerals not only used for location purposes but also to identify the designated agency of the government and the type of publication. These numbers and letters are called "Su Doc" (Superintendent of Documents) numbers, which typically look like: A 13.66/2:M 31. "Su Doc" numbers are used in shelving government documents in the library. Note the additional information in the following example of a *Monthly Catalog* entry, produced through the computer terminal (Figure 3-5):

Figure 3-5

A 13.66/2:M 31

89-9680

```
Management development program. --[Portland, OR?] : Pacific
Northwest Region, USDA Forest Service, [1989]
     1 sheet : col. ill. ; 43 x 56 cm. folded to 22 x 14 cm.
Shipping list no.: 89-142-P. "August 1988." *Item 79-C
     1. United States Forest Service--Management. 2. Assess-
ment centers (Personnel management procedure) 3. Execu-
tives--Training of--United States. I. United States. Forest
Service. Pacific Northwest Region. OCLC 19358728
```

EXPLANATION OF A 13.66/2:M 31

1. **A** Department of Agriculture

2. **13** Forest Service

3. **66/2** Publication of a subordinate office in the Forest Service in series form, such as a magazine or newspaper, **66** denotes the office — Pacific Northwest Forest and Range Experimental Station. **2** is a designated number indicating the type of publication — in this example, **2** represents general publication.

4. **89-9681** The report number. The first two digits **89** indicate the year 1989. This was the date the publication was listed in the *Monthly Catalog*.

5. The remaining numbers represent the sequential listings during the year. In the library, this document is listed under **A.13** on the shelves. (Remember, most libraries shelve government documents separately.)

When the individual researching locates a title, the document classification number (Su Doc) should be noted and then searched for in the library. As stated earlier, libraries designated as "depositories" receive most published government documents free, and many locate government documents separately. Some libraries keep these documents on microfiche. If the library does not have a specific document, a librarian can borrow the document from another library, using an inter-library loan arrangement. Other policies used include the following:

1. The author of a government document is the official body, agency, or administrative unit that writes the publication. This is unlike the classification of other books in the library. For example, a bulletin of the United States Office of Education will be entered under that heading in the

library card catalog and in the Education Index but under the Education Office in the *Monthly Catalog* and the *Document Catalog*.

2. Smaller libraries may catalog, shelve, and designate government documents with their other collections. If this is the case, the researcher will locate them using the card catalog.

3. Some libraries may keep government documents separate, especially in the case of depository libraries, and use the Su Doc numbering system.

4. Some libraries may have separate sections or rooms for this material or treat it as a separate collection, using a separate card catalog.

State and Local Documents. Information about the publications of states, counties, localities, and cities can be difficult to locate nationally. *The Book of the States*, published by the Council of State Governments in Chicago, is a good initial starting point for locating references. Another document published by the United States government is the *Monthly Checklist of State Publications*. In a majority of states, the secretary of state publishes legislative manuals or "Blue Books," which list published materials for that state. State universities, archives, and historical associations also maintain collections of relevant publications in each state.

City and county publications are issued regularly in great numbers and extensive volumes. In many cities and local communities, various publications, official statements, findings, deliberations, and reports are generally collected by local libraries or archives and kept in scrapbooks. It is best to ask the area librarians for assistance to become familiar with their practices and collection methods. A good reference source for older county documents is the publication by James Goodwin Hodgson, *The Official Publications of American Counties, A Union List* (Fort Collins, CO: Colorado State College, 1968). Another reliable reference source is the *Municipal Year Book*, published by the International City Management Association.

Classification of Public Documents

Another method of classifying federal, state, and local government documents is by the type of publication and the intended content. These include the following:

1. Directories and Registers. These are numerous and, as the names suggest, list such things as names, titles, addresses, telephone numbers, brief biographies, and other important pieces of information. The federal government's *Congressional Directory* is a good example.

2. Journals. Almost all government organizations at the federal, state, and local levels have some type of "journal" in which speeches, debates, and deliberations are regularly printed. The *United States Congressional Record* is a journal devoted to U.S. Senate meetings, speeches, and hearings.

3. Rules, Policies, Procedures, and Directives. These are issued frequently by various bureaus under varied titles, such as handbooks, manuals, and instructions.

4. Legislation and Laws. These include legislation, laws, and codes that are enacted. These are published and put together in bound volumes. There

are various branches and agencies for which the government often issues a compilation of the myriad laws and governances pertaining to its work. Examples include the Internal Revenue Service Code and the Fire Codes for a municipality.

5. Reports. Periodic reports are commonplace for almost all government organizations, including the annual report by the President of the United States, *The State of the Union Address*. These are published in a format varying from the local newspaper reports to bound volumes of the state and federal government reports.

6. Special Investigation, Funding, and Research. These include special problems, research projects, and commissioned studies for, or by, the governments themselves. They may be exhaustive and detailed; for example, dealing with resource availability by the year 2000 and beyond; or they may deal with the findings of an appointed commission investigating a criminal matter.

7. Promotional and Public Relations Publications. These promote points of interest, such as travel guides to the various states. They may inform consumers about topics ranging from the dangers of smoking to better hog pasturing. These are easily found and are dispensed by Chambers of Commerce and other groups. They may vary in publication format, from mimeographed sheets and pamphlets to books with elaborate color illustrated diagrams and pictures.

8. Statistics. Various publications are periodically produced at the local, regional, and national levels, providing access to statistical information. These vary in application and importance, and they contain a great deal of information on trends, analysis, facts, figures, and statistics. The *Statistical Yearbook of the United States* is an example of such a publication.

Note: For additional help in locating government documents, see Figures 3-6 and 3-7.

INDEXES

An index, such as the one found at the end of a book, is an alphabetical list that includes all or nearly all items (topics, names, places, issues) considered relevant, fully or partially covered in the written or printed work. Various indexes are the key to the storehouse of information on an array of subjects including the subject that has been selected for study by the researcher. Comprehensive and constantly revised indexes not only contain detailed information about author and subject, but provide bibliographies that will guide one to other sources on the same topic in a library. Some indexes may be consulted for content; others constitute an excellent source for bibliographies, such as the *Bibliographic Indexes*. There are many specialized and general-purpose indexes for various disciplines covering a vast array of topics. The importance of these books as sources of information cannot be overemphasized. There are three types of indexes: indexes to materials in periodicals, indexes to newspapers, and indexes to literature.

Periodical Indexes

The literature contained in journals is indexed regularly, sometimes within two weeks of publication. Books containing these indexes are called Periodical or

Figure 3-6

GOVERNMENT DOCUMENTS

Government documents are any publications printed at government expense and or by government authority. These publications come from local, state, and federal governments and consist of pamphlets, books, statistics, laws, court cases, magazines, bibliographies, indexes, maps and Congressional hearings.

Government documents are arranged by their own classification system and are generally located in a separate section of the library.

HOW TO FIND GOVERNMENT DOCUMENTS

A.   Pick subject and subheadings.
B.   Look up in index or bibliography.
C.   If unable to find subject, try subheadings.
D.   Copy title and call number.
E.   Find document in documents area or in microfiche area.
F.   Ask for assistance from a librarian as needed in this process.

EXAMPLE OF A CITATION INDICATING A GOVERNMENT DOCUMENT

```
1 ──────→   CHILD ABUSE
2 ──────→      LAW AND LEGISLATION
3 ──────→    Child abuse and day care:-joint hearing        ←──── 6
            before the subcommittee on Oversight of the
            Committee on Ways and Means, and Select         ←──── 7
            Committee on Children, Youth, and Families,
            House of Representatives, Ninety-eighth
            Congress, second session, September 17, 1984    ←──── 8
            Washington:-U.S. G.P.O.,:-1985                  ←──── 9
            Distributed to some depository libraries in
            Microfiche.; "Serial 98-109." Item 1028-a,12-b
4 ──────→   (microfiche) MC # 85 85-22359                   ←──── 10
5 ──────→   Su Doc # Y 4.W 36:98-109
```

1.   Main heading
2.   Subheading
3.   Title of the document
4.   Library will have on microfilm
5.   Call number (Superintendent of Documents)
6.   Document is a Congressional Hearing
7.   Name of committee
8.   Number of Congress and session/Date of hearing
9.   Date hearing was published
10.   Monthly Catalogue entry number

Note: For further assistance in locating government documents, refer to Illustrations 4.

Figure 3-7

HOW TO LOOK UP GOVERNMENT DOCUMENTS USING
GOVERNMENT DOCUMENTS SUBJECT HEADING (GDSH)

1. Find <u>Government Documents Subject Bibliographies (GDSB)</u> located at index tables. Find index in the back of GDSH catalogue 300-599. Look up topic.
   Example: Business and Business Management 4. Number 4 is the appropriate subject number.

2. Look up topic in correct catalogue.
   Example: Look up subject Number 4 in GDSB catalogue 1-100's.

3. Find subject number.

4. Find specific document related to your topic.

5. Look up call number in Government Documents section of library.

   Example: C61.2:T22

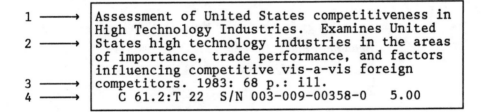

```
1 ──→ │ Assessment of United States competitiveness in
      │ High Technology Industries.  Examines United
2 ──→ │ States high technology industries in the areas
      │ of importance, trade performance, and factors
      │ influencing competitive vis-a-vis foreign
3 ──→ │ competitors. 1983: 68 p.: ill.
4 ──→ │   C 61.2:T 22  S/N 003-009-00358-0    5.00
```

1. Title of the document
2. Annotation.
3. Date of publication, pages and illustrated.
4. Call number (SuDoc), Stock number (needed only for purchase), purchase price.

General Indexes. Many general and specialized indexes are available including: the *Art Index, Book Review Index, Catholic Periodical Index, Education Index, Humanities Index*, and the *Social Sciences Index*. Through practice, one will learn which periodical index will be the best for certain research.

Some periodical indexes cover only a specialized area, such as art, business, education, or science. In general, there are two types of periodicals covered; the first being the popular periodicals written for the general public. Examples of these periodicals include: *Reader's Digest, Time, Hot Rod, Newsweek*, and *Sports Illustrated*. These give superficial treatment to the subject material and should be consulted whenever one wants a quick overview of the subject. Popular periodicals generally include photographs and advertisements and are published regularly and distributed weekly or monthly. Such periodicals are commonly found in doctors' offices, in private homes, and on newsstands. The following are three important indexes that give extensive coverage to popular magazines:

Access. Syracuse, Evanston, IL: J.E. Burke Publishing Company, 1975 to date, 3/yr.

Popular Periodical Index. Camden, NJ: Rutgers University, Camden Library, 1973-date, semiannual.

Readers' Guide to Periodical Literature. New York: H.W. Wilson, 1980-date, annually.

The second type of periodical is authoritative, professional, or academic, often called *journals*. Their content includes essays, reviews, and research findings. The information contained in these journals is written by scholars and experts in their fields. Examples of these include: *Political Science Quarterly, American Economic Review*, and *Journal of Marketing Research*. These are technical journals that specialize in certain disciplines. In contrast to popular journals, professional journals are not widely read, because most of the included information is academic in nature. In these journals, authors are identified, and pictures and advertisements are excluded. The articles are specialized, technical, and relatively long, with footnotes and bibliographies. They are, in general, published less often than are the popular periodicals. Important indexes include the following:

British Humanities Index. London: Library Association, 1963 to date, quarterly.

General Science Index. New York: H.W. Wilson, 1978-date.

Humanities Index. New York: H.W. Wilson, 1974-date, quarterly.

International Index. New York: H.W. Wilson, 1907-1965.

Social Sciences Index. New York: H.W. Wilson, 1974-date, quarterly.

The basic arrangement of materials in most indexes is similar. It is important to become familiar with the key, guide, and explanatory sample page of an index. These are usually given at the beginning of the various indexes. The *Readers' Guide to Periodical Literature*, frequently called *Readers' Guide*, is a very useful index. This enormous index is second only to the library's card catalog in popularity among library patrons. This cumulative index covers over 200 popular magazines of general interest. Its broad coverage of the social sciences includes business, economics, history, political science, and sociology. It also includes reviews of books, films, television shows, and other arts. The *Readers' Guide* is published bimonthly except for the months of July and August, when it is published monthly. Comprehensive issues are bound yearly and every two years, and are called *The Cumulative Index*. It is worthwhile to know about the inclusion of particular journals in the index. It is also beneficial to become familiar with the system of indexing and the arrangement of the included material in the *Readers' Guide*. The arrangement of materials in many scholarly indexes is alike; as a result, one could learn the indexing methods used by similar volumes.

To assist the reader, introductory guides and illustrations are included in the front of each issue. These guides familiarize the reader with the arrangement of information and the efficient use of the index. Whenever an index is consulted, review the included explanatory material that explains its uses, organization, abbreviations, and symbols.

The *Readers' Guide* arranges its material similarly to the card catalog. The material is classified alphabetically by author's name, by subject, and by title.

The most common practice is to list covered information by subject and title. One reason for this arrangement of entries by subject rather than by author is that many popular magazine articles do not have by-lines. In the index under the broad subject heading, important related subheadings are listed as well. Additional details are given about the authors, page numbers, inclusion of bibliographies, and date of publication. The subdivision headings are helpful when one is looking for an interesting topic for a research paper. In the example below, observe the listing details of additional subdivisions under the broad subject of "Management."

MANAGEMENT	MANAGEMENT
Management - Design	Management - Classical School
Management - Styles	Management - Behavioral School
Management - History	Management - Systems School
Management - Organization	Management - Contingency School
Management - Hierarchy	

The *Readers' Guide*, in addition to the listing of articles by author, subject matter, and subject subdivision, uses cross references ("see also" and "see" references). An example of a complete entry is presented below:

1. Title of the article
2. Author (if known)
3. Name of the magazine
4. Volume number of the magazine
5. The page numbers where the article appears
6. The date of publication

Typical introductory pages from the *Readers' Guide* are presented in Figures 3-8, 3-9, and 3-10. Figure 3-8 presents a key to abbreviations; Figure 3-9 presents a key to periodicals indexed; and Figure 3-10 presents a typical page explaining the notations of an entry. In addition, a list of noted indexes appears at the end of this chapter.

The *Guide to Reference Books* lists all kinds of reference books, whether they are published in the United States or in foreign countries, including encyclopedias, dictionaries, concordances, and indexes. This comprehensive guide lists subjects such as humanities, history, social sciences, and others together within a discipline. Some important and widely used indexes to various periodical literature are listed below.

ART
Art Index. New York: H.W. Wilson, 1929-date.
BUSINESS
Business Index. Menlo Park, CA: Information Access Corp., 1979-date.
Business Periodicals Index. New York: H.W. Wilson, 1958-date.
Consumer Index. Ann Arbor, MI: Puritan Press, 1973-date.

Figure 3-8

Key to Abbreviations

+	continued on later pages of same issue	Ltd	Limited
Ag	August	m	Monthly
ann	annual	Mr	March
Ap	April	My	May
Assn	Association		
Aut	Autumn	N	November
Ave	Avenue	no	number
bi-m	bimonthly	O	October
bi-w	biweekly		
bibl	bibliography	p	page
biblf	bibliographic footnotes	por	portrait
bldg	building	pt	part
Co	Company	q	quarterly
cont	continued		
Corp	Corporation	rev	revised
D	December	S	September
Dept	Department	semi-m	semimonthly
		Spr	Spring
ed	edited, edition, editor	Sr	Senior
		St	Street
F	February	Summ	Summer
f	footnotes	supp	supplement
il	illustration,-s	tr	translated, translator
inc	Incorporated		
introd	introduction	V	Volume
Ja	January	W	Weekly
Je	June	Wint	Winter
J1	July		
Jr	Junior	yr	year
jt	Joint author		

Source: *Readers' Guide to Periodical Literature*, Oct. 10, 1990, vol. 90, no. 11.

BIOGRAPHY

Biography Index. New York: H.W. Wilson, 1947-date.

Biography and Genealogy Master Index. Detroit: Miranda C. Hebert and Barbara McNeil, 1990.

BOOKS

Cumulative Book Index. New York: H.W. Wilson, 1900-date.

General Catalogue of Printed Books. London: Trustees of British Museum, 1881-date.

The National Union Catalogue: A Cumulative Author List. Ann Arbor, MI: Edwards, 1953-date.

Figure 3-9

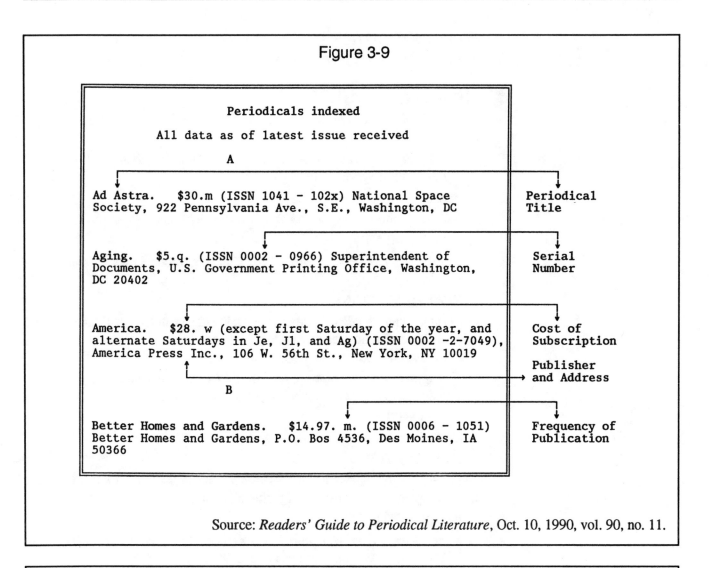

Periodicals indexed

All data as of latest issue received

A

Ad Astra. $30.m (ISSN 1041 - 102x) National Space Society, 922 Pennsylvania Ave., S.E., Washington, DC — Periodical Title

Aging. $5.q. (ISSN 0002 - 0966) Superintendent of Documents, U.S. Government Printing Office, Washington, DC 20402 — Serial Number

America. $28. w (except first Saturday of the year, and alternate Saturdays in Je, Jl, and Ag) (ISSN 0002 -2-7049), America Press Inc., 106 W. 56th St., New York, NY 10019 — Cost of Subscription / Publisher and Address

B

Better Homes and Gardens. $14.97. m. (ISSN 0006 - 1051) Better Homes and Gardens, P.O. Bos 4536, Des Moines, IA 50366 — Frequency of Publication

Source: *Readers' Guide to Periodical Literature*, Oct. 10, 1990, vol. 90, no. 11.

Figure 3-10

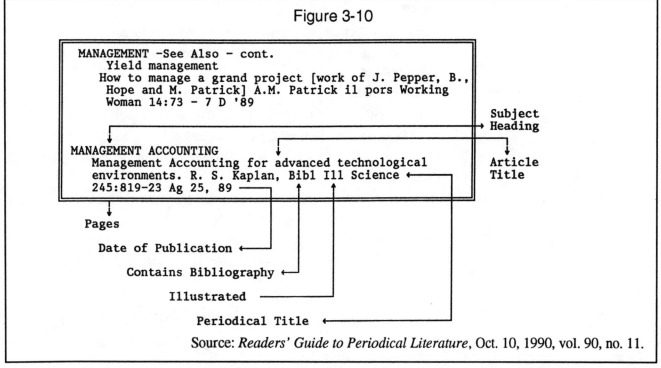

MANAGEMENT –See Also – cont.
  Yield management
  How to manage a grand project [work of J. Pepper, B., Hope and M. Patrick] A.M. Patrick il pors Working Woman 14:73 - 7 D '89

MANAGEMENT ACCOUNTING
  Management Accounting for advanced technological environments. R. S. Kaplan, Bibl Ill Science 245:819-23 Ag 25, 89

Subject Heading
Article Title
Pages
Date of Publication
Contains Bibliography
Illustrated
Periodical Title

Source: *Readers' Guide to Periodical Literature*, Oct. 10, 1990, vol. 90, no. 11.

CRIMINAL JUSTICE

Criminal Justice Periodical Index. Ann Arbor, MI: Indexing Services, 1990-date.

CURRENT TOPICS

Alternative Press Index. College Park, MD: Alternative Press Center, 1969-date.

Public Affairs Information Service (PAIS) Bulletin. New York: Public Affairs Information Services, 1915-date.

EDUCATION

Education Index. New York: H.W. Wilson, 1929-date.

GOVERNMENT

Index to U.S. Government Periodicals. Chicago: Infodata International, 1972-date.

HEALTH/MEDICINE

Abridged Index Medicus. Bethesda, MD: U.S. Dept. of Health, Education, and Welfare, Public Health Service, National Institute of Health, National Library of Medicine, 1970-date.

Cumulative Index to Nursing and Allied Health Literature. Glendale, CA: Adventist Hospital Association, 1977-date.

HUMANITIES

Humanities Index. New York: H.W. Wilson, 1074-date.

ILLUSTRATIONS

Illustration Index. Metuchen, NJ: Scarecrow Press, Inc., 1980. (This is a compilation of thousands of pictures of various subjects and objects.)

INTERNATIONAL

Social Sciences and Humanities Index (formerly *International Index*). New York: H.W. Wilson. Various issues, 1965.

MUSIC

Music Index. Detroit: Information Coordinators, 1949-date.

Sears, Minnie E., and Phyllis Crawford. *Song Index.* Reprint of 1926 ed. Reprint Services, 1990.

LITERATURE

Book Review Digest. New York: H.W. Wilson, 1905-date.

Book Review Index. Detroit: Gale Research Co., 1965-83.

Short Story Index. New York: H.W. Wilson, 1900-84, periodic supplements.

PAMPHLETS

Vertical File Index: A Subject and Title Index to Selected Pamphlet Material. New York: H.W. Wilson, 1932-date.

PHYSICAL EDUCATION/SPORTS

Physical Fitness/Sports Medicine. Washington: President's Council on Physical Fitness and Sports, 1978-date.

RELIGION

Catholic Periodical Index. Chicago: Religion Indexes Association, 1939-date.

Religion Index One: Periodicals. Chicago: American Theological Library Association, 1952-date.

SCIENCES

Applied Science and Technology Index (formerly *Industrial Arts Index*). New York: H.W. Wilson, 1913-date.

Biological Index. Biological Abstracts. Philadelphia: Bio Sciences Information Service, 1926-date.

General Science Index. New York: H.W. Wilson, 1978-date.

SOCIAL SCIENCES

Social Science and Humanities Index. New York: H.W. Wilson, various issues.

Social Science Index. New York: H.W. Wilson, 1974-date.

Newspaper Indexes Newspaper indexes are second in use to periodical indexes in the library. There are no comprehensive indexes covering all newspapers such as those for periodicals. However, an index of one newspaper, such as *The New York Times*, provides clues to coverage in other papers on events and happenings during a particular period. For localized research, one should look for information in local newspapers. Most local libraries maintain a vertical file for area newspapers, containing select articles, illustrations, statistics, and photographs on events pertinent to the community. The material is clipped, classified, and arranged by subject in special folders. The following represents a select list of important indexes:

Atlanta Journal/Atlanta Constitution Index. Ann Arbor, MI: 1982-date.

Chicago Tribune Index. New York: New York Times Co., 1972-date.

Facts on File. "Weekly World News Digest with Cumulative Index." New York: Facts on File, Inc., 1940-date.

Index to Times. London: London Times, 1907-date.

National Newspaper Index. Los Altos, CA: Information Access Co., 1979-date.

The New York Times Index. New York: New York Times Co., 1913-date.

Newsbank Index. New Canton, CT: Newsbank, Inc., 1982-date.

The Newspaper Index. Wooster, OH: Bell and Howell, 1979-date.

Newspapers on Microfilm. Washington: Library of Congress, 1967-date. (A comprehensive listing of thousands of newspapers.)

Wall Street Journal Index. New York: Dow Jones and Co., annually.

To use newspaper indexes, it is important to select the appropriate one, such as the index for *The Wall Street Journal, The Washington Post, The New York Times, USA Today,* or any other relevant newspaper. If the topic is covered by the newspaper, it will be found in its index. The index will provide information about the topic, the page number, and the date of publication. Libraries keep most newspapers for at least two weeks before they are reproduced on microfilm. For broad coverage, the *National Newspaper Index* is kept on microfilm by many libraries.

Whenever a search involves a broad topic, computerized systems, if available, are practical to use. Computers can search among thousands of stories and other items to locate precise information in a matter of minutes. Traditional methods require hours of searching in a library.

Indexes to Literature in Collections

Whenever a specific poem, play, speech, quotation, or selection from an essay or other source is called for, it is practical to look in specialized indexes. A variety of indexes covering certain fields is published. The comprehensive *Essay and General Literature Index* is noted for its detailed coverage of materials in humanities and social sciences. Included entries cover arts, economics, education, history, religion, law, linguistics, literature, and political science. This index is regularly revised, including periodic comprehensive editions. The included entries are indexed by author and subject to essays published in collections. It covers articles, essays, speeches, and a variety of other subjects published in books. Each index includes directions for its use. The following are examples of some of these indexes:

Biography Index. New York: H.W. Wilson, 1947-date.

Essay and General Literature Index. Ed. John Greenfieldt. New York: H.W. Wilson, 1990.

Granger, Edith. *Granger's Index to Poetry*, 8th ed. New York: Columbia University Press, 1986.

Illustration Index. Metuchen, NJ: Scarecrow Press, Inc., 1980. (This is a compilation of thousands of pictures on various subjects and objects.)

Play Index. New York: H.W. Wilson, 1949-date.

Sears, Minnie E., and Phyllis Crawford. *Song Index*. Reprint of 1926 ed. Reprint Services, 1990. (An index to more than 12,000 songs in 177 song collections comprising 262 volumes.)

Short Story Index. New York: H.W. Wilson, 1979.

Sutton, Roberta Briggs. *Speech Index*, 4th ed. Metuchen, NJ: Scarecrow Press, Inc., 1966-80. (An index to various collections of speeches and orations.)

BIBLIOGRAPHIES

Historically, the term *bibliography* meant writing other books. A bibliographer was a person who "copied books." Today, the word *bibliography* has many meanings, such as a list of works by a certain author and a listing of literature on a certain subject. A bibliography provides a description and history of books, including details such as dates published, authors, and other literature that may be relevant to a desired topic.

Bibliographic books vary in such features as depth, material coverage, content, and description. While some are short lists, others are lengthy and may contain thousands of entries on a single subject. There are comprehensive bibliographies that cover many disciplines, subjects, authors, time periods, and geographic areas. Others may be restricted to content, author, publisher, subject form, location, and time period. Bibliographies include description, annotated material, and other information on the included subject. The information within a bibliography may be arranged by author, subject, title, edition, or imprint, or in chronological order by the date published. Some bibliographies may list books, periodicals, and unpublished material in different sections.

Bibliographies are valuable for their brief factual information. Facts about authors, subject titles, publishers, dates of publication, prices, and descriptions of the content of the cited material found in them are useful. Bibliographies also cite for the reader parts of a book that may not be indexed in the card catalog. Some bibliographies such as *Books in Print, Cumulative Book Index, Paper-*

bound Books in Print, and *Subject Books in Print* are good sources for locating publications that are not listed in the card catalog or in other bibliographies. These publications also inform one of whether a desired book is currently available for purchase through publishers.

Through experience and familiarity with one's field of interest, the researcher will become knowledgeable about the use and benefits of these helpful reference sources. In the card catalog, these books are listed below the subject's subdivision "Bibliography." For example, United States - History - Bibliography; Art - Bibliography; Mathematics - Bibliography. Published bibliographies exist for most disciplines and subject areas. The following are three well-known classifications of bibliographical materials: General Bibliographies, Periodical Bibliographies, and Trade Bibliographies.

General Bibliographies

General bibliographies, published by book sellers and libraries, are good sources for locating books that are not listed in the card catalog or other bibliographies. General bibliographies are comprehensive in their coverage of authors, subject areas, geographical regions, and periods of time. Some well-known national, international, and specialized general bibliographies include:

Besterman, Theodore. *A World Bibliography of Bibliographies and of Bibliographical Catalogues, Calendars, Abstracts, Digests, Indexes, and the like.* 5 vols. 4th ed. Geneva, Switzerland: Societas Bibliographica, 1966.

The Bibliographic Index. New York: H.W. Wilson, 1938-date.

Books in Series. Ed. Gertrude Jennings. 3rd ed. New York: R.R. Bowker Company, 1988.

Public Library Catalog. 8th ed. New York: H.W. Wilson, 1979.

Sheehy, Eugene P. *Guide to Reference Books.* 9th ed. Chicago: American Library Association, 1986.

Wynar, Christine G. *Guide to Reference Books for School Media Centers.* 2nd ed. Littleton, CO: Libraries Unlimited, 1986.

Periodical Bibliographies

Periodical bibliographies provide descriptions and critical annotations, as well as information about content, frequency of publication, names of publishers, and other important material about published newspapers and periodicals. Some are very helpful in selecting periodicals for a library, while others are beneficial in providing information on selected topics. Examples of periodical bibliographies include:

Ayer Directory of Publications. Bala Cynwyd, PA: Ayer Press, 1969-date.

Classified List of Periodicals for the College Library. 5th ed. Boston: The F.W. Faxon Company, 1948.

The Standard Periodical Directory. Ed. Matthew Manning. New York: Oxbridge Communications, Inc., 1988.

Ulrich's International Periodicals Directory. 26th ed. New York: R.R. Bowker Company, 1987-88.

Union List of Serials in Libraries of the United States and Canada. 3rd ed. New York: H.W. Wilson, 1987.

Trade Bibliographies

A variety of trade bibliographies furnishes information on the availability of books for sale, locating publishers for a manuscript, and maintaining professional relations with publishers and editors. People, institutions, and libraries use some of these guide books to make purchases; others are consulted for technical preparation of manuscripts for printing. Publishers, book sellers, and prospective authors scan these guides for information on titles, prices, and availability of similar books. Examples of these trade and publishing guides include *The Reader's Catalog*, which lists over 40,000 books for sale in over 200 categories with brief discussions of most entries. *Writer's Market: Where & How to Sell What You Write* offers an efficient method of locating and evaluating prospective publishers by cataloging 4,000 places for the selling and publishing of manuscripts on virtually any topic. The *Prentice-Hall Author's Guide* is a welcome small volume for any beginner. It offers not only a collection of friendly tips for aspiring authors concerning relations with publishers, but also provides detailed technical aspects on the development of a manuscript from submission to printing. Authors desiring the evaluation of appropriate journals for submission of articles in business will find *Cabell's Directory of Publishing Opportunities in Business and Economics* an important source. Additional noted books include:

American Book Publishing Record. New York: R.R. Bowker Company, yearly.

Books in Print. New York: R.R. Bowker, yearly.

Cumulative Books Index. New York: H.W. Wilson, 1928-date.

Forthcoming Books. New York: R.R. Bowker Company, 1960-date.

Gale Directory of Publications: An Annual Guide to Newspapers, Magazines, Journals, and Related Publications. Detroit: Gale, 1869-date.

Paperbound Books in Print. New York: R.R. Bowker Company, 1971-date.

Publisher's Trade List Annual. New York: R.R. Bowker Company, 1957-date.

Subject Guide to Books in Print. New York: R.R. Bowker Company, 1957-date.

Ulrich's International Periodicals Directory. New York: R.R. Bowker, 1932-present.

Weekly Record. New York: R.R. Bowker Company, 1974-.

International Business and Economics Sources

Increasingly, reliable information on international business, economics, social conditions, science, and technology is needed. This situation calls for familiarity with sources that regularly list materials covering international subjects. For general background information on a nation, the *Area Handbook* is a good starting point. Then, in order to pinpoint the area of business, *Overseas Business Reports* supplies both current and historical business information on international topics. Computer databases under the listing *General Business File* are another good source offering a great deal of relevant information. Many governments, including the United States, and international organizations such as the United Nations publish materials that include this information. The following list provides some important sources:

Dun & Bradstreet's Principal International Businesses. New York: Dun & Bradstreet.

Europa Year Book: A World Survey. Detroit: Gale, annual.

Overseas Business Reports. Washington: Government Printing Office.

Ulrich's International Periodicals Directory. New York: R.R. Bowker, annual.

United Nations Yearbook of International Trade Statistics. New York: International Publications Service.

CONCORDANCES

The concordance is a specialized book resembling a dictionary, in that it is a cumulative index of the important words in a book as they occur in context. A good example is the *Concordance of the Bible*, which details hymns, passages, dates, names, and places. If one wanted to locate the unknown author of a quotation, a poem, or a specific quotation, the concordance would be an appropriate first choice. Many well-known authors of the 19th century, such as Emerson and Poe, are represented by concordances. Examples of some concordances are:

Cruden's Unabridged Concordance. Alexander Cruden. Westwood, NJ: F.H. Revell, 1953.

Holy Bible Concordance. C.I. Scofield, ed. New York: Oxford University Press, 1989.

Judson Concordance to Hymns. Thomas B. McDormand and Frederic S. Crossman. Valley Forge: The Judson Press, 1965.

A New and Complete Concordance of the Dramatic Works of Shakespeare. John Bartlett. London: St. Martin's Press, 1989.

Tatlock, John, and Arthur Kennedy. *Concordance to the Complete Works of Geoffrey Chaucer.* Washington: The Carnegie Institution of Washington, 1927.

DIRECTORIES

A directory is a classified list that serves as a guide to names, addresses, telephone numbers, rules, organizations, sources, products, and places. When one is looking for a dentist's address or a friend's telephone number, one looks it up in a telephone directory. Accordingly, when one is searching for a prominent person's place of residence, a current issue of *Who's Who in America* is consulted. Specialized directories exist for various purposes, such as the *School Supply and Equipment Directory*. Product, service, industry, profession, government, business, and miscellaneous directories are published periodically. A directory of directories, the *Guide to American Directories*, exists, which has over 6,000 listings for such books. Examples of some directories include:

Directory of American Scholars. 8th ed. Ed. Jacques Catell Press. New York: R.R. Bowker Company, 1982.

Directory of Japanese Companies in the U.S.A. Hideaki Miyake, ed. New York: Economic Salon, 1978.

Hoffberg, J.A., and S.W. Hess. *Directory of Art Libraries and Visual Collections.* New York: Neal-Schuman Publishers, Inc., 1978.

1988 Summer Employment Directory of the United States. Ed. Pat Beusterien. Cincinnati: F. and W. Publications, 1987.

The Standard Periodical Directory. 9th ed. Ed. Margie Domenech. New York: Oxbridge Communications Inc., 1985.

White, Jack, et al. *The Angry Buyers' Complaint Directory.* New York: Peter H. Wyden, 1974.

UNION CARD CATALOG

The Library of Congress publishes printed author cards with periodic supplements in the form of a book. These books include cards supplied by other libraries in the United States and Canada that represent the combined holdings of many libraries. The Library of Congress maintains a *National Union (Card) Catalog*, generally called NUC. There exists a pre-1956 NUC catalog and another NUC catalog from 1956 to the present. In 1968, the Mansell Publishing Company published the *National Union Catalog: Pre-1956 Imprints* bibliography. This catalog includes all cards of the Library of Congress and other libraries supplied from 1898 to 1956. The following are the three most important union catalogs:

Library of Congress Catalogs: National Union Catalog. Washington: Library of Congress, 1973.

Library of Congress Catalogs: Subject Catalog 1950-1973. Washington: Library of Congress, 1955-73.

The National Union Catalog: Pre-1956 Imprints. London: Mansell Publishing, Limited, 1968-81.

GOVERNMENT REFERENCE RESOURCES

The U.S. government is a major publisher of books, reports, and pamphlets. Listed below are some important bibliographies and sources of reference material for government documents.

American Statistics Index. Washington: Congressional Information Service, 1973-date.

Index to Publications of the United States Congress. Washington: Congressional Information Service, 1970.

Leidy, W. Philip. *A Popular Guide to Government Publications.* 4th ed. New York: Columbia University Press, 1978.

Morehead, Joe. *Introduction to United States Public Documents.* 2nd ed. Littleton, CO: Libraries Unlimited, 1983.

Palic, Vladimir M. *Government Publications: A Guide to Bibliographic Tools.* 4th ed. Washington: Library of Congress, 1976.

Popular Names of the U.S. Government Reports: A Catalog. 3rd ed. Washington: Library of Congress, 1976.

Schmeckebier, Laurence F. and Roy B. Eastin. *Government Publications and Their Use.* 2nd rev. ed. Washington: The Brookings Institute, 1969.

U.S. Library of Congress. *Monthly Checklist of State Publications.* Washington: Government Printing Office, 1910-date.

U.S. Superintendent of Documents. *Monthly Catalog of the United States Government Publications.* Washington: Government Printing Office, 1895-date.

U.S. Superintendent of Documents. *Selected U.S. Government Publications.* Washington: Government Printing Office, 1928-date.

Computers in Library Research

4

INTRODUCTION

The introduction of computer-based technology has proven a major advancement in library research and reference work. The past ten years have seen significant developments in the application of computers in many aspects of library operations. Computers have opened doors to fundamental changes in the way we access, analyze, and communicate information. They provide an alternate mode that affects all aspects of modern life and is more efficient for scholarly research and communication. The scope and impact of computers have yet to be fully realized. Computers have placed massive amounts of information at everyone's fingertips through the availability of databanks on thousands of topics.

The capability for high speed searches makes computers more efficient and time-saving than traditional methods of library research. Library computer systems locate and present desired information quickly and accurately. As sophisticated tools, computers reduce the amount of time spent on mundane details, allowing more time for creativity and concentration on research. Computers also eliminate going back and forth among indexes, periodicals, and card catalogs. Traditional indexing and information retrieval systems are marked by time lags between dates of publication and indexing for public use. Time saved, combined with accuracy and the ability to navigate through the vast quantity of library materials, has made computerized systems popular. Future technological progress and falling prices will make the systems more desirable. Once users become familiar with their ease of operation, library computer systems are likely to attain even more widespread use.

Computers have become popular for storing, retrieving, and manipulating information. Some computers can search or execute more than fifty million instructions per second. This speed and precision has made them ideal instruments for quickly locating and retrieving needed research materials. Computers are useful for other library practices. At checkout desks, computers quickly read bar codes, expedite checkouts, and assign due dates based on the library's policies and borrowers' requests. Computers provide a statistical paper trail, notify users of overdue books, and show the availability of returned books. While technology in the development and use of computers is rapidly changing, systems in use have already significantly enhanced information retrieval. The two widely used functions of computers in library use are: online bibliographic searches and access to various information databases.

The uses of computers in writing include creating, revising, storing, and presenting documents. A computer is more efficient than a typewriter in text layout, spelling, and word-checking abilities. Their layout features include setting margins, tabs, and spacing, centering, underlining, and boldfacing, all of which enhance the appearance of the text. Computers make writing easier by saving time spent on revisions, additions, typing, editing, and proofreading.

Any writer will find time spent learning how to operate a computer well worth the effort.

COMPONENTS OF THE COMPUTER

Computers are electronic devices that work according to the commands programmed into them. The user manipulates these commands with external instructions directing the computer to execute various desired tasks. Operations are performed speedily, with accuracy, precision, and reliability. These characteristics make them ideal instruments for many uses, including storing, retrieving, and manipulating information. Essentially, all computers perform the following four operations:

1. *Input operations*, in which the user places data into the computer for processing.

2. *Arithmetic and logic operations* for processing mathematics and comparison of values with others, where they are less, equal to, or greater than a specific value.

3. *Storage operations*, in which information and data are stored for future retrieval and processing.

4. *Output operations*, which avail processed information to the user as desired.

In order to carry out the above operations productively, several internal and external components are needed. The quality and sophistication of these components depend on how and for what purpose the computer is used. All personal computers must have at least the following components to perform for their users: (1) The central processing unit, which contains the complex electronic circuits called the microprocessor. This unit performs the logic and arithmetic processing tasks and coordinates the input and output of operations. (2) Input devices enter data into the computer's main memory; examples include the keyboard, the mouse, and the modem. (3) Output devices provide processed information to the user in a desired, understandable manner. Examples of these include the computer screen (monitor) and the printer. (4) Special instructions developed for specific application, such as word processing, make up the software programs. (5) Auxiliary storage devices include the floppy disks, hard disks, and tapes, used for storing information separately or within the computer.

The System Unit

The system inside a computer includes the central processing unit, various electronic circuits, wiring, the memory, and various boards. The central processing unit (CPU) is the mind of the computer. This is where all the analytical, computational, and logical operations are performed. The CPU controls all applications of the computer based on the permanent instructions that are encoded into it at the time of manufacture. The CPU is a complex integrated circuit composed of thousands of transistors on a single chip called a *microprocessor*. The versions of this microprocessor, from oldest to most recent, are 8088, 286, 386, and 486.

In 1981, IBM introduced a PC that was built around the revolutionary 8088 processor. This 8088 microprocessor was used in most popular IBM XT personal computers. In 1984 advanced personal computers, designated as the AT class, were introduced. They contained the newer 80286 microprocessors. The innovative 80286 chip was a 16 bit processor. The bit is the unit for storing data; the smallest unit of data that a computer works with. A bit cannot store a number, letter, or character such as the $ sign. When groups of bits are put together in different order, they can be designated to represent letters, numbers, or characters. Eight bits arranged for this purpose are called a *byte*. A byte is the amount of memory space needed to store a single number, letter, or character. A computer's storage ability is measured in thousands of bytes.

The AT class of computers was adequate for storing information, writing long documents, and performing detailed tasks at home and in the office. The advent of the 80386, 32 bit processor made newer generation computers versatile, speedier, and able to run advanced programs and applications. The arrival of the newer powerful 486 class computers are perhaps a luxury for most personal applications at home. The 386 is a computer of choice in terms of value and use for most people. The newer generation units can perform essentially the same tasks as larger expensive computers referred to as minicomputers or mainframes, except they have smaller storage capacity. They are also smaller in physical size and much less costly. A computer's speed is measured in megahertz (Mhz), which is the frequency with which the microprocessor gathers and distributes data. These speeds range from 4 to 50 Mhz. Typical speeds for 386 personal computers are 16, 20, 25, and 33 Mhz. As computers advance, these speeds will increase.

Memory. There are two types of memory in the computer, ROM and RAM. ROM stands for "read only memory" and contains the computer's permanent instructions built into the circuitry when it is manufactured. ROM contains the guides that direct the computer to start operations, check internal components, and load the DOS (disk operating system) into RAM (random access memory). Other commands built into the memory include instructions for performing mathematical and logical operations. Instructions can be called upon from ROM, but no data can be entered or stored into ROM by the user. The phrase "read only" notifies the user that the information cannot be changed, erased, or supplemented.

The random access memory (RAM) represents the computer's volatile memory capacity, where current information is stored or retrieved from other sources, such as the hard disk. It is the total work area of the computer at the time of use, where information is temporarily stored until the user decides what to do with it. If electricity is interrupted for any length of time, this volatile memory is erased. RAM represents memory available to the user. One can enter, store, erase, or change information in RAM. The total RAM capacity of a computer limits which software programs can run on it. If a user purchased a program requiring 3 Mb (megabytes) of memory, the computer must have this much RAM to hold all this information available and current in its memory while performing operations.

The RAM capacity of a computer is measured in megabytes. A typical personal computer with 1 Mb can store about 1,024,000 bytes of data. A byte represents one character: a number, letter, or symbol. A kilobyte is equal to 1,024 bytes. A typed page of text uses approximately 2,000 kilobytes (2k) of storage. Popular capacities of RAM in personal computers are 1 Mb, 2 Mb, and 4 Mb.

Software programs may require a certain amount of memory, such as 1 Mb of RAM, to be able to operate. For example, the popular Microsoft Windows 3.0 program needs at least 2 Mb RAM to run satisfactorily. One who wishes to buy a computer or software should be aware of this critical limitation before making a purchase.

Permanent Storage. It is necessary to have sufficient RAM and permanent memory to perform the desired computer operations. Most software packages specify how much RAM is needed for operation. RAM holds information temporarily for as long as electricity is available. Information that is being worked on, such as drafted letters and other created files, needs to be saved for future use. This calls for transferring this information from RAM to a permanent storage device. There are two popular devices for this purpose: the floppy disk and the hard disk.

A floppy disk is somewhat similar to a reusable phonograph record and will quickly become an important part of a computer user's life. The disk has become a popular computer storage medium because of its convenience, flexibility, reusability, and cost. One can easily remove a floppy disk from the system to work on at home or elsewhere if another computer is available. At least one floppy disk drive is needed on any computer to load programs from it to the hard disk and vice versa. Floppy disks are commonly available in 5.25-inch and 3.5-inch sizes. Since one size can only fit in its corresponding disk drive, it is worthwhile to have a computer with both size drives. A single disk can store up to 1.44 or 1.2 bytes, or more than 360 pages of typed text.

A hard disk, or fixed disk (also called a hard drive), is another storage device that is normally installed within the computer. It can store thousands of times more information than a floppy disk can. Without a hard disk, programs have to be reloaded constantly, making the system exceedingly cumbersome and time consuming. Most current popular programs will not work without hard disks. Also, without a hard disk, floppy disks are more likely to be damaged and misplaced due to constant use. Any serious user should not consider purchasing a computer without an internal (hard) disk. The storage capacity of hard disks is measured in megabytes. A book of over 500 pages and a popular word-processing program may require ten megabytes of storage. The total storage capacity of hard disks can be used up very quickly. Although a 20 Mb hard disk is adequate for most users, it is preferable to purchase at least one 40 Mb hard disk, which has the capacity to hold over 20,000 pages. Another advantage of hard disks is their speed of locating information quickly, measured in milliseconds. Speeds of over 50 milliseconds are considered slow, so it is good to have a unit with speeds of less than 20 milliseconds.

Computer Software

Although some people are intimidated by computer jargon, it is worthwhile to become familiar with these machines, the necessary software and hardware, and some aspects of their operations. In order to operate a computer, two kinds of materials are needed: hardware and software. The necessary hardware discussed above includes the actual internal and external physical components of the computer.

Software includes the important instructions that dictate what the computer will do. The software device stores specialized information called a *program* similar to the way phonograph records "store" music. Just as a phonograph is useless without records, a computer is useless without software. Software is the operational plans that control the computer's input, processing, output, and storage operations. It is the component that performs desired tasks for the user, such as writing a letter, spell-checking, playing a game, or designing a birthday card. Since software governs the sequence of operations within the computer, a user instructs the computer to perform such tasks as entering data into its memory from the keyboard, performing as a calculator, or printing a document. These programs are written by computer programmers and sold by vendors to users. Two major classifications of computer software are *system software* and *application or operating software.*

System Software. The operating or system software is the first kind of software that a computer requires to operate. The computer hardware, such as the CPU, does not understand the language or codes of the application programs that a user want to perform. The operating system works as a translator between the computer and the application program. It contains a collection of instructions that tell the computer how to interact with the keyboard, the monitor, other hardware, and the user. These are programs that load, or "boot," the computer and then execute, store, retrieve, copy, erase, and perform other utility functions. These programs have a variable part and a fixed part. The variable part, called BIOS (basic input/output system), is a part of the control system that transfers information back and forth between the physical peripheral devices such as the screen, the keyboard, and the printer. The fixed part, commonly called the disk operating system (DOS), works with the application programs in the performance of such tasks as opening and reading stored documents. A program developed by Microsoft Corporation for IBM, called MS-DOS, has been a most popular program used for this purpose. Personal computers that use this language are referred to as IBM-compatible. Software programs that run on IBM-compatible computers will not work on non-compatible machines such as the Macintosh models of Apple Computer Inc., and vice versa.

Application Software. Application software enables the user to perform desired tasks on the computer. Application software programs instruct the computer to perform meaningful end-user tasks like writing a report, playing a chess game, or processing a customer's order. The most important applications of software programs include word processing, spreadsheets, database management, desktop publishing/graphics, and other specialized applications.

Word Processing Software. This category of software is the most common, with an estimated 60 to 80 percent of microcomputers purchased for this task. Word processing is typewriting with a computer. It manipulates words, letters, and numbers electronically, making it easy to copy and edit text. Also, it can create, edit, format, and print letters, memos, reports, and documents of any length. In addition, word processing can correct spelling, present alternate words from a thesaurus, check writing styles, and correct grammar. Some very good software packages include WordPerfect, Multimate Advantage, WordStar Professional, Microsoft Word, PFS:Professional Write, and DisplayWrite.

Spreadsheet Software. Spreadsheets use a matrix consisting of rows and columns in order to do calculations on numerical data. Spreadsheets have long been used in business calculations, teachers' grade-books, and decision-making. Whenever tedious executions of math, quantities, numbers, and their arrangement in rows and columns are involved, spreadsheets are the ideal tools to deal with them. Computers can remember formulas and changes associated with them. Whenever one number is changed, the computer incorporates an associated change in all the rest of the numbers quickly and accurately. The computer's ability to answer "what-if" questions (for example, what would be the effect of a 13.031 percent increase in the cost of supplies?) saves time in decision-making. Spreadsheets are very helpful in preparing budgets and taxes and in creating statistical reports. Some popular spreadsheet software includes Lotus 1-2-3, VisiCalc, Quattro, Microsoft Excel, and Plan Perfect.

Database Software. Database software carries out the task of storing large volumes of information in a database and retrieving information from that database for updating and reorganizing. Once stored in the database, data can be retrieved for use in a variety of ways, including sorting a list or preparing a mailing list. Police officers who want information on the ownership of any automobile may telephone in the tag number and immediately get this information. Other examples include maintaining employee records and preparing payroll, customer lists, parts order lists, and levels of inventory. PerfectData, dBase, Q&A, and Paradox are among the outstanding database software programs available on the market.

Desktop Publishing/Graphics. Desktop publishing programs are computer programs that convert normal documents, pictures, and graphics into professional-looking publications. Examples of these include newsletters, pamphlets, brochures, bulletins, and reports. Graphic capabilities enable users to create color and black-and-white high quality charts and illustrations. These programs are used in the publication of all kinds of in-house mass-distribution materials by business, government, and educational institutions. Some popular desktop publishing programs include: PageMaker, Ventura Publisher, PFS:First Publisher, and Harvard Graphics.

Specialized Programs. Specialized software programs are used for a great variety of purposes. Computer-aided design (CAD) is one such program developed to perform complex drawings for engineers and architects. Some programs exist for such business applications as time and resource management. One very popular line of software incorporates several different programs into a single package. Such a package may be one that integrates word processing, database, and spreadsheet into one versatile program. Examples include: AutoCAD, Harvard Project Manager, Q&A, Smart, and Symphony.

ONLINE INFORMATION

The term *online* means the computer has access to collections of organized and stored information called *databases*. These databases may be located in other computers with which it is linked, located on or off the premises. Great advances in the combination of computers and telecommunication equipment have resulted in storing, retrieving, and manipulating information from place to place. Desired information can be retrieved quickly using computers. For example, the New York Stock Exchange has databases on commodities, bonds, and stocks that contain enormous amounts of information. A broker may want to retrieve stock prices and other information through the use of computers from his office. People and institutions are accustomed to using online systems.

Libraries subscribe to get access to various databases. Some databases are specialized; for example, including only bibliographic information. The information in bibliographic databases is similar to traditional printed index books. Computerized online access databases provide more information and detailed indexing of reference materials than do traditional card catalogs. Patrons also may retrieve abstracts of journal articles and documents in many fields through author, subject, date of publication, and other key word searches. Online use eliminates time-consuming searches through large numbers of books, periodicals, and other materials to find needed information. Some databases have the complete text of articles and other materials. Specialized systems developed primarily for library use are already an integral or supplementary part of large libraries. One such system is the LS/2000 online technology developed to provide access to library reference materials. This technology includes online databases, automated circulation, and other features. The LS/2000 is "user friendly" and simple to operate even by those with no prior computer experience. Citations are classified under specific headings and subheadings. Users can quickly produce printed, customized bibliographies of articles and documents published on the topics of their choice. Most academic libraries are interconnected with member libraries into networks of information retrieval systems. In these networks, members have access to each other's vast sources of information. These systems may allow patrons to search for bibliographic or other information from their offices, homes, or other convenient locations outside the library. It also may allow for access to library material beyond the library's regularly scheduled hours.

Another technological device involves the availability of information on disks called Computer Designed Read Only Memory (CD-ROM). Bibliographical references and other information are placed on small disks sold to libraries for use by their patrons. These disks are periodically replaced with updated copies. An example of a CD-ROM disk is COMPACE DISCLOSURE, which contains information on over 12,000 publicly traded companies. The Digital Equipment Corporation sells disks that hold tens of thousands of abstracts, including technical publications on health, safety, and other related areas. Another company, The Grolier Corporation, has a disk on the market that includes the 9 million-word *Academic American Encyclopedia*. Datatex Corporation has four disks that hold one million pages of information on more than one thousand U.S. companies. This information is gleaned from many private and public sources, such as company annual reports and Securities and Exchange Commission publications. Presently, the largest bibliographic database sold by Dialog Information Services contains over four million summaries of articles, books, and other documents. The following general categories are covered by Dialog:

- Corporate News
- Agriculture
- Business Information
- Medicine
- Government Publications
- Education
- Computers and Electronics
- Magazines
- Engineering

In its January 16, 1989 issue, *Business Week* reported the following companies and their products as leaders in the vending of online information of the following products:

The Leaders in Online

Company

LEXIS, NEXIS, MEDIS — MEAD CORP.

Abstracts and full text of articles on legal, financial, medical, and general interest topics

DOW JONES NEWS/RETRIEVAL SERVICE — DOW JONES & CO.

Historical stock quotes, corporate information, business articles

DIALOG, INFORMATION SERVICES CO. — KNIGHT-RIDDER INC.

340 databases with abstracts and full-text articles on the sciences, technology, business, and medicine

COMPUSERVE, INFORMATION SERVICES CO. — H&R BLOCK INC.

Abstracts and text of business and general articles, historical stock quotes, on-line shopping, dozens of user bulletin boards

Source: *Business Week*, January 16, 1989, p. 92.

Reproduced material is copied and sold at so many cents per page, or at a flat fee for an entire article. The impact of these databases for reference purposes is just being realized. As availability increases and prices decline, databases may become less a supplement and more a primary means through which to access specific information.

The database DIALOG is the world's largest bibliographic database, covering over 4 million articles, books, reports, and other information. The Dow Jones includes a full text of all printed material in *The Wall Street Journal, Barron's Weekly*, and the *Dow Jones News Service. Easylink* is another large online database. *ERIC* indexes materials in education. *Psychlit* contains articles in psychology. The *Monthly Catalog* is a comprehensive index of U.S. government documents. *Medline*, produced by the National Library of Medicine, specializes in biomedical literature and related areas of health and medicine. It covers journal articles in the United States and over seventy foreign countries.

THE LS/2000 ONLINE PUBLIC ACCESS CATALOG

Increased interest in and reduced cost and availability of personal computers have led to an increase in their use in all facets of library functioning and research. Efficient computer systems are developed to compete with and often replace the traditional card catalogs. These systems make it possible to search a library's entire collection from the confines of one's office or dormitory room, or from the library itself.

The LS/2000 system is one system used by many libraries. This system offers online access to various collections contained in a library and also may offer access to other national or regional libraries. Although some familiarity with the use of computers may be beneficial, it is not necessary for use of the LS/2000 system. Its "user-friendly" design makes the LS/2000 catalog system easy to operate. Guides for its use, a list of explanations of abbreviations, and various keys are found near the terminal. Time is saved by learning some of the commands (words, phrases, or codes entered to access information), thus skipping the menus for help. For those unfamiliar with the system, the menus provide a simple, step-by-step means to access the desired information.

To Begin the Search

The library systems are normally turned on. When the Return key is depressed, the Main Menu will appear on the screen, allowing one to specify the type of search desired. The search can be made from the databases by subject, author, title, or key words. In computer use, it is critical to spell and punctuate correctly while typing. Corrections are made using the CLEAR and CLEAR/DEL keys. Capital letters do not have any bearing on searches in the LS/2000 system. If assistance is needed during operations, go back to the main menu, type (?), and depress the Return key for instructions. Additional guidelines for use and explanations of abbreviations are found near the terminal or with the librarian. Once seated in front of the LS/2000, by depressing the Return key, the following Main Menu screen will be presented (Figure 4-1):

FIGURE 4-1

```
PUBLIC CATALOG                    Searching: APPALACHIAN STATE UNIVERSITY


          Enter the NUMBER of search you wish to perform

          1 - By AUTHOR
          2 - By TITLE
          3 - By MAIN SUBJECT HEADING
          4 - By PERSONAL NAME AS SUBJECT
          5 - By FACULTY/COURSE RESERVES
          6 - For OTHER Searches


              OR

          Enter a KEY WORD to see possible matches

CHOICE:

  Enter ? for GENERAL INSTRUCTION.  To ENTER, type number then press RETURN.
```

Typing the number (1) on the keyboard and depressing the Return key will produce the following message on the screen:

Enter author's full or partial name in this format: Last, First

Type in "Maslow, Abraham" and depress the Return key. The computer screen will present the following information (Figure 4-2).

From the "REF" column, one selects the item. The "TITLES" column indicates

FIGURE 4-2

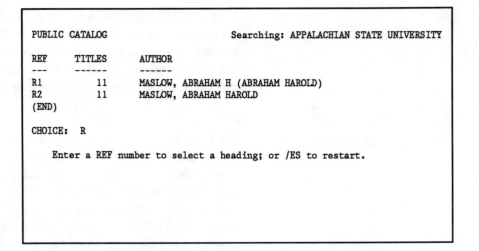

```
PUBLIC CATALOG                        Searching: APPALACHIAN STATE UNIVERSITY

REF      TITLES        AUTHOR
---      ------        ------
R1         11          MASLOW, ABRAHAM H (ABRAHAM HAROLD)
R2         11          MASLOW, ABRAHAM HAROLD
(END)

CHOICE:  R

    Enter a REF number to select a heading; or /ES to restart.
```

the number of available books. Type the "REF" number 1 and depress the Return key (when selecting from a list, type the number only, not the letter "R"). The first page of the information on the screen will present the following ten titles (Figure 4-3):

FIGURE 4-3

```
PUBLIC CATALOG                        Searching: APPALACHIAN STATE UNIVERSITY

PERSONAL AUTHOR:  MASLOW, ABRAHAM H (ABRAHAM HAROLD)
                  FOUND:   11

REF     DATE     TITLES                        AUTHOR
---     ----     ------                        ------

R1      1987     Maslow's hierarchy of needs
R2      1973     Dominance, self-esteem, self-act   Maslow, Abraham H
R3      1972     The farther reaches of human nat   Maslow, Abraham H
R4      1971     Humanistic psychology:             Frick,  Willard B.
R5      1968     Toward a psychology of being       Maslow, Abraham H
R6      1966     The psychology of science;         Maslow, Abraham H
R7      1965     Eupsychian management;             Maslow, Abraham H
R8      1964     Religions, values, and peak-expe   Maslow, Abraham H
R9      1959     New knowledge in human values.     Maslow, Abraham H
R10     1954     Motivation and personality.        Maslow, Abraham H
(MORE)

CHOICE:  R

  Enter a REF number to see details of a title; or /ES to restart.
```

To view additional titles, when (MORE) is below the last reference, depress the Return key. If the number 7 is typed and the Return key is depressed, the following information will be presented with the availability of the material in the library (Figure 4-4):

FIGURE 4-4

```
PUBLIC CATALOG                          Searching: APPALACHIAN STATE UNIVERSITY

   Maslow, Abraham H
     Eupsychian management; a journal, by Abraham H. Maslow.
   Homewood, Ill., R. D. Irwin, 1965.
      xvi, 277 p. 23 cm.
     The Irwin-Dorsey series in behavioral science
      Bibliography: p. 267-277.
     Psychology, Industrial

   LOCATION        CALL#/VOL/NO/COPY          STATUS

   ASU/BLK/STK     HF5548.8  .M374 c.1           Available
   ASU/BLK/STK     HF5548.8  .M374 c.2           Available
   ASU/BLK/STK     HF5548.8  .M374 c.3           Available

   (END)  Press RETURN to continue or /ES to start a new search:
```

Depressing the Shift and PrintScreen keys will print the above reference for the operator. Searches can be started from the Main Menu by typing the corresponding number and depressing the Return key, or they can begin at any time by typing one of the following commands:

/ AU = [Name of Author]

/ TI = [Title of Book]

/ SU = [Library of Congress Subject Heading]

/ KW = [key word]

Prompts After a selection is made, the computer presents four choices called *prompts*. These prompts and their associated functions are:

1. CHOICE: The *prompt* occurs at the Main or the Other Searches menu. One enters the number of the desired search or types a key word, then depresses the Return key.

2. CHOICE: The *R prompt* will present a list of terms, titles, or names. When Return is depressed, a list of alternative choices is presented on the screen with a REF column. At this time, one types the number of the desired choice and depresses Return.

3. CHOICE: The *R1 prompt* occurs only when one selection is available for the search topic of the selection. At this point, one depresses Return to continue.

4. (MORE): If the list retrieved on the selected topic exceeds the screen display capacity, the *prompt (MORE)* will direct the user to press Return to examine the rest of the list. If a return to the previous screen is desired, type /B and depress Return.

Moving Around and Basic Commands

The LS/2000 system uses a few keys to aid in quick searches and to assist or instruct the user. One can quickly learn the function of these keys to perform desired operations.

IF YOU WANT TO...	PRESS KEYS:
Begin a new search	/es
Correct typing errors	CLEAR or CLEAR/DEL
See additional part of the list, when the list ends with (MORE)	RETURN
Go back one step in a search process	"^" (shift 6)
See the previous list	/b RETURN
See information about the next title (without going back to list)	/n RETURN
Get help	? RETURN

You must return to the main menu in order to use the "?" command for instructions.

Note: If a mistake is made at any time during the process, it can be corrected by simply pressing the CLEAR or CLEAR/DEL key, which will backspace to the error, and then type over the error. This is called a strikeover.

Methods of Searching

Search by Subject. In order to search by subject, one must define the subject. A subject can be a person, place, topic, or corporate body. If one is not sure about the exact wording of the desired subject, it may be checked in the Library of Congress Subject Headings for accuracy. This book is normally placed near the online public access computers (OPAC). If not, ask the librarian for assistance. To search by subject, select number (3) from the Main Menu or (/SU) at any point, and then depress Return. The name or heading is then entered, followed by depressing the Return key. In the following example (Figure 4-5), the word "basketball" was typed followed by depressing the Return key.

FIGURE 4-5

```
PUBLIC CATALOG                          Searching: APPALACHIAN STATE UNIVERSITY



        ENTER SUBJECT:
        BASKETBALL



Enter a term that describes the subject you are interested in.



```

Note: The screens are constantly changing due to additions and subtractions in the library collection.

The screen will instantly show the following listing including the number of titles and the main subject headings for basketball (Figure 4-6).

FIGURE 4-6

```
SUBJECT:     BASKETBALL              Searching: APPALACHIAN STATE UNIVERSITY

REF    TITLES     MAIN SUBJECT HEADING
---    ------     --------------------
R1       61       BASKETBALL
R2       14       BASKETBALL FOR WOMEN
R3       11       BASKETBALL PLAYERS
R4        1       BASKETMAKERS
R5        2       BASKETS
R6        4       BASKETWORK
R&        1       BASQUE AMERICANS
R8        3       BASQUE LANGUAGE
R9        1       BASQUE LITERATURE
R10       3       BASQUES
(MORE)


CHOICE: R

Enter a REF number to select a heading; or /ES (Enter Search) to start.
```

If "basketball players" is the subject desired, typing the number 3 and depressing the Return key will present the following information (Figure 4-7):

FIGURE 4-7

```
PUBLIC CATALOG                      Searching: APPALACHIAN STATE UNIVERSITY

MAIN SUBJECT HEADING:    BASKETBALL PLAYERS

REF    TITLES     MAIN SUBJECT HEADING
---    ------     --------------------
R1       16       Basketball players
R2       12       - Biography
R3        2       - Juvenile literature
R4        2       - Periodicals
R5        1       - Recruiting
R6        2       - Statistics
R7       14       - United States
(END)

CHOICE:  R

Enter a REF number to see the title list; or /ES to (Enter Search) to
restart.
```

This process is continued until the desired information is located. For example, if number 1 is typed, the following titles on "basketball players" are presented (Figure 4-8):

FIGURE 4-8

```
PUBLIC CATALOG                    Searching: APPALACHIAN STATE UNIVERSITY

MAIN SUBJECT HEADING:    BASKETBALL PLAYERS
              FOUND:   13

REF    DATE    TITLES                      AUTHOR
---    ----    ------                      ------
R1     1991    David Robinson :            Miller, Dawn M.
R2     1990    Forever's team /            Feinstein, John.
R3     1990    Kareem /                    Abdul-Jabbar, Kareem,
R4     1990    Raw recruits /              Wolff, Alexander,
R5     1989    Drive :                     Bird, Larry,
R6     1989    Sports great Magic Johnson / Haskins, James,
R7     1987    Heir to a dream /           Maravich, Pete,
R8     1986    Honey Russell :             Russell, John,
R9     1983    Giant steps /               Abdul-Jabbar, Kareem,
R10    1983    NBA register.
(MORE)

CHOICE:  R

Enter a REF number to see details of a title; of /ES (Enter Search) to
restart.
```

This list indicates (MORE), so to continue to see the next part of the list, press the Return key.

FIGURE 4-9

```
PUBLIC CATALOG                    Searching: APPALACHIAN STATE UNIVERSITY

MAIN SUBJECT HEADING:    BASKETBALL PLAYERS
              FOUND:   16

REF    DATE    TITLES                      AUTHOR
---    ----    ------                      ------
R11    1982    Basketball my way /         Lieberman, Nancy,
R12    1982    Official NBA guide.
R13    1979    Second wind :               Russell, Bill
R14    1978    They call me "The Big E"/   Hayes, Elvin,
R15    1977    Hondo :                     Havlicek, John
R16    1973    Pro basketball's big men.   Klein, Dave.
(END)

CHOICE:  R
Enter a REF number to see details of a title; or /ES (Enter Search) to
restart.
```

To view the first list again, enter "/b" and depress Return. If the "Kareem" book is wanted, type the number 3 from the first list and depress Return. The following reference will be presented (Figure 4-10):

FIGURE 4-10

```
Abdul-Jabbar, Kareem, 1947-
  Kareem / Kareem Abdul-Jabbar ; with Mignon McCarthy.
New York : Random House, 1990.
  233 p., [16] p. of plates : ill. ; 24 cm.
  Abdul-jabbar, Kareem, - 1947-
  National Basketball Association.
  Basketball players - United States - Biography.


LOCATION           CALL#/VOL/NO/COPY        STATUS

ASU/BLK/STK        GV884.A24 A3 1990 c.1    Date due 03/20/92



(END)  Press RETURN to continue or /ES to start a new search:
```

HELPFUL HINTS

- When entering a name or heading, type all internal punctuation, but omit any initial punctuation (LAWRENCE, D. H).

- When typing names, enter last name first.

- Type only one part of a subdivided subject heading at a time and then scan the subdivisions. (VIRGINIA or CIVIL WAR, not VIRGINIA-HISTORY-CIVIL WAR). If the Library of Congress subject headings are used, phrases must be entered exactly as they appear, e.g., POETRY, AMERICAN.

Author Search. Searching by author is very similar to searching by subject. Number (2) is selected from the main menu or (/AU) at any point. Next enter the person, the corporation, or the conference name and depress Return. Select the corresponding REF number for the desired choice, then depress RETURN. This will present all available titles on the author in the library. Typing "Eliot" or "Eliot, T. S) produces the following examples (Figures 4-11 and 4-12):

FIGURE 4-11

```
PUBLIC CATALOG                    Searching: APPALACHIAN STATE UNIVERSITY

AUTHOR:    ELIOT,
REF     TITLES    AUTHOR
---     ------    ------
R21         1     ELIOT, MARTHA M
R22         4     ELIOT, ROBERT S
R23         1     ELIOT, SAMUEL, 1821-1898
R24         1     ELIOT, SUSAN B
R25        84     ELIOT, T. S (THOMAS STEARNS), 1888-1965
R26         1     ELIOT, THOMAS DAWES, 1808-1870
R27         3     ELIOT, THOMAS HOPKINSON, 1907-
R28        84     ELIOT, THOMAS STEARNS, 1888-1965
(END)

CHOICE:  R
Enter a REF number to select a heading; or /ES (Enter Search) to restart.
```

FIGURE 4-12

```
PUBLIC CATALOG                          Searching: APPALACHIAN STATE UNIVERSITY


AUTHOR:   ELIOT, T. S

REF     TITLES     AUTHOR
---     ------     ------
R1        46       ELIOT, T. S (THOMAS STEARNS),  1888-1965
(END)


CHOICE:  R1/

     Enter a REF number to select a heading; or /ES to restart.
```

Note: Author searches not only list the desired author, but also retrieve names spelled closely. This aids the search if only a last name is known.

HELPFUL HINTS
- The last name should be entered first, then a comma, then a space and the full or partial first name (ELIOT, T. S).
- Choose the name by which the person is most commonly known, such as MARK TWAIN.
- Various forms of names should be checked (MCCLENDON or MACCLEDON).

Title Search. Titles can be searched under main title, various subtitles, or uniform titles. To begin searching by title, select number (3) from the main menu, or (/TI) at any point, and then depress Return. Type as much of the title as is known.

HELPFUL HINTS
- It is important to exclude letters and words such as A, AN, THE, LE, LES when searching by title. If a title is entered in a foreign language, uniform titles will retrieve the English as well as any foreign editions. This will lead to the desired title and/or others that may be helpful.
- Internal punctuation should be included and final punctuation omitted.
- Subtitles should be omitted or entered separately (Hurricanes or Charleston, not Hurricanes: Charleston).

A title search for *Gone With the Wind* or *The Three Musketeers* generated the following screens (Figures 4-13 and 4-14):

FIGURE 4-13

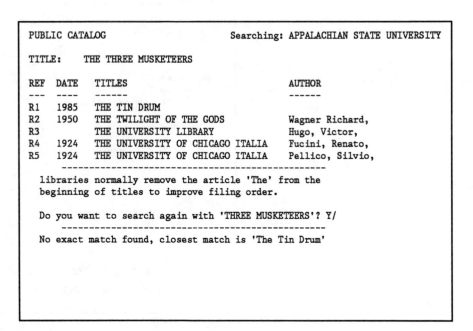

```
PUBLIC CATALOG                           Searching: APPALACHIAN STATE UNIVERSITY

TITLES:   GONE WITH THE WIND
REF  DATE   TITLES                                AUTHOR
---  ----   ------                                ------
R1   1986   GONE WITH THE WIND                    Mitchell, Margaret,
R2   1985   GONE WITH THE WIND
R3   1975   GONE WITH THE WIND                    Mitchell, Margaret,
R4   1954   GONE WITH THE WIND                    Steiner, Max,
R5   1936   GONE WITH THE WIND                    Mitchell, Margaret,
R6   1989   GONE WITH THE WIND  : Definitive      Bridges, Herb,
R7   1989   GONE WITH THE WIND AND ITS FEMAL      Taylor, Helen,
R8   1983   GONE WITH THE WIND AS BOOK AND F
R9   1953   GONE WITH THE WIND GERMAN             Mitchell, Margaret,
R10  1976   GONE WITH THE WIND LETTERS 1936       Mitchell, Margaret,
(MORE)

CHOICE:  R
Enter a REF number to see the title list; or /ES (Enter Search) to restart.
```

FIGURE 4-14

```
PUBLIC CATALOG                           Searching: APPALACHIAN STATE UNIVERSITY

TITLE:    THE THREE MUSKETEERS

REF  DATE   TITLES                                AUTHOR
---  ----   ------                                ------
R1   1985   THE TIN DRUM
R2   1950   THE TWILIGHT OF THE GODS              Wagner Richard,
R3          THE UNIVERSITY LIBRARY                Hugo, Victor,
R4   1924   THE UNIVERSITY OF CHICAGO ITALIA      Fucini, Renato,
R5   1924   THE UNIVERSITY OF CHICAGO ITALIA      Pellico, Silvio,
     ------------------------------------------------
  libraries normally remove the article 'The' from the
  beginning of titles to improve filing order.

  Do you want to search again with 'THREE MUSKETEERS'? Y/
     ------------------------------------------------
  No exact match found, closest match is 'The Tin Drum'
```

Key Word Search. A key word search is a useful and time-saving device when one is not sure of the exact term, author, name, or title of the search. A key word is a particular word or phrase that appears in a name, title, publisher, or subject. The key word may be entered from the main menu or (/KW) at any point during the search. Typing the word "basketball" under (/KW) search produced the following screen (Figure 4-15):

FIGURE 4-15

```
PUBLIC CATALOG                    Searching: APPALACHIAN STATE UNIVERSITY

KEY WORD:    BASKETBALL

REF     TITLES     KEY WORD
---     ------     --------
R1        352      BASKETBALL
R2         10      BASKETBALL'S
(END)

CHOICE:  R
         Enter a REF number to see search contexts; or /ES to
         restart.
```

In the above example, 352 titles are too many to search. In order to deal with a manageable and precise list, the following limiting menu is used (Figure 4-16).

FIGURE 4-16

```
PUBLIC CATALOG               Searching: APPALACHIAN STATE UNIVERSITY
KEY WORD: BASKETBALL                     FOUND:  142

Your search has identified many citations.  What would you like to do next.

1. Narrow search

2. View citations sequentially

3. Start new search

 Enter one of the numbers above; or /ES to restart.
 CHOICE:
```

To narrow the search, from the above menu number 1 is selected, followed by the Return key. The system then produced the following screen (Figure 4-17):

FIGURE 4-17

```
PUBLIC CATALOG                   Searching: APPALACHIAN STATE UNIVERSITY
KEY WORD: BASKETBALL                        FOUND:  142

         Enter the NUMBER of the limitation search you wish to
         perform

                  1 - Limit by PUBLICATION YEAR
                  2 - limit by LANGUAGE
                  3 - Limit by PERSONAL AUTHOR
                  4 - Limit by SUBJECT
                  5 - Limit by Other Searches
                     OR

Enter a KEY WORD to see possible limiting matches

CHOICE:
```

The above list allows several options including selection by publication year, language, author, subject, or key word. When number 1 was selected and requested to limit the search to the period 1988-1990, the following screen was produced (Figure 4-18):

FIGURE 4-18

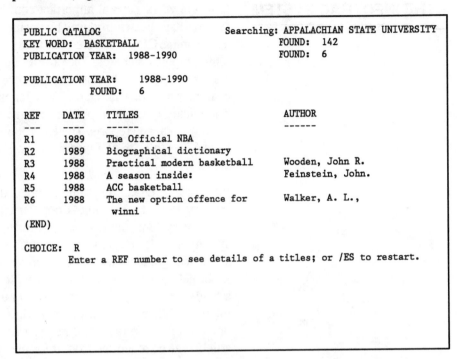

```
PUBLIC CATALOG                    Searching: APPALACHIAN STATE UNIVERSITY
KEY WORD:  BASKETBALL                        FOUND:   142
PUBLICATION YEAR:   1988-1990                FOUND:   6

PUBLICATION YEAR:      1988-1990
          FOUND:   6

REF     DATE    TITLES                       AUTHOR
---     ----    ------                       ------
R1      1989    The Official NBA
R2      1989    Biographical dictionary
R3      1988    Practical modern basketball  Wooden, John R.
R4      1988    A season inside:             Feinstein, John.
R5      1988    ACC basketball
R6      1988    The new option offence for   Walker, A. L.,
                   winni

(END)

CHOICE:  R
         Enter a REF number to see details of a titles; or /ES to restart.
```

After making an initial selection using key words, one may continue the search until the precise topic is located. If a search retrieves more than twenty items, it is better to narrow the search by the year of publication, key word, subject, title, author, or language. The researcher should follow these steps to narrow the search by matching another word of interest:

1. Enter #1 from the limiting menu (Narrow Search)
2. Depress Return
3. Enter key word
4. Depress Return
5. Enter new search (dates, type of publication, subject, other)
6. Depress Return
7. Enter R number at the far left of the item if desired to combine with the first search, and depress Return again.

Two additional items are important for the LS/2000 computer user to remember: (1) If one sees "NO MATCH TO THIS ENTRY," check spelling, spacing, and punctuation or ask for assistance. (2) If the computer suggests narrowing the search, follow the guidelines given on narrowing searches. (3) Keep in mind that by depressing the shift key "^", one is able to return to the last screen to find another possible match.

Conclusion
The LS/2000 is an efficient online catalog system that is simple to use. It can locate appropriate material quickly and accurately. In addition, several institutions may be linked through the system, providing greater information access.

Members throughout the system lend books, periodicals, and other materials to system users.

THE INFOTRAC SYSTEM

In recent years, several important computer reference searches and database systems have been introduced by business firms and publishers for library use. These online CD-ROM reference materials range from library catalogs to large bibliographic databases. The proliferation of full-text databases has led some research journals to be published exclusively in electronic formats. Important examples include Dialog, the Dow Jones Database, and the InfoTrac System. The Dialog database provides information on several million abstracts, articles, books, and reports. The Dow Jones Database includes texts of material from *The Wall Street Journal, Barron's Weekly*, and *The Dow Jones News Service*.

InfoTrac, a CD-ROM system introduced by Information Access Company in January 1985, has become a popular choice for use by many libraries. The InfoTrac system simple to use, requiring no prior computer experience. This system provides references on many subjects covering the contents of thousands of periodicals, newspapers, government documents, and other materials. Its broad coverage includes information on over half a million individual articles drawn from more than 1000 business, technical, legal, and general interest publications. It covers materials published at the national and international levels by private and public institutions. The entire text of magazine articles can be requested from Information Access Company. The most useful features of the InfoTrac database system include:

- It is a self-contained supplemental system, designed for library use and research. It can search millions of articles for desired information in seconds.

- No prior computer training or knowledge is required for the use of this system.

- It is a regularly updated comprehensive database with coverage of topics across the disciplines.

- It is a cost-effective system with its own storage capacity. Speedy access, search options, and simultaneous multi-user capability make this a very efficient system.

- Its indexing of the covered material is organized alphabetically, based on the standard Library of Congress subheading and cross reference method of arrangement.

- It provides a thesaurus, which is helpful in locating precise search terms.

- It is possible to off-line and online to remote databases with downloading and editing capabilities.

How to Use the InfoTrac System

The InfoTrac system is simple to operate, with on-screen instructions that guide the user through the step-by-step process of using the system. The examples of screens, functions of the keys, and other information in this section are from the computer terminal to which the author had access. Certain statements and examples will be different in other libraries because of the inclusion of different databases, improvements, and periodic updating. However, the basic working of all InfoTrac systems is alike, and with some initial practice one can become knowledgeable about its operation.

Once seated in front of the computer and the monitor, one will communicate with the InfoTrac through a typewriter-like keyboard. Begin by depressing the START/FINISH key, which will turn on the database system (or terminate the operation). Next, the InfoTrac will present a list of available databases. By depressing the HELP key, the "SELECT THE TOPIC YOU NEED HELP WITH" screen will appear. Depressing the Arrow keys, which move the cursor to the desired topic, and then depressing the SEARCH/ENTER (Return) key, will present information related to that topic. At any point in operations, one can go back to this screen by depressing the HELP key. Depressing the BACKTRACK key will return the operator to the point at which exit was made. The following information will appear on the Help screen (Figure 4-19):

Figure 4-19

```
SELECT THE TOPIC YOU NEED HELP WITH:
    WHAT DATABASES ARE AVAILABLE
    HOW TO SEARCH
    HOW TO PRINT
    SAMPLE CITATION
    COLOR-CODED FUNCTION/MOVEMENT KEYS
    HOW TO FIND PUBLICATION INDEXED
    WHAT PUBLICATIONS ARE INCLUDED
```

Figure 4-20

```
WHAT DATABASES ARE AVAILABLE

    ACADEMIC INDEX
    GENERAL PERIODICAL INDEX
    HEALTH INDEX
    LEGALTRAC INDEX
    MAGAZINE INDEX
    NATIONAL NEWSPAPER INDEX
    TOM
```

By choosing the first topic, the user will have access to the available databases provided by the library. The following databases were available in the InfoTrac system used by the author (Figure 4-20).

InfoTrac has many databases, some of which are specifically prepared for library use. The following represents some widely used InfoTrac databases.

ACADEMIC INDEX. Designed for research in the humanities, social sciences, general science, and current events, it provides bibliographic reference to over 400 scholarly and general interest journals, as well as covering the last six months of *The New York Times*. It covers the most current three to four years of information and is updated monthly. There is an EXPANDED ACADEMIC INDEX, which provides bibliographic references to and abstracts of articles from over 960 scholarly and general interest publications.

GENERAL PERIODICALS INDEX. This is the largest, most comprehensive database available on the InfoTrac system. It covers over 1,100 general purpose and scholarly publications as well as abstracts in art, business, economics, current affairs, and social sciences. *The New York Times, The Wall Street Journal,* and *The Christian Science Monitor* newspapers are covered. This database is available in two versions: academic library and public library editions.

HEALTH INDEX. This database indexes over 130 publications on health, fitness, and nutrition, including consumer-oriented magazines, newsletters, and professional journals. Also included are selected health-related articles from over 3,000 magazines and newspapers. Another database, HEALTH REFERENCE CENTER, is comprehensive in coverage of topics related to medicine and medical journals. Both databases span over four years with monthly updating.

LEGALTRAC INDEX. This comprehensive index covers legal periodicals. The sources include major law reviews, seven legal newspapers, specialty publications, and bar association journals. It presents subjects, titles, authors, cases, and statutes. This database covers the period from 1980 to the present and is updated monthly.

MAGAZINE INDEX. This database indexes close to 400 popular magazines. The subject areas encompass current affairs, consumer information, travel, arts, and entertainment. It is updated monthly and spans four years.

NATIONAL NEWSPAPER INDEX. This is a comprehensive index of five newspapers: *The New York Times, The Washington Post, The Los Angeles Times, The Wall Street Journal*, and *The Christian Science Monitor*. It covers four years and is updated monthly.

TOM. This text on microform database is prepared for use in secondary schools. It includes articles from over 100 popular magazines that are most frequently used in schools and covers materials from 1980 to the present. It is updated monthly.

GOVERNMENT PUBLICATIONS INDEX. This is an index to the *Monthly Catalog of the United States Government Printing Office*. It indexes public documents generated by the legislative and executive branches of the U.S. government. Its coverage dates to 1976 and is updated monthly.

GENERAL BUSINESSFILE. This database provides current public and private information on all aspects of trade, finance, management, and industry. It covers 800 publications and provides information on over 150,000 companies in fifty-three industries. Many business topics, including forecasts on national and international companies and industries, are covered.

To exit from the database screen or to select a different database, depress START/FINISH. Depressing the HELP key will present the Help menu. Selecting the "HOW TO SEARCH" option from this menu will enable one to learn about the initial steps involved in the search process. When a database is selected, the user will then enter the selected subject, name, or author. When the SEARCH/ENTER (Return) key is depressed, InfoTrac will begin the search. If additional and operational information is desired at this stage, the HELP key is depressed. InfoTrac will provide a menu of desired information choices on the screen. Some familiarity with the use of the two types of Movement and Function keys discussed later in this section is useful at this stage for these operations and further searches.

The arrangement of InfoTrac reference material is alphabetical by subject headings, corporate or personal names, and titles of books, movies, and plays. The subject headings are broken into subheadings and related subject headings. If the subject cannot be found, the closest alphabetic match is shown on the screen. For many topics, some related subjects are also indicated under the "see also" listing. The references include other information on publisher, inclusion of illustrations, and the length of the article. Bibliographic references are displayed in reverse chronological order, allowing for browsing through earlier materials and gaining historical perspective on a selected topic. This also permits the researcher to prepare an initial customized bibliography on a chosen topic. Some may find this useful when prospecting for desirable topics for term and research papers.

When a desired topic is located, it may be noted from the screen or printed. The selection of HOW TO PRINT guides the user through printing out the material. With the noted or printed information, one may proceed to locate the materials in the library.

Searching a Desired Topic

Type the desired search topic and then depress the SEARCH/ENTER (Return) key. The screen will present the Subject Guide that lists topic headings and subheadings, with cross references ("SEE" and "SEE ALSO" references). Typing in upper or lower case letters makes no difference. If the exact topic is not located, the nearest alphabetical matched headings will be displayed. The top of the screen will indicate the subject and which database is being searched. The movement keys are then used to position the cursor next to the desired item and the Return key is depressed. A smaller screen at the lower left titled CITATIONS will be displayed; the heading will indicate what number citation this is and how many others exist (1 of 7, for example). In this window, complete bibliographic information for the found reference will be presented. One can browse through each of the seven found references one at a time. The up and down arrows are used for this. This information is given at the bottom of the Citations window. If the cursor is placed next to the citation and the PRINT key depressed, the item will be printed. The BACKTRACK key is used to return back to an earlier topic on the screen. This is useful when attempting to prepare a bibliography.

Searching for a Periodical

Enter LIST PUB at the topic request screen and depress the Return key. An alphabetical list of the publications indexed will be presented. To obtain information on a specific periodical, position the cursor at the individual title and depress the Return key. One can also request information on a specific periodical by typing in the name of the publication after the LIST PUB is entered and prompted to enter a subheading. Information on the periodical can also be obtained by requesting searching under the topic. The displayed citation will include information on the periodical's publisher, frequency of publication, location, and subscription price.

Help Features

An important feature of the InfoTrac system is the HELP key. At any point, the user can request assistance by depressing the HELP key. One is returned to the point of search from the Help screen by depressing the BACKTRACK key. The Help screen will present a menu of the following choices:

What Databases are Available — This request provides brief profiles of the information available in the included database.

How to Search — This will furnish a brief tutorial.

How to Print — This option provides instructions for printing.

Sample Citation — This function explains specific notations for a reference.

Color-Coded Function/Movement Keys — It details the important function and use of these keys.

How to Find Publications Indexed — An alphabetical list of the indexed publications is provided by this choice.

Keyboard Use

InfoTrac uses only a few basic keys for its operation so that individuals with no prior computer experience can use the system. The keys are color coded with the function of each key printed on top of the key. There is also a printed description of each key located right above the keyboard. Any user will quickly learn the various uses of the function and movement keys. The uses for each key are as follows:

F1: START/FINISH — This key is used to start, search, finish, or select a different database.

F2: HELP — This key presents instructions on how to use the InfoTrac system.

F3: PRINT — This key is used to print out selected references for the user.

F4: MULTI PRINT — This key is used to print up to fifty references under a specific heading/subheading. (This option is not usually available to students.)

F5: SUBJECT GUIDE — This key presents an alphabetical list of subjects and related items.

F6: BACKTRACK — This key backtracks the user one step to the previous subject term. It is also used to go from HELP to the previous location in the program.

HOME: This key will take you to the first reference of the topic you are searching.

END: This key takes the user to the last topic being searched.

[↑] PRIOR LINE: This key scrolls the screen backward one reference in the database being searched or one line in the SUBJECT GUIDE.

[↓] NEXT LINE: This key scrolls the screen forward one reference in the database being searched or one line in the SUBJECT GUIDE.

[PGDN] FAST FWD: This key scrolls fast forward, useful when the user is working with a large list of references.

[PGUP] FAST REV: This key moves the search backward a number of citations.

[←]: This key will move from citation to SUBJECT GUIDE citation (right to left).

[→]: This key will move from SUBJECT GUIDE to citation (left to right).

[↵] SEARCH/ENTER: This (Return) key will search the desired database for the subject entered. It also accesses to the reference positioned at the pointer and the Citation windows.

InfoTrac Examples

SEARCH HEADING

Enter the subject or name you wish to find:

```
Basketball
```

There are a large number of references under this subject. To narrow your search, you may enter a subheading.

```
Jordan, Michael
```

(then depress the Enter key)

or to search the original subject only, depress the Enter key.

The following information will appear on the screen if you type Jordan, Michael as a heading, not a subheading, under Basketball.

JORDAN, MICHAEL (ATHLETE)

-biography

-accident

-achievement

-competition

-endorsements

-finances

-interviews

-selection

-training

If the researcher wanted information on interviews from the above list, when requested, the screen would display the following information.

Challenges facing Jordan: New rule and new Bulls' role. (Michael Jordan; Chicago Bulls; basketball) by Sam Goldspar 19 col in. V137 The New York Times Nov 4 '87 p55 (N) pA21 (L) col 4.

Once the desired information is located, it may be copied from the screen or printed by depressing the PRINT key. This information is then used to search and locate the material in the library.

Sample of Newspaper Indexes

The information that appears on the screen will include newspaper titles, date, edition, and column number. A typical newspaper citation from the *National Newspaper Index* would look like Figure 4-21.

Sample of Journal Citation

The citations on journals include information for volume number, name of publication, date of publication, page where article begins, number of pages in the article, illustrations, and location code. Figure 4-22 is an example.

Sample of Government Publications and Documents

The Government Publication Index covers the *Monthly Catalog* of the United States Government Printing Office and other public documents generated by the various departments of the United States government. Included material is listed alphabetically by subject, author, and issuing agency. This information is updated and accumulated monthly. The InfoTrac citation gives the author, the issuing agency, the Su Doc number, the item number, and the *Monthly Catalog* entry number. A typical entry on acid rain will provide the following information (Figure 4-23):

Figure 4-21

```
MANAGEMENT
-BUSINESS APPLICATIONS
The non-profits quiet revolution.
(institutions adopt sound management
practices ) (column) by Peter F.
Drucker 32 col in.  The Wall Street
Journal Dept 8 "88 p26(W) P30(E) col 3.
    LIBRARY SUBSCRIBES TO THE JOURNAL
```

Figure 4-22

```
MANAGEMENT
-ECONOMIC ASPECTS
Run the government like the best American
corporations. (Business, Economics and
Oval Office) by Ralph Nader il v66 Harvard
Business Review Nov-Dec "88 p81 (6).
47C4430                          41U3323
    LIBRARY SUBSCRIBES TO JOURNAL
```

Figure 4-23

```
AN:  90004250
SU:  Y 1.1/7:
SU:  Y117
CA:  United States.  Office of Management
and Budget.
TI:  Cumulative report on recessions and
deferrals:  Communication from the Director
the Office of Management and Budget,
transmitting the Cumulative report ...
pursuant to 2 U.S.C. 685 (e).
```

How to Print

To print a citation, the up and down arrow keys on the numeric pad, or the movement keys, are used to position the cursor next to the item, and then the PRINT key is depressed. This operation will provide a printout of that reference and its abstract. If one wishes to print the entire page of the citation, move the cursor to the top of the screen and enter the PRINT PAGE key. This will print all the information contained on the screen. For additional instruction on printing, request help from InfoTrac.

Conclusion

InfoTrac is a high speed automated system that retrieve with computer efficiency references and bibliographic materials placed on its disks. It is a popular and extensive self-contained reference system for use by libraries. The availability of any specific InfoTrac database with the system in a library is critical for a researcher. Specialized and comprehensive databases are available from the Information Access Company for library and institutional use. Some of these databases are fairly expensive and not available in some libraries. Currently, a four-station InfoTrac database system with the General Periodicals Index costs more than $14,000 annually. It is foreseen that because of technological advances, future prices will decline. In this case, many libraries, institutions, and some private individuals will be able to afford the InfoTrac system. It is important that students and other interested individuals become familiar with the use and features of this system.

WORD PROCESSING

Today, a broad range of activities is used to expedite the processing and writing of documents of various sizes and descriptions. Word processing programs, because of their flexibility, allow for quick and efficient alteration of documents. Word processing may be defined as creating and modifying text files such as letters, documents, and memos with great ease and then printing them on paper. People discover that when the fear of the unknown has been overcome, computers are practical, full of exciting possibilities, and simple to operate.

The use of personal computers is increasing as a tool for research and writing at all levels. Computers and word processors are useful tools for any serious researcher or writer. Any student, writer, manager, secretary, or household that does not use them will be functioning at a great disadvantage. Word processing saves time spent on revisions, additions, retyping, editing, and proofreading. Word processing has become a major function not only in the business world but in the homes of many people. It has taken the place of the typewriter in many areas, with the possible exception of typing certain kinds of envelopes and contracts. Word processing is not only a convenience but almost a necessity for authors, researchers, students, and others.

The purpose of this discussion is not to provide a working knowledge of computer and word processor use; rather it is to provide information on some aspects of word processing. As prices of computers have decreased, one may affordably purchase a computer with tutorial software and learn easily at home. Many training sessions, most of which are free, are available throughout the country, permitting beginners to learn basic skills.

A word processing machine may be described as a super typewriter package or a system of inter-connected machinery that produces typed words on a screen. A user may correct and delete, and add words, sentences, or paragraphs to a document as desired. Other features include setting margins, tabs, and spaces between lines while enhancing the appearance of the final text through customized boldfacing, centering, and underlining. All this makes the traditional job of typing easier, worthwhile, and even intriguing. The word processor can cut, paste, re-format, store, reproduce, and print documents with maximum flexibility. It is very helpful and time saving in numbering sections of a chapter, making an index, creating a table of contents, and checking spelling and grammar.

Word processing packages allow for the use of templates. Templates help in the writing of contracts, memos, documents, and forms. Thus, all one has to do later is fill in the blank spaces instead of retyping the whole document. Templates are a convenient feature for typing form letters and mailing labels. These operations deliver high quality and professional results.

Some word processors contain a thesaurus to aid in selecting alternate words. Using a word processor, one may easily create charts, graphs, bars, logos, illustrations, letterheads, or mailing lists. After some familiarity with word processing, programs of all sorts can be purchased to explain and prepare legal documents, term papers, and sales contracts.

The expression "word processing" parallels the term "data processing" and refers to the writing, storing, manipulation, and retrieval of text. It is associated with the first word processing machine introduced by IBM in 1964. The machine was called Magnetic Tape Selectec Typewriter (MT/ST). It was a major invention in that it recorded every keystroke a typist made and automatically made a new recording after further corrections, insertions, and deletions were made. Also, it could print multiple copies of letters and insert different addresses on each letter. A large number of improvements have been incorporated into the technology of word processing since that time.

Elements of a Word Processing System or Unit

Word processing technology has branched out to include many systems such as software, hardware, and electronic typewriters. A typical word processing system consists of a video terminal, the CPU, the keyboard, and other devices such as floppy disks and a printer. The various systems fall into three main categories: (1) stand-alone systems supporting one operator; (2) local area network (LAN) or clustered systems, which enable several operators to share software, printers, etc.; and (3) files and hybrid systems, attached to mainframe or microcomputer systems that are able to perform additional functions.

Features of the Word Processor

Although a wide variety of word processors exists to meet different needs and purposes, the basic way in which they all operate is very similar. Word processing devices perform five main functions: (1) inputting, (2) processing, (3) editing, (4) storing, and (5) outputting.

Inputting is the process of entering information into the computer.

Processing enables one to make deletions and additions and format changes in a document.

Editing and writing become effortless in that it is easy to change words, add lines, delete whole paragraphs, and replace text. The traditional tasks of cutting, pasting, and rewriting are made very convenient, requiring only a few key strokes.

Storing is the preservation of documents one is working with internally or externally. A hard drive or a floppy disk stores documents for future needs and further changes.

Outputting and communicating involve the production of the documents in any one of many different formats, such as on the display terminal or by printing.

Notable changes and improvements are taking place in the technology of word processing. Some recent changes include programs that present on screen exactly what will be printed. Another is "windows," which display portions of different documents on the screen simultaneously. Other improvements are paperless word processors, laser printers, and voice recognition. Handwriting and voice recognition already exist. Indeed, the great challenge of the 1990s will be bridging the gap between paperwork and electronics.

Countless word processing programs are available. Some are easy and less costly, while others are intricate and expensive. The costs of these programs range in price from about $15 to over $2,000 for multipurpose packages prepared for use by professional print shops. Among the popular word processing software packages available on the market are WordPerfect, Multimate, WordStar, PC-Write, Microsoft Word for Windows, and PageMaker. One should postpone purchasing expensive programs until one becomes familiar with the less expensive variety, or until one develops a need for a particular system. All too often, one can purchase too many accessories and never get their full potential or use out of them.

Reading and Outlining

5

INTRODUCTION

This section serves as a guide for preparing lengthy written documents. Knowledge of the basic mechanics of writing is a prerequisite for the composition of formal documents such as reports, term papers, books, and other manuscripts. Research and writing without the use of proper techniques may become a source of frustration and failure. These techniques consist of gathering information, making an outline, writing within acceptable legal conventions, and composing the final draft.

Researchers are investigators in search of knowledge that has been presented by others as a path to the formulation of new thoughts, views, and ideas, which can be expressed in writing. They become students of the writings of others, learn from their findings, and discover what the authors have found to be true. Concurrently, researchers can become conceptual thinkers and associate their knowledge and experience with newfound information to formulate an integrated new *whole* or *truth*. Having knowledge of the facets of the writing process and carefully following proper techniques to avoid plagiarism and violation of copyright laws are the responsibility of the author of any written document.

Prior to writing, the researcher must understand how to "give credit where credit is due," through proper acknowledgment. One must know where to draw the line between original thinking and the thoughts expressed or implied by others. Being knowledgeable about the critical details of plagiarism and copyright laws is essential to any writer.

ACCEPTABLE LEGAL CONVENTIONS

Plagiarism

Writers, students, researchers, public speakers, inventors, artists, and others often misunderstand plagiarism. The crime of plagiarism frequently occurs without the perpetrator's realizing it. One of the mistakes made by some people during writing formal papers is thinking that changing a few words in a paragraph or simply paraphrasing is acceptable. Some people presume that only copying entire sentences, paragraphs, or phrases is plagiarism. *Encyclopedia Americana* defines plagiarism as the "reproduction in whole or essential part of a literary, artistic, or musical work by one who falsely claims to be its creator." This example would be considered plagiarism if the reference to the source was not included. Other forms of expression are included in this definition of plagiarism as well. Senator Joseph Biden, a contender for the Democratic nomination for the Presidency of the United States in 1988, withdrew from the race after the discovery that one of his speeches was plagiarized from a speech of the British Labor Party Leader, Neil Kinnoch. Another of Biden's speeches contained passages from a speech delivered by President John F. Kennedy. The *World Book Encyclopedia* explains that "a work need not be identical to the original to be plagiarism. However, it must be so similar that it has obviously been copied."

Plagiarism is a serious offense and should not be taken lightly. Detection of plagiarism can have terrible consequences, such as dismissal from school, loss of a job, professional ruin, and possible lawsuits. Criminal and civil penalties can lead to further punishment, including imprisonment. Statutory damages and fines of up to five thousand dollars can be issued depending on the nature, type, and extent of plagiarism.

Many writers are influenced by scholarly research and publications. Therefore, on occasion they may inadvertently articulate similar thoughts and ideas. The synthesis of one's own reasoning with a fresh arrangement of newly discovered thoughts may be a solution to "improving" previously expressed statements. Synthesis is one reason people write. One's own style and harmony of words are what makes writing worthwhile and creative. One should use quotations, citations, or paraphrases with proper documentation when an idea cannot be expressed in a better way than in its original form. Authors, students, and speakers must be careful not to give any basis for the charge of plagiarism. One would not expect professional journalists to plagiarize due to possible discovery by vast readership. Yet, according to an article entitled "Ethics Violation," in *Editor and Publisher* (April 26, 1986), the American Society of Newspaper Editors found that one-sixth of editors surveyed had encountered plagiarism during their previous three years on the job.

Copyright Regulations

Copyrighting is defined in *Webster's Ninth Collegiate Dictionary* as "the exclusive legal right to reproduce, publish, and sell the matter and form of a literary, musical or artistic work." Copyright statutes cover and protect almost any type of original expression: artistic, dramatic, literary, musical; as well as photographs, lithographs, poems, novels, postcards, jewelry, architecture, motion pictures, translations, and condensations. Copyrighting also includes the structure, sequence, and organization of computer programs. All these examples of original expression known as *intellectual property* are covered by copyright statutes. Trademarks that can be represented by words, logos, or symbols are also covered as intellectual property.

Civilized societies have laws to protect tangible property and the physical well-being of their citizens, as well as laws to protect intellectual property. Through copyright laws an owner has statutory rights to protect his or her work. These laws restrict the use of copyrighted work owned by others in any medium of expression. Without the authorization of the owner, copyrighted work may not be published, translated, adapted, broadcast, or exhibited legally. In effect, copyrighting gives the owner a monopoly over the reproduction and sale of the work. However, it does allow the legal possessor — someone other than the copyright owner — to use the item for personal and authorized use.

The origin of copyright laws can be traced back to 15th century England during the early stages of printing technology. Advances in printing technology made it easier to reproduce prohibited religious and political matter; therefore, laws were enacted to control the dissemination and printing of designated books and other material. Copyright laws were considered a form of censorship. The failure of these laws led to literary piracy, plagiarism, and the reproduction of other people's work for profit. In England in 1710, the Statute of Anne went into effect and prohibited unauthorized printing of certain books for a limited number of years. The owners were given a fourteen-year copyright protection by the British Parliament in 1979.

The Constitution of the United States of America recognized the unauthorized duplication of literary property and invention in 1789. Since that time, Congress has developed a fairly comprehensive copyright law to include various additions, interpretations, and reorganizations. This law finally came into effect in 1978. The Universal Copyright Convention in Geneva, Switzerland made it possible to obtain copyright protection in all signatory countries of the convention. In March of 1989, the United States officially subscribed to the Berne Convention. As a result, if one registers a work in the U.S., one will automatically own copyright protection under the laws of other signatory countries.

Types of Copyrights. There are two forms of copyrights: the statutory law and the common law. A statutory copyright is secured upon publication of literary works with the insertion of the notice in an appropriate location. This copyright notice must include the following information:

- The name of the copyright owner
- The word "copyright" or its abbreviated form "cop," or the symbol "©", and
- The year copyrighted, although common law protection governs unpublished literary work for the duration of the time that it remains unpublished.

Any type of original work can be protected under copyright laws. In the United States, the following fourteen categories of creative authorship are eligible for copyright protection:

- books
- periodicals
- lectures and sermons
- musical compositions
- dramatic and musical compositions
- maps
- works of art
- original reproductions of works of art
- drawings or plastic works
- photographs
- prints and pictorial illustrations
- motion pictures
- photoplays and motion pictures other than photoplays
- computer programs

Registering a Copyright. Authors of dissertations, reports, books, poetry, translations, computer software, and other similar works of value should register their work by writing to the Publication Section, Copyright Office, Library of Congress, Washington, DC 20559, and request an application form for copyright registration. The copyright is obtained through sending the completed application that will contain description of the material to be copyrighted with a fee of twenty dollars. One copy of the original work, or two copies if the work is published, must be sent with the application. It is permissible to request registration for several works; an example of this would be a group of articles under one application for the single fee of twenty dollars. However, in this case the work must be assembled in a binder, bearing a single title, representing the work of the author or the collaborators.

The Copyright Office issues the applicant a Certificate of Registration that may be used as evidence of ownership in court. Copyright protection lasts for the life of the author plus fifty years, with heirs receiving the remaining benefits. If the copyright was obtained by several collaborators, protection is provided for the life of the last survivor plus fifty years. After the copyright expires, the material reverts to the public domain.

Copyright protection does not include works completed for others under the provisions of "work for hire." The person or organization commissioning the work owns the copyright. If the work is not registered, ownership rights of the creator are still protected under common law provisions. However, this makes it difficult for people to know that a work is copyrighted and for the holder to prove ownership. For this reason, it is advisable to obtain a copyright through registration. Unpublished material sent to prospective publishers should include a copyright page with the author's name. Doctoral theses and dissertations are considered published upon acceptance, at which time they are put on microfilm for distribution. For additional protection, the author should register the thesis manuscript and obtain copyright protection.

At least three criteria are needed to obtain a copyright registration. First, the material must be able to be perceived, reproduced, and/or communicated. Second, it must promote creativity and inventiveness. Third, it must demonstrate the expression of an idea. Ideas themselves cannot be copyrighted; it is only the development and arrangement of ideas that are protected. Names, words, slogans, and titles cannot be copyrighted because they cannot be registered and are protected as trademarks. The federal copyright laws protect against infringement and give statutory rights to authors over their work. This work is considered the intellectual property of the author until this right is transferred to a publisher upon publication. Publishers can obtain copyrights for manuscripts and transfer ownership to themselves. Copyright laws protect one's own work, as well as the work of other people. Without authorization from the copyright holder, no work may be published, translated, adapted, broadcast, or exhibited.

Work for Hire. Work for hire is the hiring or commissioning of someone to accomplish an assignment for others. Copyright ownership is forfeited over material created under this type of agreement. Publishers regularly commission and assign authors to write articles and other material for them. When a professor publishes an article or a book, using institutional time and resources, the university does not own the copyright. On the other hand, if the professor is asked under contract to engage in a research project or write an article or a book, then copyright ownership belongs to the institution. This applies to works created in private as well as other institutions. The disputes over the ownership of copyrights covering material created during normal work hours resulted in the "work for hire" provision in the new copyright laws. This provision requires an employer to include in the agreement "work for hire" or a similar phrase in order to gain ownership over copyrights. One should be aware of the loss of ownership rights over any material produced during normal work by signing such agreements in advance.

Stipulations of Copyright Laws. Some exclusionary rights for personal, limited use are provided under the "fair use" provision of the copyright laws, which allows the public limited use of copyrighted material without authorization. Scholars, journalists, teachers, and critics are allowed to copy portions of works for non-commercial purposes. This encourages free exchange of ideas, creativity, and research. Students may quote, copy, and reproduce limited materials for personal use or writing term papers. However, if the material is to be published, authorization is needed. Instructors are not allowed to copy articles from journals for student distribution without authorization. Libraries obtain prior authorization for copied materials that are put on reserve by instructors for students. The owner of a computer program is not allowed to make copies of personal software for distribution to friends and family members. Quotations with more than 150 words may require payment. If a lesser number of words is used, and they constitute a substantial or significant segment from the original work, authorization is needed. Finally, after authorization is received, it must be recognized either in the copyright or in the acknowledgment section of the manuscript. Infringement of copyright laws usually takes the form of a substantial appropriation of content for use in other media or through copying the arrangement and setup of a certain work. The effect of the use on the potential commercial value of the work may restrict copyright material usage and reproduction.

A lawsuit for copyright infringement cannot be initiated if the work is not registered. If an infringement occurs, and the creator of the work subsequently registered the material, and then a lawsuit is instigated, certain rights may be lost. This will include recovering attorney's fees and statutory damages. However, lost income and other benefits can be recovered as a result of infringement. Registration before infringements makes for a stronger legal case. Although incidents of infringements are rare, the nature and importance of the work should guide the author in the undertaking of the efforts and expenses involved in obtaining a copyright. Penalties for infringement include liability for lost profits, civil and statutory damages, fines, and imprisonment. Publishers regularly scrutinize materials for infringement of their copyrights, and the Copyright Office screens other copyrights for duplication. The final policing of the copyright is the obligation of the holder. When a violation of copyright law occurs, it is the responsibility of the owner to prove infringement and file for court injunction and other damages.

Finally, care should be exercised in the reproduction of written materials, charts, pictures, illustrations, graphs, computer software, and other such material without authorization. Copyright protection is essential for the protection of the rights and creativity of authors. Copyright laws ensure the preservation of original works and acknowledge their historical significance. Without such security one would not know who wrote, composed, invented, or painted an original work. Creativity in research, arts, writing, and invention would be seriously affected if people could not safeguard their work from duplication. Copyright laws encourage creativity and innovation. Typical copyright pages that should be included with a manuscript are shown in Appendix H.

READING

Introduction

Some people assume that they are able to read proficiently. Instructors trust that most students know how to read. When reports, projects, and papers are returned by instructors, students begin to realize that they know the mechanics of reading but fail to read productively.

Speaking, writing, and reading are perhaps the most distinguished forms of communication. Reading allows one to become knowledgeable and informed about people, ideas, cultures, and the environment. Without reading, people would not be able to perform simple tasks, such as observing traffic signs. Most people can learn to read on a basic level, understanding both the form and meaning of printed and written characters. However, few people are able to comprehend reading on a professional level. Still, some students take reading abilities for granted, which ultimately affects their performance on examinations and research projects and in their careers.

A person's ability to write will be greatly enhanced through better reading skills. Reading abilities improve through preparation, planning, and practice. Studies have indicated that most people use only a small part of their total reading capabilities. Reading is regarded by some as an art. It is rare that an artist becomes talented without preparation and practice. To become accomplished in the art of reading, as in any art, preparation and practice are necessary.

A Brief History of Reading

The history of reading dates back over 3,000 years to the ancient Orient. Although the Phoenicians were originally credited with the invention of the alphabet, they are now credited only with its popularity. Recently an old alphabet script was discovered in northern Syria. It was concluded that people in the Syrian-Palestinian regions were the first to discover the practicality of using symbols to represent simple sounds. The Phoenician merchants, on their economic sojourn to other regions, carried these symbols and scripts to other parts of the world. These merchants influenced the Greeks, who in turn invented a better alphabet that allowed greater flexibility in writing.

The first English alphabet was written by early Christian missionaries using modified Latin letters. In the Middle Ages, reading was a skill possessed only by the clergy. Surprisingly, most kings and nobility were illiterate. The only way to reproduce books and other manuscripts at this time was to copy them by hand. This practice made books and other materials rare and expensive. Advancements in technology during the 17th and 18th centuries led to the invention of the printing press. The printing press increased interest in reading by making books both attainable and affordable. In time, Western countries became interested in universal education as well. Finally in 1850, a bill was passed by the English Parliament that provided minimum schooling for children. This act was later modified in the United States, resulting in wider interest in education, reading, and writing.

Types of and Purposes for Reading

Reading is the ability to comprehend, not simply to recognize, letters, forms, and symbols. Some animals learn to recognize letters but not actually understand their meaning. Without comprehension, reading may prove to be almost useless. There are three levels of reading comprehension. (1) Literal reading is the ability to follow directions and understand exact words, meanings, and characters. (2) Aesthetic reading is the ability to appreciate artistically the style and overall quality of what is being read. (3) Critical reading consists of making factual distinctions between common ideas, facts, and opinion. This capability is needed for valid interpretation and analysis. Total comprehension requires reading at all of the above levels. Thus, to comprehend a chapter in a textbook well, one must have the ability to read at all levels.

Reading for different purposes requires a reading level suitable for that intention. Literal reading is required for all purposes, but all three types are required for total comprehension. There are at least five main purposes for comprehensive reading. These purposes include: (1) reading for specific information, (2) reading for application, (3) reading for pleasure and entertainment, (4) reading for ideas, and (5) reading for understanding. All these purposes require necessary skills in order to be accomplished efficiently.

Reading for Specific Information. Reading for specific information is a common form of reading used to discover specific or limited information. It is reading at an elementary level through the recognition of simple symbols, words, and sentences. Reading for this purpose involves looking for specific information and finding it quickly. This type of reading occurs upon observing traffic signs or checking television listings. Looking up a word in the dictionary or a number in the telephone book is another example of reading for specific information. Some forms of magazine and newspaper reading may also involve this type of reading.

Reading for Application. Reading for application is used to accomplish a special task. This type of reading may consist of reading a cake recipe or following instructions to make or fix something. Reading how a word processing program is run on a computer is also a form of reading for application. Most repair manuals and guide books are read to learn how to apply written information to accomplish some desired task.

Reading for Pleasure and Entertainment. Individuals read for many pleasurable reasons. This includes reading popular magazines, newspapers, novels, and other similar materials. It is a slower form of reading, which allows the reader to envision the scenery and contemplate the background and characters with enjoyment and appreciation. This form of reading calls for the total involvement of the reader. A child may spend a great deal of time reading pleasurable stories like *Winnie the Pooh, Peter Rabbit*, and *Beauty and the Beast*. College students may read certain history books, adventure books, or plays for entertainment. Scholars may recall reading classics such as *Moby Dick* or *David Copperfield* for pleasure.

Reading for Ideas. This type of reading requires paying special attention to main ideas and concepts and the nature of the presented information. The reader skims through major topics, headings, illustrations, and conclusions in order to obtain a general idea of the content. A college student selecting several journals or books from the library may skim through them, section by section, to obtain a general idea of their contents. Reading for ideas is enhanced through familiarity with the overall field of study, related topics, facts, and discussions.

Reading for Understanding. Reading for understanding requires comprehension of the relationship between the information introduced and overall knowledge of the subject. It requires understanding the relationship of topics to sentences, paragraphs, and the main idea. The reader must observe the associations between facts, data, and other details. For example, students reading an economics textbook must carefully compare and contrast similarities and differences of the facts and data presented in order to understand the subject. To comprehend the material, the reader must possess the ability to understand the author's level of presentation. Reading for understanding requires critical attention and mental evaluation.

Methods of Reading

There are at least six methods of fulfilling these purposes of reading. These methods include: (1) previewing, (2) skimming and scanning, (3) reading for study, (4) critical reading, (5) reading for critical evaluation, and (6) speed reading.

Previewing. Previewing is an advance evaluation and brief examination of the material. To preview a book, one may look at the preface, table of contents, and chapter headings. Previewing is used for looking over a chapter in a textbook before studying it. This is done to get a general idea of the information included and how much effort is required to read the chapter. One may read a few pages of a novel or a book to decide whether or not to read it. If necessary, the reader can return to the selection and read it in greater detail. The knowledge gained from previewing helps to determine whether the document is a worthwhile source to read. In general terms, previewing is like warming up in sports; it prepares one to read productively.

Skimming and Scanning. Skimming and scanning, also called *survey reading*, are appropriate when the reader is too pressed for time to read an entire selection. In skimming it is helpful to become familiar with the words used by the author or those frequently used in a chosen discipline. This is accomplished by glancing over material quickly, or reading bits and pieces of material. People skim books, newspaper articles, magazine articles, and essays to select appropriate information by obtaining a general understanding of the work. The concept of looking quickly at a selection and picking out key words, ideas, phrases, and sentences helps one save time. In essence, skim reading is looking quickly for main ideas and the overall content that supports them. A person with a larger vocabulary has an advantage in skim reading and comprehension.

In scanning, unlike skimming, one knows what one is looking for in advance. Some examples of scanning are when one scans catalogs or a telephone book to locate an item or a number that is listed. Scanning is involved when one looks for specific facts, names, dates, words, or any other exact information.

Reading for Study. Study reading is undertaken carefully at a rate allowing the individual to assimilate the information. This form of reading requires a good deal of concentration. Study reading is necessary during schooling, training for a specific job, or preparing for examinations. It is also undertaken to further oneself in a profession. An engineer who wishes to learn about the latest developments in nuclear waste disposal could read a magazine article and then apply the information to his job. Study reading is characterized by the reader's ability to comprehend and retain key ideas and information from the material. This type of reading will be productive only if one takes time to pose questions about the content of the material that was read. One should try to remember to test one's understanding of the key concepts of what was read, and to take some notes. A well-known formula for study reading involves the memory-enhancing characters "SQ3R" (survey, question, read, recite, and review). Remembering and using these five steps will greatly benefit one's comprehension and retention during study.

Critical Reading. Critical reading requires the ability to comprehend accurately what is written by the author. Critical reading requires reasoning between facts, opinions, and references, and their presentation. Most college classroom assignments involve this type of reading, such as writing a term paper or preparing for an essay examination. The student must be able to comprehend the material and evaluate it thoroughly. Lack of critical reading often results in failure to succeed in taking objective tests, such as multiple-choice or true-false type examinations. The reader must critically judge the author's information, biases, facts, and conclusions against all available evidence. This type of reading requires adequate preparation and familiarity with the subject matter.

Critical reading is not merely comprehending the meaning of something written or printed, but a methodical endeavor to understand the significance, intent, and relationship of written concepts. Most college students can read *Moby Dick* and follow the plot as it applies to a story about whaling, but only the critical reader will be aware of the underlying themes and ideas in the story. Most managers can read and understand a proposal for divestiture, but only the critical manager will be able to examine the argument and determine whether it is valid for the circumstances. A college student may understand an article on financial management, but only the reader who is able to evaluate concepts in the context of overall business objectives will gain insight from such reading. Critical reading is a requirement toward scholarship, professional development, and creativity, all of which demand a thorough understanding of content.

Other aspects of reading are useful as well. These include reading for critical evaluation, the importance of vocabulary, and some other helpful hints. It is important to observe all methods of reading in order to find what works best for oneself.

Reading for Critical Evaluation. Reading for critical purposes can be undertaken in two stages. These two stages consist of the introductory stage and the intensive stage. The introductory stage includes previewing articles, books, and other material in order to gain necessary background information on a subject. The preview should be short yet productive. The introductory stage involves developing a plan of attack. Questions to be answered in the introductory stage are: (1) How much time will be required? (2) How extensive will be the total effort and for what purpose? (3) When will it be finished? (4) What methodology will be used in both research and writing? (5) Where will most of the activities take place? Introductory preparation calls for some initial mental exercises. Start reviewing unabridged dictionaries, encyclopedias, popular magazine articles, and chapters in books, histories, and appropriate reference works. When looking at the material, preview the work, while flipping through page by page. Observe interesting aspects of the topic. Read the preface, evaluate the table of contents, graphs, tables, appendices, and illustrations. Find out how extensive or brief the book is. What topics are discussed? What are the titles? Take special notice headings of chapters, sections, and paragraphs. Observe the organization and presentation of the material. Headings, opening sentences, and first paragraphs normally present main ideas from an entire section. Skim sections and read any interesting sentences or paragraphs. If summaries are included, read them and take notes. These notes may be about interesting aspects of the topic, or the location or availability of material. It is important to take some time to consider the topic and the challenges of the endeavor while planning for the second stage.

The second stage in critical reading requires intensive reading, analysis, and note-taking. According to a prepared plan, the reader looks for specific information that will be used in research and writing. The focus of reading should be on newly discovered information and subject specialization. If it is a personal book, take notes in the margins, and/or mark important information by underlining. For critical reading, such as preparing for examinations, take notes on a separate sheet of paper or on index cards. Take at least one page of notes for each chapter. When finished, reflect and review the highlighted parts of the chapter to observe what has been learned. Set the chapter aside and come back later for review. Reading marathons should be avoided. Distributing reading throughout the day or week with brief breaks is more effective than reading all at once. Finally, learn from the reading and ask yourself, "If *I* were the examiner, what would *I* include on the examination?" The examiner is probably most interested in the main ideas, key terms, and significant concepts.

Speed Reading. The increasing need to read a great deal of material faster in our everyday life requires one to read quickly. Speed reading is the ability to read at a high rate of speed while comprehending the material being read. Skill in speed reading is beneficial to those who must continually read a great deal of material in a short time. It is useless to read faster without retention or understanding. A skilled speed reader is able to understand the meanings of sentences at a glance, much as one would recognize a word. The average reader reads 250 to 350 words per minute. A skilled speed reader may read over 6,000 words per minute. Speed reading is based on skimming and scanning and is improved through practice. Most colleges and universities offer speed reading courses that include a wide variety of styles and learning approaches.

Several different approaches are recommended for proficiency in speed reading, one of which is based on *decreasing regression*. This refers to eye movement and rereading of words. Emphasis is placed on a rhythmic eye movement from left to right and greater concentration on the subject matter. Beginners start reading with a 3 x 5-inch card in one hand, covering words and lines as they are read. After some initial frustration, speed reading is achieved through lessening regression and avoiding rereading. Another method called *clustering* is accomplished through reading several words at once instead of reading word for word. Progressively, whole lines are read at a glance, much like recognizing a word at a glance. Still another technique involves reading every second, third, fourth, and subsequent words by moving a pencil, pen, or finger in a constant rhythmic movement across lines until the desired level of speed reading is achieved.

It is debatable whether speed reading is suitable for reading a complex subject critically. Understanding what is read is important, regardless of the rate of speed. Although one can learn to read faster, it is always better to read slowly with comprehension.

Vocabulary   Good reading requires an adequate vocabulary. Poor vocabulary and lack of proper skills in reading are among the major causes of poor comprehension and lack of appreciation of reading. The readers of this book are likely to deal with complex reading material that demands a large vocabulary. It is beneficial to develop such a large vocabulary. This will save time in looking up individual words, a process that would cause loss of concentration and a misunderstanding of critical meanings. It has been estimated that an average college student is skilled in the use of approximately 5,000 words. However, the active vocabulary, which consists of words used in speaking and writing, is considerably smaller. Through habitual exercise one may gain a larger vocabulary. Readers should make note of unknown words in the field of interest and learn their definitions. Unrecognized words that are frequently encountered in a text should be looked up in a dictionary or thesaurus. Failure to comprehend certain words may result in misunderstanding sentences, paragraphs, or entire sections. Too frequently in reading and writing, people neglect the use of the thesaurus and the dictionary. These references are consulted for correct spelling, pronunciation, grammar, and various definitions. The thesaurus is a useful book that contains meanings, antonyms, and synonyms of words. A handy notebook should be kept to record meanings of newly discovered words. It should be used for alternative word usage and vocabulary. Also, individuals may enhance vocabulary by consulting a special list of difficult words such as the list included in Appendix B. Appendix C presents a list of words that are often misspelled. In some cases, vocabulary enhancement may be achieved through reading one of the many brief books written for the subject. A person can understand words and develop a good vocabulary by observing the following recommended approaches: (1) familiarity with words through increased reading; (2) skeletal clues (breaking words into identifiable parts, such as (auto-bio-graphy); and (3) contextual clues — guessing what the word means from the way it is used.

The more one sees unfamiliar words in context while reading, the better one understands the meaning of the words. It is well established that reading on a wide range of subjects is the best way to build up a good vocabulary. It is a good practice to read several works of the same author, and to read in the same discipline in order to gain increased vocabulary in one's field of interest. People recognize more words than they realize through their ability to break down words into component parts. On many occasions one does not have the time or a handy dictionary to look up a word. In skeletal clues, if one were to encounter the word "circumvent," from the existing knowledge of the words "circle" and "vent," one could establish that it means "circulating around" something. This method is facilitated through memorizing the meanings of frequently used prefixes and suffixes. The contextual clues approach is to observe and decipher the meaning of a word by paying attention to the context in which words are used. For example, "While looking out the window of the 17th floor, Maria had an acrophobia relapse," indicates that acrophobia is fear of high places.

Reading: Helpful Hints   Reading requires practice just as all other skills do. When it is said that one reads well, it means that one encompasses several different skills at a variety of levels, for a number of purposes. Most adolescents are capable of informational reading for pleasure the moment that they enter high school, but serious reading involves more advanced skills than most students have at the high school level. These skills are learned and acquired through practice. Productive reading requires planning, discipline, organization, and a suitable environment. Two factors crucial to serious reading are alertness and the ability to concentrate.

When reading for enjoyment, one may prefer light music in the background, a comfortable armchair, or lying in bed. On the other hand, serious reading disallows such distractions as radio, television, music, friends, and telephone calls. Lack of preparation, emotional preoccupation, poor physical health, lack of time, and a poor location hinder serious reading. A reader should experiment to discover the best suitable circumstances for reading. First, one should determine the preferred times for reading. Some individuals may prefer to read at night, while others like the early morning hours or the afternoons. The second important item to consider is a proper location for reading. Some people prefer secluded areas where their friends and others cannot find them, such as the reading cubicles in the library. It is also recommended to read habitually at the same time periods and at the same location.

Another important factor for efficient reading is quality lighting. Quality lighting consists of appropriate illumination, type of light, and position of the light fixture. When illumination is too intense, eyes become fatigued. The source of light should be placed where it will not disturb the reader's eyes. It should be strong enough to light the pages clearly, yet not so strong as to produce a glare on the text. The best position for a reading light is above one's shoulder, as it reduces eye strain. An indirect light fixture is recommended for intensive reading purposes.

In summary, the environment in which one reads should encourage concentration and discourage distraction. There is no foolproof method for improved reading comprehension. Each person should find his or her most efficient and effective approach to reading. In serious reading it is recommended to apply oneself so as to get as much read as possible at one sitting before losing interest. Occasional breaks may enable one to return with fresh vigor and enthusiasm. Different habits should be developed and used according to the type of reading involved. To say one reads critically and with understanding is to say that one has mastered one of the finest arts devised for education. The art of reading is a skill that must be developed through planning and good organizing. In order to read with comprehension and recollection, a plan based on an approach similar to the following suggestions will prove productive.

PREVIEW THE MATERIAL
- Examine the document with interest, curiosity, and some enthusiasm. Notice the publication date, title, author, and publisher. Skim through any included introductory, dedication, and preface material. Observe included drawings, illustrations, pictures, graphs, and statistical data. Ask yourself the following questions: How extensive and thorough is the material? How much time and effort will be required to read the material for the intended purpose?

- Notice secondary titles, subheadings, and any itemized details. These indicate organization of the presented material and their relevance throughout the discussions. Information printed in color, different print, italics, underlined, or boldfaced calls attention to prominent discussions and facts.

- Scan any introductions and summaries that are included in the chapter. Become familiar with what the reading presents. Pay special attention to the first and last paragraphs. Principal thoughts are presented by most writers at the beginning and repeated at the end.

- Read and understand the leading sentence of each of the other paragraphs. These are generally the topic sentences that summarize the complete paragraph.

- Scan any questions that may be included at the end. They inform the reader about important concepts and ideas to learn and remember.

READ ATTENTIVELY
- Choose a fitting time, place, and environment. Concentrate on the reading material without distractions.

- Be aware of the reason for the reading and the author's purpose. Ask yourself, is this reading for pleasure, to study for an examination, or to evaluate new ideas and facts?

- Take notes on a sheet of paper. Underline or write in the margin of personal books significant and freshly discovered information. Become judgmental in the evaluation of important and insignificant information. It is a wasteful practice to underline passages indiscriminately.

- Comprehend words and build your vocabulary. Become familiar with words in your field of interest or discipline and the expressions that are frequently used by the author.

- Read critically and with challenge. Debate and reason the presented facts, opinions, and references. Be judgmental concerning the author's information, biases, facts, and conclusions. One should not readily accept any information just because it is written.

- Whenever the assignment is read, reflect and quiz yourself about the facts, concepts, and nature of the information. Ask yourself, what were the main and supportive theses? Reread and locate any missed or significant information.

THE OUTLINE

Introduction

An outline is a preliminary sketch representing the principal features, structure, and content of a written work, essay, story, speech, or other type of material. Before writing the outline select an appropriate subject and topic. A hypothesis or thesis statement should then be formulated to focus on the topic and the subject. Creating and following a numbered format for the material to be presented will make the subject more clear and will guide the writer through the composition process. A properly written outline structure will give the writer confidence and motivation throughout the research effort. Overall, the outline will form the basic plan of the final paper.

Outline Development

In writing, the outline is a preparatory sketch that includes the principal features of what is to be written. The chief value of an outline in writing is its ability to facilitate the organization of research and writing. An outline, like a blueprint of a building, is a preliminary systematic sketch. It is essential for the development and writing of a logical and cohesive paper.

Three essential parts to any formal essay or written document are the introduction, the body, and the conclusion. In the outline, the introduction and conclusion labels are not used. These are too vague to assist the writer when beginning to write. Instead, one of the topics in the outline is used to start the introduction and the conclusion.

The introduction identifies the purpose and specific topics of the written material. It should point out the importance of the material, arouse the reader's interest, and indicate the direction of the writing. In the introduction, the author should briefly state the current views and the status of research on the topic.

The body of the paper presents the writer's research findings and observations through presentation, expansion, and clarification of the discussions.

The conclusion should not be a simple summary or restatement, but rather a presentation of the findings and implications of the research effort. The author should take a stand and express a point of view within this section. The position taken should be stated forcefully and indicate the value of the effort by the author.

Writing and following a numbered format makes the plan of writing easier, while guiding the author through the creative process. The outline will indicate clearly and logically the main ideas of the written material and their relationship to each other in a brief format. A good outline helps the writer "navigate" and allows for concentration and focusing on the thesis of the paper. Writing without an outline frequently leads to disorganization, impatience, postponement, and even desertion of the writing effort.

Overall, an outline is a tool for maintaining effective organization of material and providing momentum to write. An outline takes the writer through the writing process step by step; from the introduction to the body, and finally, the conclusion of the paper. Once a proper outline is constructed and followed, it will produce a satisfactory final paper. Effective outlining requires writing a clear and concise thesis statement. This is followed by the development of a structure through the use of numbers, letters, and headings that facilitate the logical presentation of the material and writing.

Thesis Statement. When proper information is gathered, the next step involves preparing a tentative or trial thesis statement, also called the *controlling idea*. This statement should indicate the topic and be organized according to the questions who, what, where, when, why, and how. In brief, the thesis should answer the questions: Why is one writing? For whom is one writing? What is the subject of writing? The thesis statement should be concise, informative, interesting, and original. Only when these criteria are present will the writing be worthwhile and important enough to sustain the composition effort.

The second step involves composing a lucid thesis statement that provides the writer with a focal point for gathering facts that will lead to valid and desirable conclusions. One clear sentence may be sufficient in writing the thesis statement (such as in the case of writing short papers). However, it is appropriate to write a full paragraph for longer papers. For best results, the subject of the thesis sentence should name the topic of the paper, while the predicate of the sentence lists the major headings or divisions of the paper. The thesis statement is like a map that leads the writer to a finished product. A polished outline and thesis statement will give the writer direction, momentum, and maneuverability. Writers who start without a thesis statement in hopes that the desired material will fall into place may frequently abandon the effort out of frustration and lack of a clear objective.

The thesis statement guides the writer in evaluating the collected relevant information by keeping him or her focused on the purpose of the paper. Suppose one is writing a paper about the Olympics; a preliminary thesis statement, such as the following, would give guidance and direction for the outline and the paper to follow:

> The purpose of the modern Olympic games is to bring the nations of the world together to promote peace and friendship. However, through intense competition, the true spirit of the games has been lost in recent years. Nationalistic and political pressures are endangering the competition's existence. This has served to dilute or diminish the true spirit of world athletic competition and caused the games to be endangered and their future uncertain.

After writing the thesis statement, it becomes necessary to develop a structure through the use of numbers and headings. This structure becomes the skeleton for the outline and presentation of the written material.

Numbering Systems. To facilitate the logical progression of discussions and presentations of written material, several numbering techniques can be used for grouping information in an outline. This combination of letters, numbers, and corresponding topics becomes the skeletal guide for use in drafting the paper. It is employed to break down major topics into decreasingly lower levels of topical relevance. For example, in the case of arranging by numbers and letters, the outline is structured by assigning Roman numerals to major headings. Capital letters are reserved for secondary subheadings. Arabic numbers are indicated for lower headings. Lower case letters are used for topics that are more specific. It is important that any heading or subheading be broken into at least two parts; thus if there is a number I, there must be a number II. If something is divided, there must be at least two parts. The three most widely used methods of numbering outline structures are: (1) alphanumeric, (2) decimal, and (3) Roman numeral.

ALPHANUMERIC METHOD

The *alphanumeric method* has become the traditional choice in the preparation of such documents as government manuscripts, publications, and reports. It is a simple method to construct, use, and understand. The following is the structure for numbering the major topics (A. B...) secondary topics (1. 2...,) and topics of lesser importance (a. b...):

A. Major Heading
   1. Subheading — 1st degree
   2. Subheading — 1st degree
      a. Subheading — 2nd degree
      b. Subheading — 2nd degree
         (1) Subheading — 3rd degree
         (2) Subheading — 3rd degree
            (a) Subheading — 4th degree
            (b) Subheading — 4th degree

3. Subheading — 1st degree

B. Major Heading

1. Subheading — 1st degree

2. Subheading — 1st degree

DECIMAL METHOD

The *decimal method* is popular in the use and preparation of scientific, technical, and book-length documents that tend to require accuracy, greater detail, and more precision. The following structure is an example of this method.

1. Major Heading

1.1 Subheading — 1st degree

1.11 Subheading — 2nd degree

1.12 Subheading — 2nd degree

1.111 Subheading — 3rd degree

1.112 Subheading — 3rd degree

1.1111 Subheading — 4th degree

1.1112 Subheading — 4th degree

1.2 Subheading — 1st degree

2. Major heading

2.1 Subheading — 1st degree

2.2 Subheading — 1st degree

ROMAN NUMERAL METHOD

The *Roman numeral method* is most commonly used in the fields of business, industry, and social science. Its simplicity makes this approach very popular for use in the writing of term papers and other reports by college students. The following example illustrates the structure of the Roman numeral method:

I. Major Heading

A. Subheading — 1st degree

B. Subheading — 1st degree

1. Subheading — 2nd degree

2. Subheading — 2nd degree

a. Subheading — 3rd degree

b. Subheading — 3rd degree

(1) Subheading — 4th degree

(2) Subheading — 4th degree

C. Subheading — 1st degree

II. Major Heading

A. Subheading — 1st degree

B. Subheading — 1st degree

Constructing an Outline

After the controlling idea has been written, a detailed outline can be constructed using one of the numerical methods. The purpose of the paper, as described in the thesis statement, suggests the skeleton of the outline by defining the main topic and specifying the ideas to be discussed in their order of presentation. A well-structured outline should develop a logical connection between the introduction, body, and conclusion of the paper. This outline should highlight major elements of the thesis statement and provide for a unity of direction.

The main function of a properly constructed outline is to create balance and continuity throughout the paper. The composition of an outline allows the writer to maintain control of the work by developing main ideas and propositions in a reasonable, flowing, structured form. These ideas may be arranged in order of importance, chronologically, by topic, or in any other logical progression. It may be appropriate in one paper to present the hypothesis, data, arguments, and strong points at the beginning, thus getting the reader's attention immediately. In another paper, it may be better to postpone the best arguments, evidence, and data on suggested points until the end, in order to build a continually persuasive and climactic resolve for the thesis. The most common outline formats and their related structures are presented in the following pages.

OUTLINE FORMAT   Thesis Sentence:

_____

_____

_____

I. (Roman numeral: First Major Topic or Sentence Heading)
   A. (Capital letter: First subtopic or sentence heading)
      1. (Arabic number: First topic or sentence heading under a topic of secondary importance)
         a. (Lower case letter: Sentence heading under second subtopic)
         b.
            (1)
            (2)
               (a)
               (b)
      2.
   B. (Capital letter: Second major subheading under Roman numeral I)
      1.
      2.
         a.
         b.
            (1)
            (2)
               (a)
               (b)
II. (Roman numeral: Second major topic or sentence heading)

Indentation. In the outline, the level of significance of the subject matter is indicated through indentation. All divisions and subdivisions should be indented according to their importance. The objective is to find a division that will produce fairly equal and comparable counterparts. Time, place, quantity, order of importance, amount of information, or topics of equal significance are the common bases for these divisions. The number of subheadings used will depend on the thoroughness and complexity of the intended writing. For reports and term papers, it is seldom necessary to use subheadings beyond the first category of small letters. However, it is important to use headings of the same degree of importance on identically designated margins with parallel rankings. There should be a logical development between major headings or ideas and subheadings or minor ideas. All major topics or sentence headings (I, II, III...) are set flush with the left margin. Capital letter subheadings are indented four to five spaces from the left. Arabic numerals (1,2,3...) moved another four or five spaces to the right are reserved for sentence headings under a topic of secondary importance. Lower case letters (a,b,c...) are used for third category subheadings, which are also respectively indented below the upper-level.

Outline Organization. In preparing the outline, it is important to arrange the structure so that it develops the initial topic of writing from conception to growth and eventual maturity. All headings and topics should have parallel grammatical structure to support this growth. Observe the error in the following topical outline:

I. CARD GAMES
   A. To play Rook
   B. Uno
   C. Bridge

"To play Rook" is obviously not grammatically parallel to the nouns "Uno" and "Bridge." To correct this, "To play Rook," must be changed to "Rook," making all subtopics nouns. The writer could also change "Uno" and "Bridge" to "To play Uno" and "To play Bridge," turning all subtopics into infinitives. Grammatical forms cannot be mixed. An example of a corrected topical outline is shown below. The headings are indented and the ideas are subordinated. It should be noted that the entry of a single subheading indicates only one major idea.

I. CARD GAMES
   A. Rook
      1. Rules
      2. Strategy
   B. Uno
      1. Rules
      2. Strategy
   C. Bridge
      1. Rules
      2. Strategy

The following outline, by contrast, is superior to the one above. This outline indicates maturity of thought, organization, and greater fluency of the subject matter.

CARD GAMES

   I. The Strategy of Rook

      A. Thinking

      B. Remembering

      C. Planning

  II. The Strategy of Uno

      A. Thinking

      B. Remembering

      C. Planning

 III. The Strategy of Bridge

      A. Thinking

      B. Remembering

      C. Planning

Types of Outlines. Many different ways of forming outlines exist; however, the following five are the most widely used methods:

1. Topical outline

2. Scratch outline

3. Sentence outline

4. Paragraph outline

5. Decimal outline

The most common outline form is the *topical outline*. This form is used when writing a paper of several pages. It consists of a series of single words or phrases that are assigned letters or numbers indicating their relative importance. The use of the outline enhances the orderly illustration and parallel progression of ideas. If the topical outline is a workable one, the main points can easily be converted into the opening sentences or paragraph topics when starting to write. For example, in the topical outline presented below under (I. C. 1.,) "The Alphanumeric Method" was used to come up with the first sentence of the paragraph: "The alphanumeric method has become the traditional choice in the preparation of such documents...." The following is the topical outline used in writing this section on outlines:

THE OUTLINE

   I. Outline Formats

      A. Introduction

      B. Thesis Statement

      C. Numbering System

         1. Alphanumeric Method

         2. Decimal Method

         3. Roman Numeral Method

  II. Outline Construction

    A. Introduction

    B. Outline Format Example

    C. Indentation

    D. Outline Organization

III. Outline Methods

    A. Topical Outline

    B. Scratch Outline

    C. Sentence Outline

    D. Paragraph Outline

    E. Decimal Outline

IV. Conclusion

The *scratch outline* consists of a few principal words or phrases in the form of notes, written primarily to refresh the memory. This form is especially suitable for those occasions when time is limited or when one must write quickly. One may easily use this method when taking an in-class essay examination or writing a three- to five-page essay. In the margin or somewhere else, one may jot down a few words or phrases that will be followed when starting to write. Scratch outlines allow the writer to condense thoughts into single words or phrases. The format is not that important; however, the arrangement should be orderly. If one were asked to write an essay on how to learn to play tennis, the following example of a scratch outline could be used:

Thesis: Learning to play tennis requires the mastery of four steps.

    I. Serve

   II. Forehand

 III. Backhand

 IV. Follow-through

The third type of outline, the *sentence outline*, is used in preparing long research papers and manuscripts. This format allows the writer to present his thoughts in an expanded manner with fully developed sentences. Each sentence must identify the topic and indicate what will be discussed about the topic.

Each of the topic sentences must be further developed with at least two subtopics or subdivisions. Sentences are written to define exactly what is stated under each heading. All subtopic sentences should be included in the outline after topic headings have been established. The subtopic sentence should be a complete statement, not a question. Also, the same tense should be used throughout the outline. The main purpose of the subtopic sentence is to restrict and control the author, and to allow him to focus on the main points of the research. Again, consistency in the development of the structure is important. If long sentences are used in one heading, the rest of the sentences should be of the same length. Having major headings as nouns and subheadings as sentences is acceptable. The following thesis statement and sentence outline provide an example:

Thesis Statement:

The purpose of the modern Olympic games is to bring the nations of the world together to promote peace and friendship. However, through intense competition, the true spirit of the games has been lost in recent years. Nationalistic and political pressures are endangering the competition's existence. This has served to dilute or diminish the true spirit of world athletic competition and has caused the games to be endangered and their future uncertain.

I. To understand the impact that politics has on the modern games, one must first understand the true purpose of the games.

    A. The Olympics were founded on the basis of competitive spirit.

        1. The ancient Greeks began the tradition of the games.

        2. The purpose of the games is not to win, but to take part and compete.

        3. Athletes are intended to be ambassadors of goodwill for their respective nations.

    B. Beginning early in the modern era of the Olympics, the political element entered the games.

        1. Competition is intended solely for the athletes, not the nations they represent.

        2. The focus on political problems surrounding the games has taken away some of the recognition the athletes deserve.

II. National, social, and political gestures surround every aspect of the modern Olympic games.

    A. Politics promotes many negative elements, which have served to slowly destroy the spirit of the Olympics.

        1. Nationalism is perhaps the biggest problem with the Olympics today.

        2. Gestures of racism and sexism are prevalent throughout the games.

    B. Many nations use the games as a stage to show the rest of the world their political power and superiority.

        1. Nations use the Olympic games as a form of political war.

        2. The drive to achieve national superiority has promoted a higher level of cheating by athletes and judges.

        3. Olympic organizers and officials must work to eliminate these problems if the Olympic games are to survive and thrive.

The fourth type of outline is the *paragraph outline*. This type is most useful in writing papers that require a great deal of detail. Major headings, as in the sentence outline, can be a noun or a phrase. The subheadings are paragraphs indicating the detailed information that will be contained in this section. The same numbering system used in other types of outlines is used for paragraph outlines. Below is an example of a paragraph outline:

I. The classical school of management (phrase)

    A. The classical school of management stresses production processes. It encourages the manager to use his time in assuring the efficiency of the production processes.

    B. The major classical theorists of management include Frederick W. Taylor, Frank and Lillian Gilbreth, William H. Leffingwell, Mary Follett, and Henri Fayol. The scientific management theorists include

Frederick W. Taylor, Frank and Lillian Gilbreth, and William H. Leffingwell. The total entity management theorists include Fayol and Follett. (paragraph)

II. The behavioral school of management

   A. The behavioral school of management proposes that humans have needs aside from monetary ones. These needs include the social, psychological, and physiological. This school of management stresses the human element of management.

   B. The major theorists of the behavioral school of management include Abraham Maslow, Douglas McGregor, and Frederick Herzberg. Abraham Maslow's claim to fame is the hierarchy of needs. Douglas McGregor is responsible for Theory X and Y. Frederick Herzberg's theory concerns motivation. All of the above stress working relationships.

The final type of outline is the *decimal outline*. This outline is used for very long business, engineering, and scientific papers, and also for detailed manuscripts and books. The decimal outline is a detailed and precise form. It uses numbers and decimals to create sub-parts. The following is an example of a decimal outline:

1. The Functions of Management

   1.1 Planning

   1.2 Organizing

   1.3 Leading

   1.4 Controlling

2. The Theorists of Management

   2.1 Classical Theorists

      2.1.1 Frederick W. Taylor

      2.1.2 Frank and Lillian Gilbreth

      2.1.3 William H. Leffingwell

      2.1.4 Mary Follett

      2.1.5 Henri Fayol

   2.2 Behavioral Theorists

      2.2.1 Abraham Maslow

      2.2.2 Douglas McGregor

      2.2.3 Frederick Herzberg

Conclusion Writing should begin with the construction of a suitable outline. The outline should be examined carefully for proper logical and structural progression. All facets of the outline should correlate and support the thesis statement. An effective outline should cover the topic, maintain a logical order of presentation, and balance all ideas equally. Sentence outlines are more suitable for term papers, while scratch outlines are ideal for brief papers, short essays, and in-class examinations. In addition, individual preferences will determine a technique that one adapts to and feels comfortable with.

Note Taking

6

INTRODUCTION

Taking notes is a systematic method of recording information gathered from books, newspapers, magazines, reports, and other sources used in writing. Note taking will help the individual learn, remember, and keep track of information gathered during research. Accurate and careful note taking reduces plagiarism and facilitates the preparation of documentation, as well as saving time in research and easing the writing effort. Careless note taking and reliance on memory result in inefficiency and forgetfulness. The use of stray sheets of paper leads to disorganization and unmanageable information. Using index cards for note taking allows for flexibility, categorization, and addition and elimination of cards as needed. It is good to experiment and practice with the methods of using index cards in gathering information for research and writing. The following discussion will help the researcher become familiar with proper methods of note taking and the organization of information on index cards.

WHY NOTE CARDS?

Taking notes on scratch pads, notebooks, or slips of paper is impractical. Photocopying creates confusion and reduces the productivity of mental participation that takes place while taking notes. When note taking, use a stack of 3 x 5 or 4 x 6 inch index cards. Some people prefer to use 3 x 5 inch cards for the working bibliography and 4 x 6 inch cards for note taking. The latter provide more space for writing. Writing on one side of cards allows for better organization. The index cards can be shuffled for preparation of bibliographies or easily replaced with newly discovered information. They can also be rearranged to conform with the framework of the research outline. Notes taken in pen, rather than in pencil, keep the material from becoming blurred and illegible due to repeated shuffling of the cards. Some people may prefer using pencils for the ease of erasure. Through practice, one will find the most practical methods of noting information. Regardless of which method one uses, it is important to write legibly and neatly. Each note card should include: (1) a heading, which will indicate the included material, (2) an index or identifying number, indicating the source, and (3) important contents, facts, quotes, summary, or other pertinent information.

WHAT TO PUT ON A NOTE CARD

Different formats are required in presenting documentation in various fields. It is beneficial to determine at the outset what style of documentation will be used in order to gather appropriate information during research. This will also simplify the eventual preparation of bibliographies. One card should be prepared for each source and include only bibliographic information. The source card should also provide information on the location of the document, such as in the local library or elsewhere. The following information is included on these cards:

1. *The library call number.* Enter the library call number in the upper lefthand corner. Beneath the call number, indicate the location of the book in the library. In the upper righthand corner of the card, note the location of the source. For example: Reserve Section, Local Library.

2. *Name(s) of the author(s).* First enter the last name of the author, a comma, the first name and middle initial, and then a period. If there is more than one author, write all their names.

3. *Editor's name.* Write the editor's name followed by a comma and *ed.* If the source is an article and is unsigned, indicate the title on the card. In cases of a translated work, the translator's name should be written.

4. *Title of the work.*

   a. *Book.* The title of a book is written and underlined followed by a period.

   b. *Edited book.* Enter the title, then the editor's name followed by a comma and *ed.*

   c. *Unsigned work.* If it is an unsigned work, the title is entered first, recorded in quotation marks and followed by a period.

   d. *Articles.* Enter the author's name, if given, followed by the title of the article.

5. *Publication information.* This includes place, publisher, edition, date, and page number(s) (*p.* or *pp.*).

   a. *Books.* In the case of a book, the city of publication is entered and followed by a colon, then the name of the publisher, a comma, the date of publication, and a period.

   b. *Periodicals.* For periodical articles, the title of the article is given first, followed by the name of the periodical, which is underlined. This is followed by a volume number in Arabic numerals (omit for popular magazines), a comma, the date in parentheses, and a colon. The page numbers are included last with the *p.* or *pp.* For newspaper articles, the name of the newspaper is underlined, followed by the date, section number, page number, and column number. Each is separated by a comma and the last entry is followed by a period.

6. *Index number and personal observation.* A number should be assigned to each work, which will then be assigned to all cards referring to the work. For reasons of convenience, a number may be assigned by the researcher to each work. This number is assigned to all cards referring to the same work. The number is entered in the upper righthand corner of the card. Documentation of personal notes can be included at the bottom of the card for additional items, such as whether the book contains a current bibliography or illustrations and charts.

TYPES OF NOTE CARDS

Three kinds of note cards are used during note taking. These are *bibliography note cards, content note cards,* and *summary note cards.* The noted information for each card should be complete and accurate. This will eliminate the need for later searches in the library and elsewhere for missed or correct information such as call numbers, dates of publication, and other details.

Bibliography Note Cards

A bibliography is the list of sources consulted on the topic during research. Two bibliography cards — the working bibliography and the final bibliography — are used. The *working bibliography* is the list of all sources consulted during research. The *final bibliography* is the alphabetical listing of all sources that provided specific information in writing the manuscript. Correct bibliography cards will simplify the preparation of citations, footnotes, bibliography, and the works cited list. The bibliography card should look somewhat like the following illustrations (Figure 6-1).

FIGURE 6-1
BIBLIOGRAPHY NOTE CARD

```
330.13                    College Library
H36
Heilbroner, Robert L.  The Worldly Philosophers:
The Lives, Times, and Ideas of the Great Economic
Thinkers.  New York: Simon and Schuster Publishing
Co., 1953.


Well-respected book that contains chapters on many
of the great economic thinkers including Karl Marx
and John Maynard Keynes.
```

Note: The call number is always placed in the upper lefthand corner. Below the call number, write the author's name (last name first), the title of the work (underlined), and the facts concerning publication (date, edition, place, publisher, etc.). At the bottom of the card, indicate brief, significant notes for later use.

OTHER EXAMPLES OF
BIBLIOGRAPHY CARDS

FIGURE 6-2

```
5438.4                              (1)
HF.F87

    Futtrell, Charles.  Sales Management.




Chicago: The Dryden Press, Holt, Rinehart,and
Winston Inc., Saunders College Publishing,
1988
```

FIGURE 6-3

```
HF 5438.4                              (2)
.J65

Jolson, Marvin A.  "A Tactical Approach."
Sales Management.




New York: Petrocelli, Chester 1977.
```

FIGURE 6-4

NEWSPAPER

```
                                       (3)

Periodical
Desk




"Small Firms Flock to Stock Market to Get
Financing" The Wall Street Journal, July 16,
1990, p. B2 (e), col. 3.
```

FIGURE 6-5

MAGAZINE ARTICLE

```
                                       (4)

     Kelley, Bill.  "When your Customer base
Changes: Lecroy's salespeople know they are
well, until management decided that the
company's future rested with a new market."
Sales and Marketing Management.  February
1990, 72-73.
```

FIGURE 6-6
ENCYCLOPEDIA

(5)

"Salesmanship." The World Book Encyclopedia.
World Book Inc, 1986. 17: 55-59.

Author unsigned.

FIGURE 6-7
PERSONAL INTERVIEW

(6)

Grant Interview   Future Management
                         Training

FIGURE 6-8
PERSONAL INTERVIEW

(7)
Grant M. Davis   Personal Interview
Dean College of Business, A S U
Boone, North Carolina. July 18, 1990

"The completion of the new business building
will provide students a unique opportunity to
test management theory in behavior laboratories.
The training of future managers will be greatly
enhanced by this facility."

Content Note Cards

The second type of card is the content note card. It contains actual information noted from articles, books, and other sources. Write only on one side of the card, since notes taken on the back of the card may be overlooked during the writing of the paper. If it is necessary to write on the back of the card, place the word "OVER" in the lower righthand corner. It is important to indicate the source and other relevant data, including a note that a bibliography card has been made. The identification may be made by author, title, or subject. The library call number is indicated in the top lefthand corner, whereas the page number on which the information is found should be noted in the top righthand corner. The noted contents include important facts and other significant information. It is important to write what can be used rather than writing indiscriminately. The prepared outline should be consulted to determine needed information. An example of a content note card is illustrated below (Figure 6-9):

FIGURE 6-9
CONTENT NOTE CARD
(FRONT OF THE CARD)

```
330.13                                          p 195
H36
Heilbroner, Robert L.  The Worldly Philosophers:
The Lives, Times, and Ideas of the Great
Economic Thinkers.

A bibliography card has been made.

"Foreign investment and foreign trade, despite
their political flavor, do not add up of
themselves to imperialism."


                                            "OVER"
```

FIGURE 6-10
(BACK OF THE CARD)

```
Imperialism is characterized by political
domination, economic exploitation, the military,
and ideas that stand in their way.
```

Note: Write the call number in the upper lefthand corner and the page number in the top righthand corner. Below, name the source of the content card followed by a note indicating that a bibliography card has been made. If you must write on the back of the card, indicate this by noting OVER in the lower righthand corner of the card.

Summary Note Cards

The third type of note card is the summary note card. Summary cards are used for important personal thoughts that one may form during research. Because the greater portion of a research paper represents one's own thinking and writing, it is wise to take good summary notes. Good judgment should be exercised when writing these summaries to avoid plagiarism and distortion of original facts. A summary card is used to write briefly what one has read at length. The following is an example of a summary card (Figure 6-11).

FIGURE 6-11

```
SUMMARY
 Heilbroner, The Worldly Philosophers: The
 Lives, Times, and Ideas of the Great Economic
 Thinkers.

 This is a very lively and highly readable book
 about inconspicuous scholarly men and their varied
 doctrines that indirectly shaped the world around
 them by "influencing men's minds for generations
 to come." They were of varied opinions and
 backgrounds but all should be noted for the
 "extraordinary power of their ideas."
```

Note: The decision to use summary note cards is a matter of personal discretion and one's own mental recall.

Conclusion

When these three types of note cards are prepared throughout the research process, they will: (1) save time and make the writing process productive and easier; (2) allow for efficient presentation and organization of thoughts; (3) prevent unintentional plagiarism; and (4) provide necessary information for the preparation of documentation and bibliography.

THE RESEARCH MATERIAL

In researching, one should carefully examine articles, books, and other materials for information pertinent to the topic. Preview any preface, introduction, table of contents, or index to get a good grasp of the contents. Investigate to see if the book provides graphs, charts, or bibliographies. Spend some time thinking through the amount, nature, and order of the included information. Review the topics in the research outline. Be selective in note taking and do not attempt to write down information from the source indiscriminately. Write down only one important concept, fact, or statement on each note card.

Beginning the Note-Taking Process

Some sources may be reviewed without taking notes; others with authoritative and relevant details may require taking notes on several cards. Careless note taking can lead to clutter and confusion. An individualized method will develop through practice and ingenuity. Following basic guidelines as discussed in this section will be helpful until a preferred personal method is developed. When taking notes, paraphrase, quote, summarize, or make personal observations about the sources researched. It is critical to distinguish between one's own ideas and those of others during the note-taking process.

Paraphrasing

Paraphrasing is the process of conveying the meaning of an author's work into a different form: expressing what has been written with clarity and enhancing interpretation. Lucid paraphrases are always preferred over long quotations. Paraphrasing from original material clarifies and enhances writing. Numerous quotations lead to dullness, lack of creativity, and a jumbled patchwork of information. Paraphrased material should blend with the context and the author's style of writing. One should carefully choose only important material for paraphrasing. The rephrasing must be authentic and not mere substitution of synonyms or rearrangement of sentences. The paraphrased material must be documented to avoid any suspicion of plagiarism.

Quoting

Carefully selected extracts should be used only when they present the best evidence on the subject and when they would lose meaning if paraphrased. They should be reserved for those occasions when one cannot express an idea better, for reasons of authoritativeness, exactness, and uniqueness, as when one must quote from literature or law. Copy the exact words of the author, including any errors in the text. Place quoted material in quotation marks and include documentation to indicate the source. Whenever words or phrases in a quotation are omitted, a three-dot ellipsis (...) should be used to indicate the omission. If words or phrases at the end of the quotation are omitted, a four-dot ellipsis (....) should be used to indicate that a sentence was not completed. Quoted information may be verbatim, i.e., word for word. Both quoted and paraphrased material should be correctly documented. The following is an example distinguishing an original writing from that which has been plagiarized. First, the source is given, followed by two versions, one correct and one incorrect. The original quote is from Ernst Cassirer, *The Myth of the State*, New Haven: The Yale University Press, 1946, p. 268.

> Freedom is one of the most obscure and ambiguous terms not only of philosophical but also of political language. As soon as we begin to speculate about the freedom of the will, we find ourselves involved in an inextricable labyrinth of metaphysical questions and antinomies. As to political freedom, all of us know that it is one of the most used and abused slogans. All political parties have assured us that they are ever the true representatives and guardians of freedom.[1]

The following construction illustrates poorly paraphrased material that, despite documentation, leads to a suspicion of plagiarism:

> Freedom is an extricable abstract word to define in philosophy and political science. Trying to define it gets us into a labyrinth of

abstraction and metaphysical arguments. It is indeed misused by every political party, almost all claiming to be the true champions of the concept.[1]

The paraphrase below is an acceptable version, well written and properly cited:

Freedom is a difficult if not tortuous word to define accurately. Historically, the word freedom has been used with uncertainty and abstraction in both philosophy and political science. Every political movement has made claims of being the real savior of the concept of freedom.[1]

---

1. Ernst Cassirer, *The Myth of the State*. New Haven: The Yale University Press, 1946, p. 268.

Summarizing

Summarizing is used to convey the message of long discussions and paragraphs in a condensed and concise form. The summary should consist of several compact sentences that restate the main points of the discussion. As soon as an entire passage is read, it should be summarized in a paragraph or two on the note cards. If notes are taken while reading for the summarizing process, it is possible to become involved in recording details rather than the main point and concepts. Care should be used in condensing and presenting facts when summarizing. Although the use of exceptional phrases and words from the original work is permissible, good judgment should be exercised to use them sparingly.

Personal comments concerning the subject may include insights, conclusions, judgments, or peculiarities. Documentation is recommended if summaries contain important points in someone else's work. If confused or worried about committing plagiarism, cite the source.

After adequate data has been gathered, examine the note cards carefully to determine whether the information is sufficient to put the research topic into proper perspective. If the information proves sufficient, arrange the cards into groups so they will conform with the prepared outline and the overall purpose of writing the paper. If any gaps or inadequacies exist in the gathered information at this stage, additional research in the library may be necessary before attempting to write.

Writing the Research Paper

7

INTRODUCTION

When the planning phase of gathering and assembling information is complete, ideas should be put on paper towards writing a first draft. This is a critical task, since a great investment of time, energy, and thought has gone into research and the gathering of information. Planning and organization are necessary in writing a satisfactory final draft. This effort includes writing the first draft, revising, documenting, editing, and proofreading the paper.

THE FIRST DRAFT

Before starting to write, review the thesis statement, the prepared outline, and the assembled information to ensure the production of a well-rounded, organized paper. Scrutinize the bibliography cards for satisfactory information, including documentation and acknowledgments. Set aside adequate time and select an appropriate environment to write a major section of the entire paper without any interruptions as soon as possible. A higher level of productivity is achieved when writing is initiated after research, while thoughts are fresh.

Quality papers are seldom created in one sitting. Some mental exercise, practice, and warmup in writing are just as rewarding as in sports. The writer is often not sure of the opening word, sentence, or arrangement of a paragraph. As a general rule, do not attempt to come up with the ideal or perfect opening statement. Start by recording simple relevant thoughts. These initial few sentences and paragraphs will produce enthusiasm and motivation. Return later for changes, accuracy, grammar, and needed revisions. Do not become discouraged and stop writing. Follow each thought through as you write. Concentrate on recording ideas while maintaining a writing rhythm.

The first draft should be written with adequate space left between sentences, paragraphs, and margins for later revisions. It is recommended to write lengthy first drafts and then return for deletions, revisions, and additions to the paper. Set aside time for verification of quotations, spellings, punctuation, grammar, style, and word usage.

Some people think that accomplished writers simply sit down and write out a perfect letter, essay, or other document from start to finish in one sitting. In actuality, writers spend a great deal of time drafting, writing, and rewriting. Effective and polished writing does not happen instantly. Writing requires time, persistence, and patience. Throughout the writing process, follow the prepared outline. Write clear sentences and maintain paragraph unity by expressing only one main idea in each paragraph. Every paragraph must represent a group of related sentences that develop one main idea. Paragraphs should start with a proper topic sentence in order to accommodate additional expansion of the main ideas. The body of the paragraph should include additional sentences that develop and support the main idea. Paragraph compatibility and flow should be observed closely, so that the reader will be able to follow written thoughts progressively. After complete paragraphs and sections are written, put this work aside and take some time to reflect upon the material and the remaining tasks. Upon returning, scrutinize each section and ask some important questions, such as: Do they introduce the aspired subject? Are they interesting? Is there continuity among sections in terms of information and the thought process? Are they conveying concepts to the reader with some force and interest? Words, phrases, and sentences that are not clear should be replaced, eliminated, or revised. It is frequently stated that the most difficult part of writing is getting started. With practice and patience, writing will become expressive, creative, and consistently easier.

REVISIONS

A manuscript is greatly improved upon revision. Providing time for this task during the writing process is very important. Following the completion of the first draft, make a guarded check of the entire paper. Make minor and major corrections and reorganize if necessary. Revisions may involve some rewriting and rearranging of sentences and paragraphs. A written manuscript should introduce thoughts in a flowing, logical order. If serious gaps are found in the presentation or structure of the information, the prepared outline should be changed. Time should be spent on correcting grammar, punctuation, and spelling. Consult a dictionary or a thesaurus for words that are inappropriate or overused. The thesaurus is a valuable tool for finding precise alternative words to help express thoughts clearly. Select words that make writing simple rather than sophisticated. Readers can quickly absorb what is read, if thoughts are communicated clearly. Through proper selection of words one can add spice, variety, and liveliness to the manuscript. Appropriate and simple words create mental images that arouse the curiosity and interest of the reader. The writer should express rather than impress with diction and rhetorical skills.

EDITING

Editing involves serious attention to surface errors as well as reorganization of certain parts of the written material. Surface errors may include punctuation, grammar, spelling, and factual errors. Parts of the draft may require rearrangement and rewriting. Edit carefully to ensure that headings are parallel and the mechanics (capitalization, punctuation, and use of numbers and symbols) are correct. Special attention is given in editing to details that will help make the manuscript more lucid and enjoyable to read. Editing eliminates the trivial while emphasizing the important. A writer should give personality and character to written information through effective substitution of words. Dictionaries and thesauruses should be used to discover new and choice words in the expression of intended thoughts.

If the writer is using a computer, spell-checking and error correction capabilities can be accomplished instantly. The availability of dictionaries and thesauruses in software can save a great deal of time looking up words. A definite advantage in the use of computers is seeing corrections on the screen. Through editing, one is able to improve the flow and the presentation of the final manuscript.

DOCUMENTATION

When writing the manuscript, provide adequate room between sentences, paragraphs, and margins for documentation and other notes. Paraphrases, quotations, and summarized ideas of others must be carefully documented with footnotes and acknowledgments. Special conventions provide for the presentation of quotations, footnotes, comments, and bibliographies. A number of styles are used for this presentation. One should become familiar with the style used in the particular area or discipline. When writing a manuscript, it is a good practice to ask what style the publisher or instructor prefers. These conventions are discussed later under the topic of footnotes and bibliographies.

PROOFREADING

Proofreading is a very worthwhile effort that will improve the final document. Careless mistakes that would require correction in the final copy are spotted and corrected through proofreading. The author must carefully examine the final manuscript. Do not submit a document without a final and thorough proofreading. The submitted manuscript should represent the best research, thought, and effort. A final check is beneficial in looking for last minute slip-ups, typographical errors, omissions, misspellings, and other mistakes. It may be necessary to read the entire manuscript word by word. Reading paragraphs or sections aloud may provide a feeling for how they sound. Some may use a pencil to follow each sentence and look at each word, while others may give the manuscript to someone else for quick proofreading. If a computer with word processing capabilities is available, use it to check for misspellings and grammatical and structural errors. If the paper is given to others for typing or word processing, proofread it carefully before and after submission. The final scholarly presentation of the paper is the responsibility of the author alone.

Proofreading Marks. Proofreading marks are symbols used in the process of proofreading. They are vivid instructions for the typist and self-reminders in making any changes in the text. Their use saves a great deal of time in making revisions in the final copy and in typing. One can quickly become proficient in their use. A list of commonly used proofreading marks is included in Appendix F. Learning a few of these marks will prove beneficial to a serious writer. Proofreading marks are placed in the margins corresponding to the written lines where errors or corrections are indicated. These marks are used in pairs, one in the text where the change is to be made and one in the margin. When there is more than one single correction in a written line, the corrections are written in order of occurrence and separated by a slash, such as (stet/ cap/ ctr.) If there are numerous errors, both margins are used.

Punctuation, Spelling, and Grammar Basics

8

INTRODUCTION

Punctuation is the use of special symbols in writing. It is used to separate words into sentences, clauses, phrases, quotations, and contractions. Correct use of punctuation assists the reader in comprehending the meanings and grammatical relationships of concepts, ideas, and words. Punctuation symbols convey meanings and thoughts to the reader that are not explicitly communicated by the words used. Writing well requires the use of proper punctuation for practical and effective communication. Punctuation marks personalize the writer's style and help the reader comprehend a subject with clarity. A working knowledge of the basic rules of punctuation helps a writer compose with ease and clarity. Writing can become difficult for an author who lacks skills in punctuation.

Many rules exist for the use of punctuation and other marks in writing. These rules should become as much a part of the author's skills as the words he uses. Those who desire a brief overview of frequently used punctuation marks will find the following discussions beneficial. Outlined below are the six major categories of punctuation marks:

IMPORTANT MARKS

I. Ending Punctuation Marks
   A. The Period [.]
   B. The Question Mark [?]
   C. The Exclamation Mark [!]

II. Principal Interior Punctuation Marks
   A. The Single Comma [,]
   B. The Pair of Commas [,,]
   C. The Semicolon [;]
   D. The Colon [:]

III. Infrequently Used Interior Marks
   A. The Dash [—]
   B. The Parentheses [()]
   C. The Paired Dashes [— —]

IV Enclosing and Other Marks
   A. The Quotation Marks [" "]
   B. The Brackets [ ]
   C. The Ellipsis [...]
   D. The Slash [/]

V. Some Non-Punctuation Symbols
   A. The Abbreviation Marks (Points) [.]
   B. The Hyphen [-]
   C. The Decimal and Percentage Marks [. , %]
   D. The Capital Letter (Proper Names) [A,B]
   E. The Underscoring [_____]
   F. The Apostrophe [']

VI. Spelling or Writing Numbers
   A. A Number Begins a Sentence [One]
   B. Time [12:45]
   C. Units of Measure [10 lbs.]
   D. Fractions [¾]
   E. Ordinal Numbers [third]

ENDING PUNCTUATION MARKS

Ending punctuation marks are symbols used to separate sentences and ideas within paragraphs. *Periods, question marks*, and *exclamation points* are marks of termination. These three marks are also called *end stops*. All complete sentences require one of these marks at the end. These ending marks cue the reader that a statement is complete, a question has been asked, or interruptions are needed. Their correct use enables the author to give written material the rhythm of natural speech.

Periods (.). Periods mark the end of all sentences that are not used as direct questions or exclamations. Among other uses, they are placed at the end of footnotes, endnotes, and bibliography entries, and with abbreviations. The following are some common uses of the period:

1. Periods are used at the end of declarative sentences that are not a direct question, a command, or an exclamation.

   It is an ideal morning for fishing.

   It may rain today.

2. Periods are used after most accepted abbreviations.

   Ph.D., Sept., Dr., Mrs., Lt. Col.

3. Periods are used before decimals and to separate dollars and cents.

   The correct length of this board is 3.15 inches.

   He is paid $5.67 an hour.

4. Periods are often omitted from abbreviations of organizational names, such as FCC, GOP, IRS, UNESCO, VISTA, and others. This usage may vary, such as USA, U.S.A.; USSR, U.S.S.R. It is a good practice to be consistent in usage throughout a document. Whenever unfamiliar abbreviations are used, spell them out the first time they are written. This will allow the reader to become acquainted with the abridgment. Example: To connect your video cassette recorder (VCR) properly, the VCR output must be connected to the television's VCR input outlet.

PUNCTUATION, SPELLING, AND GRAMMAR BASICS

A current dictionary will contain a list of abbreviations and indicate whether periods are to be used with them.

5. Only one period is used at the end of a sentence, even if the sentence ends in an abbreviation. If a sentence ends in an exclamation or a question mark, then the end punctuation follows the period after the abbreviation, as in the following examples:

   John is studying for his Ph.D.

   Did John ever finish his Ph.D.?

6. If a phrase or sentence ends with a quotation, the termination marks are placed *inside* the quotation marks. If a parenthetical statement is dependent, the termination marks are placed *outside* the quotation marks.

   "What luck!"

   "Am I right?" he shouted.

   "Tell me."

   Follow instructions in the text (see page 102).

7. Use periods after *numbers* and *letters* that introduce items in a stacked list, as in an outline.

   1. Management Functions

       A. Planning

       B. Organizing

       C. Controlling

8. Listed below are common errors that occur using the period.

   a. Run-on sentences contain two or more complete ideas without the use of a period.

       Matilda went to the ball game she wore a blue dress to town.

   b. Fragments are sentences that do not complete an idea or statement.

       Matilda in a blue dress.

Question Marks (?). Question marks are used at the conclusion of a sentence to indicate a direct question. They are also used in parenthetical statements to show uncertainty. The following are some principal uses of the question mark.

1. A question mark is used at the end of a sentence that asks for information or requires a direct response.

   What time is it?

   When will I see you again?

2. A rhetorical question is also followed by a question mark.

   How will we learn to play tennis without tennis balls?

3. Question marks may be used in parentheses to show uncertainty about correctness of a number, word, or date.

   John was born in 1975(?) somewhere in England.

   Score: Home Team 17, Visitors ?

4. When a question mark and a quotation mark fall together and the quotation is a question, enter the question mark inside the quotation. If the entire sentence is a question, place the question mark outside the quotation mark.

He was shouting, "Should I quit college?"

Do you believe that he said, "I should quit college"?

5. Demand statements in the form of indirect questions do not require a question mark. For example:

They all wanted to know why I left.

I wonder if the total message is objective, tactful, and worthwhile.

Exclamation Marks (!). An exclamation mark signals that the preceding word, phrase, or sentence is an emphatic utterance, an interjection, or a surprise.

1. Exclamation marks are used when the statement is intense with strong emotion. (Oh! No! Help! Why!)

2. Exclamation marks are frequently found in writing dialogue.
(Interjection)
The people in that country have truly suffered!
(Surprise)
What a beautiful morning! David, Come here: Look!
(Utterance)
Oh! The building had disappeared overnight.

3. Observe the following sentences where the change of the marks makes them a request, question, or command.
(Request)
Will you answer the telephone.
(Question)
Will you answer the telephone?
(Command)
Will you answer the telephone!

4. The exclamation mark can be placed within the quotation marks that occur in a sentence:

"I am through!" he shouted.

5. The exclamation mark can be placed outside the quotation marks when the entire sentence is exclamatory:

He looked mad and shouted, "I am through"!

PRINCIPAL INTERIOR PUNCTUATION MARKS

Punctuation marks used within sentences are intricate, requiring knowledge and skill of the writer. Writers should study their purpose critically. Effective improvements in writing can be credited to the correct use of interior punctuation marks. These marks include the comma, semicolon, and colon.

Comma (,). The comma is the most frequently used mark in punctuation. Some important uses include: (1) to create a slight pause or an interruption in a statement or sentence, (2) to introduce a new idea and to separate lists and elements, and (3) to mark words out of normal order. Other major uses of commas are listed below:

1. Use a comma to separate words, phrases, or clauses in a list.

   Volleyball, tennis, soccer, swimming, and jogging are my favorite forms of recreation.

   Percussion instruments include: bass drum, cymbals, gong, orchestral bells (Glockenspiel), snare drum, timpani (kettle drums), and xylophone.

2. The use of a comma before and, and/or in a series of three or more is optional, but the use must be consistent.

   The height, width and depth of that box are the same.

   You can write with a pen, pencil, or crayon.

3. Use a comma to set off an introductory word, if that word is being emphasized.

   Amazingly, Lori spoke after eight months of silence.

4. Use a comma with introductory and transitional words.

   Sam, however, did go home.

   Finally, you graduated from college.

5. Two commas surround words that interrupt a sentence.

   That reference, in our opinion, is not worth quoting.

6. Appositives must have commas on both ends. An appositive is a word or phrase that comes after a noun and identifies or supplements the meaning of a preceding expression.

   My doctor, Dr. Jones, recommended I exercise more, but my supervisor, a smart man, recommended rest and vacation.

   We will go, you and I, to the show.

7. Place a comma before a phrase that gives additional and incidental information on the noun mentioned. Place a comma before a phrase or clause that is tacked at the end of the stated sentence.

   We plan to visit Mount Washington, which is more than 6,500 feet high.

   I graduated from college in five years, thanks to my mom.

8. A comma is used before the introduction of a direct quotation, an introductory *yes* or *no*, or noun of address. The latter is the listener we are talking to directly.

   Dr. Wolf said, "Wait for me."

   No, I will not come today.

   Yes, Sophia can watch TV, if she cleans her room.

9. Use a comma to set off words that address someone directly.

   Lori, go find Kitty.

10. Commas are used to separate elements in dates, addresses, and place names, to group numbers into units of three from the right, in author references, etc:

    March 10, 1981

    March, 1981 (optional when only month and year are given)

    Boone, North Carolina, U.S.A.

    I am worth $3,756,013.

    Oliver Twist, by Charles Dickens

11. Use a comma after a name followed by titles or degree.

    See Stanley Isaacs, Ph.D., for a consultation.

12. In informal or personal correspondence, use a comma after introductory salutations and the complimentary closing of the letter.

    Dear Mom,

    Sincerely yours,

13. Use a comma to separate parts of a sentence, especially a long introductory clause or phrase.

    I make it a habit to go to all home football games, especially the Davidson game.

14. Place commas in sentences where slight pauses occur.

    When we went hiking, Lori got lost.

15. The comma is inserted before the end of quotation marks.

    "I will not come back today," she said.

16. A comma is used with contractions, such as *etc., i.e., e.g.,* when they are not at the end of a sentence.

    I will bring the ball, glove, bat, etc., to the game.

17. Use commas to separate contrasting elements.

    I am mad, not drunk.

    He needs discipline, not a car.

18. Use a comma with coordinating conjunctions. A coordinating conjunction is a word that joins two or more independent clauses (clauses that can stand alone as sentences) into one. At the joining point, a comma signals that one independent clause is closing and another one is about to begin. These independent elements or phrases are linked by coordinating conjunctions, such as *and, but, or, for, yet, nor,* preceded by a comma.

    He looked, stared at the tables, and sat in the first available place.

    No one in particular said anything, yet you had to get mad and leave.

    He went to the ball game, but his wife refused to go.

    Going to college is becoming very expensive, and getting a scholarship is hopeless.

19. Commas should not be used in account numbers, street numbers, page numbers, and the like. A comma is not used before the first item in a series, nor is it used when a conjunction does not connect two phrases.

    This year the trees have good blossoms and rich green leaves.

Paired Commas (, ... ,). Paired commas are used to separate words in a sentence from the rest of the sentence. The omission of the closed part would not change the sentence's meaning. The following are some rules for using paired commas.

1. Paired commas are used to separate a phrase or a word, especially between the subject and the verb.

   The game, played yesterday, was boring.

2. Paired commas are also used to include words or word groups that comprise transitional words in the middle of an idea.

   The game, for the most part, was very boring.

3. To separate a contrasting phrase, use two commas.

   Lake Success, not Geneva, is where United Nations headquarters is located.

Semicolon (;). The semicolon, also called a *super comma*, is used instead of a period to separate short, related sentences. Semicolons provide more separation than a comma but less than a period. Semicolons are used to separate independent clauses that are not connected by coordinating conjunctions such as *and, but, nor, so, for, yet*, and others. They are also used to separate long lists of items and elements in a series. However, a semicolon is not used to introduce a list. A colon is used for that purpose.

1. A semicolon is used to separate a list that contains commas.

   The congressional committee includes: Helms, N.C.; Kemp, N.Y.; Reagan, Cal.; and Pardue, Fla.

2. A semicolon is used to separate two independent clauses joined by a conjunctive adverb.

   Joe played ball for four years; however, he was never a starter.

3. A semicolon is used to separate several related phrases.

   He needs her; she needs him; and the child needs both of them.

4. Whenever a semicolon is used with quotation marks, it is placed outside of them, unless it is part of the quote.

   I was listening to Beethoven's "Fidelio"; I did not wish to go out.

Colon (:). Proper use of colons makes writing clear and emphatic. Colons are used to make the reader stop and look at a word, phrase, clause, list, or quotation. They signal explanation of what is stated in the first part of the sentence. They inform the reader to "watch what follows." A colon is also used to introduce a string of ideas or a list separated by commas. In addition, a colon is used after an opening salutation in a business letter. There are many rules for the use of colons.

1. A colon is used to introduce a list of items or to illustrate and amplify stated material. If the preceding clause is a complete sentence, begin with a capital letter.

   I have visited the following campuses: Columbia, Dartmouth, Harvard, and Chapel Hill.

2. A colon is used to introduce a quotation.

   On the game show "The Price is Right," it is Rod Roddey, not Bob Barker, who entices game show participants with the statement: "Come on down!"

3. A colon is generally used after a statement that describes what you are about to do.

   On page four define: marketing, management, and finance.

4. Use a colon before a statement that is going to introduce a new idea.

   I smelled a delightful fragrance: a rose.

5. A colon is used after an introductory salutation, in writing a business letter, and in other special situations, such as between the chapter and verse of biblical sources.

   Ladies and Gentlemen:

   Dear Mr. Brown:

   (Psalm 25:2-3)

6. A colon is used between hours, minutes, and seconds when time is expressed numerically. It is also used to indicate proportions or to write ratios.

   2:17:35 AM

   The proportions of sugar: water were 1:5.

7. A colon is used between titles and subtitles of the written works. It is also used between the name of the city and publisher for "works cited" entries.

   The Leadership Game: Matching the Man to the Situation

   New York: Columbia University Press

8. A colon is placed outside a final quotation mark.

   You will most likely enjoy the writings of "Mark Twain": The stories are adventurous.

INFREQUENTLY USED INTERIOR MARKS

Dash (—). The dash, typed as two hyphens (- -) with no spaces before or after, informs the reader that there is a pause. The dash is more intense than a comma. Uses of the dash include indicating interruptions, thoughts, actions, clarification, and summaries, and for parenthetical remarks and special emphasis.

1. Use a dash to explain something in the middle of a sentence.

   My professor — not Judy Martin, but Dr. David Kelly — is a nice person.

2. A dash is used to indicate a sharp change of thought.

   Let's shoot pool — no, let's pitch softballs.

3. A dash is used to express an interrupted statement.

   He was — to me at least, if not you — a figure less memorable than pathetic.

4. Except in formal writing, a dash can replace a colon in an opening remark.

   There is one thing Bob enjoys more than eating — golf.

5. Use a dash in summarizing phrases.

   The four P's of marketing are as follows:

   — Place

   — Price

   — Product

   — Promotion

6. The final summarizing clause of a sentence beginning with a series of nouns should be preceded by a dash.

   Oranges, grapefruits, tangerines, and nectarines — these are my favorite fruits.

7. Dashes are used after introductory words that are to be repeated after each of the lines following.

   We pledge

   — to take pride

   — to be timely

   — to be serious.

8. Dashes are used to omit letters of a name or something that needs to remain anonymous. They are also used in older writings and in omissions in profanity.

   J—— said, we are going to win the game.

Parentheses ( ). Common usage of parentheses includes the introduction of secondary information. They are also used for the inclusion of numbers or letters to show numerical sequence of written items. Parentheses are used to enclose details or incidental information not directly related to the sentence. In fact, parentheses deemphasize, whereas colons emphasize information. Parentheses are used to enclose references and cross references. In business and law, parentheses are used to enclose monetary values in digits after they are written. Following are some common uses of parentheses:

1. Parentheses are used to give secondary information related to the subject in a sentence.

   Harry did not know what to do (poor fellow); therefore, he did nothing.

   Niccolo Machiavelli (1469-1537) is the author of *The Prince*.

2. Paired parentheses are used to enclose numbers or letters that indicate items sequentially.

   The four P's of marketing are: (1) price, (2) product, (3) promotion, and (4) place.

3. Paired parentheses are used when monetary values are indicated.

   The bill was ninety-eight dollars ($98.00).

4. Use parentheses to give additional information.

   He is the director of United Nations Relief and Rehabilitation Administration (UNRRA).

5. Use parentheses to give references and cross references.

Brown found similar results in his research (212).

For further explanation see Brown's comments (Appendix A, page 14).

6. Punctuation marks go inside the parentheses when they just punctuate the words inside, otherwise they follow the parentheses.

He spoke about his cars (he has five of them) the entire trip.

You have written a good term paper. (Show it to your instructor, or better, sell it to a publisher.)

Paired Dashes (—...—). Paired dashes are used to enclose ideas related to the subject but not so closely associated as to require the use of paired commas. In addition, if the related part is heavily punctuated with commas, the paired dashes are more appropriate.

1. Paired dashes are used to separate ideas less significant than those presented with paired commas.

His record collection — mostly rock — contained 10,000 records.

2. Paired dashes are used to show related materials that are heavily punctuated.

The instruments — cello, double bass, viola, and violin — are all members of the violin family.

ENCLOSING PUNCTUATION MARKS AND OTHERS

Quotation Marks (" "). Quotation marks — "quotes" — are used when the writer takes material word for word from another source. Quotations are also used to enclose titles of plays, essays, and songs, names of ships, or to emphasize something in writing. Open quotation marks are placed at the beginning of the quoted material, while closing quotation marks are placed at the end. A quotation within a quotation is usually set off by single paired quotation marks ("..'..'..."). Periods and commas go inside the quotation marks. Semicolons and colons are placed outside the quotation marks. The following examples include normal uses of the quotation mark.

1. Use paired quotation marks around direct quotes.

"I like you!" she said.

2. Paired quotation marks are used to enclose the title of short works.

"Dover Beach" is Matthew Arnold's best-known poem.

3. Paired quotation marks are one way to indicate specific words in a sentence.

An "erg" is a unit of energy.

Note: Italics or underlining could be used instead of quotation marks.

4. Quotation marks are used to emphasize sarcasm.

Tim's "beautiful" blind date was a little girl.

5. Quotation marks are used to set off slang expressions.

You looked "spaced out" last night at the party.

6. Use quotation marks to indicate thoughts within hypothetical thoughts.

   "If I only had love," I thought.

7. Use single quotation marks within double quotation marks to enclose originally quoted material within a quotation.

   John said, "I really like 'To an Athlete Dying Young,' as a poem."

8. Use single quotation marks within double quotation marks to enclose a title within another title.

   The article was titled "Exodus in 'Insight' magazine."

9. Question marks go within quotation marks if the question is contained within the marks. This also applies to exclamation points, periods, question marks, and commas.

   John said, "Who are you?"

   "Tackle him! Tackle him!" the coach shouted from the sidelines.

10. Colons and semicolons are placed outside quotation marks.

    There are four important characters in the "Open Boat": the cook, captain, sailor, and correspondent.

Brackets [ ]. Brackets are used for inserting something in a quotation and for enclosing pronunciation. If a typewriter does not have brackets, write them in by hand. Do not use parentheses instead of brackets. Following are some uses for brackets.

1. Place brackets in a direct quote to make the meaning clear.

   Sophia said, "She [Emily Dickinson] is the best female poet America has produced."

2. Brackets are used whenever pronunciation is inserted.

   The normal pronunciation of palm is [pahm].

Ellipses (...). Triple-spaced period marks, or ellipsis, are used to indicate omission of letters or words. They create a pause for the reader to imagine, or "help to get the entire picture." They are used when the writer quotes parts of a long passage and omits the rest of the material. Quadruple periods (....) are used if the quotation or omission ends at the end of a sentence. If paragraphs are omitted, three to five asterisks (*) are placed in the middle of the page indicating the omission. Following are some examples.

1. " ... time is ... the imagination of the age."

2. "Our cereal contains fruit and ...."

3. It was a beautiful morning ... a cloudy afternoon ... and a stormy evening.

4. Martin Luther King, Jr. wrote: I have traveled the length and breadth of Alabama, Mississippi, and all the other states ....

5. Unprintable words and expletives are indicated by the use of asterisks, daggers, or ellipsis dots.

   The lieutenant shouted to the troops, "I will kick ... if you do not dress properly."

   The **** dog barked all night.

The Slash (/). The slash (also known as a solidus or virgule) is a slanting line (/). In keyboarding, it is referred to as a *diagonal*. It is used to indicate two alternatives, as in *and/or* and to set off phoneme symbols. The slash is placed between two words to indicate that either word is appropriate under the circumstances.

John and/or Sue will take you to the game.

Make productive use of your thought/speech advantage.

Each of the students should do his/her homework.

SOME NON-PUNCTUATION SYMBOLS

Abbreviation Marks (.). Abbreviation marks, also called points, are used with words that are common and where they are appropriate for the context. Accepted common contractions such as FBI, MD, rpm, and kwh do not need abbreviation marks. To be on the safe side, consult a recent dictionary for the accepted usage format. Following are some guidelines for the use of abbreviations.

1. Use abbreviation marks before common titles, for designations after names and dates, and for times, names of businesses, organizations, countries, states, and acronyms.

   Dr. Jones

   David Carter Esq.

   John Gray, Jr.

   342 B.C.

   9:23 A.M. (or a.m.)

   U.S. (or U.S.A.)

2. Days of the week, if used with dates, are correctly abbreviated as following:

   Sun., Mon., Tues., Wed., Thurs., Fri., Sat.

3. Abbreviate only the following months. The abbreviated forms are used only if written with dates:

   Jan., Feb., Aug., Sept., Oct., Nov., Dec.

4. The following Latin terms are abbreviated:

Abbreviation	Latin	English Equivalent
a.m. (or am)	ante meridiem	before noon
p.m. (or pm)	post meridiem	after noon
e.g.	exempli gratia	for example
cf.	confer	compare
et al.	et alii	and other people
etc.	et cetera	and others
i.e.	id est	that is
loc. cit.	loco citato	the place cited
vs.	versus	against
ibid.	ibidem	in the same place
A.D.	anno Domini	since Christianity
op. cit.	opere citato	in the work cited

Hyphen (-). The linking hyphen is used to compound figures, words, and word elements. Hyphens are used with most compound words that begin with *all*, *ex*, and *self* (all-inclusive, ex-wife, self-educated) and others. It is safe to consult a dictionary if not certain. Some general rules for hyphen use are listed below.

1. The hyphen is used in compound figures.

   A two-thirds majority will be required to pass the bill.

2. A hyphen is used within compound words.

   Attorney-at-law

3. Use a hyphen when compound adjectives are used directly before a noun.

   Ex-champion Ali was a good boxer.

   Anti-German feelings are still common.

   Player-coach relations help athletes.

4. Hyphen are used to split words at the end of a line, indicating that the word written is to large to fit in the given space. Divide the word at the end of a syllable. If unsure about the division, consult a dictionary.

   After working very hard, I received a good grade on my punc-

   tuation paper.

5. A hyphen is used when a word is divided into syllables.

   Gentlemen, I probably will not run for re-election this year.

6. A hyphen can express stuttering or sobbing.

   P-p-please b-b-bear with m-m-m-me.

Decimal and Percentage Point (. %). A period (decimal point) pertains to and is based on the number 10. A fraction with an omitted denominator of 10, or some power of 10, is indicated by a period (decimal point) before the numerator. For example, .25 = 1/4. Percent gives the part or amount in every hundred. Percentages and decimals are indicated in Arabic numerals even when they are less than one hundred. The word *percent* is used with a number. The word *percentages* is commonly used when a number is not indicated. The symbol (%) is used in tables and with figures. Below are some examples of the use of decimal points.

1. A decimal point is placed to separate dollars and cents.

   .59

   59¢

   less than 59 cents

   $3.59

2. A decimal point is used to indicate fractions of less than one. When accuracy is important, a zero is placed after the decimal point.

   413.7

Capital Letters. The use of capital letters signifies the importance of a word in a sentence or paragraph. When the reader sees a capital letter at the beginning of a group of words, it marks the beginning of a new sentence. The first noun or pronoun encountered after this capital letter may well be the subject of the sentence.

Capitalize names, including people, places, countries, religions, languages, events, publications, documents, associations, brands, months, and days of the week. Do not capitalize if the nouns do not indicate specific names such as a university, church, or management association. Principal uses of capitalizations are shown below.

1. The first word of a sentence, a quotation, and often a statement within quotation marks is capitalized.

   Mozart is perhaps the greatest composer of all time.

   He addressed the dead Hamlet saying, "Good night, sweet prince, and flights of angels sing thee to thy rest!"

   He said yearningly, "All I wanted was to have finished college."

2. Capitalize proper nouns, names, and official titles preceding a name.

   Mr. Jones

   Reverend Jones

   Dean Jones

3. Specific names of associations, businesses, organizations, buildings, and institutions are capitalized.

   General Motors Corporation

   Boy Scouts

   Empire State Building

   New York Public Library

4. The first word in the complimentary closing in a letter of correspondence is always capitalized.

   Very truly yours,

   Sincerely yours,

5. Whenever the titles of books, newspapers, or movies are written, the first, last, and all important words (nouns, pronouns, adjectives, adverbs, verbs) are capitalized. The first word after a colon in a title is always capitalized. Articles, conjunctions, and prepositions of fewer than five letters are not capitalized. These may vary in the preparation of footnotes and bibliographies.

   The Iliad of Homer

   The Christian Science Monitor

   Gone With the Wind

   Conceptual Blockbusting: A Guide to Better Ideas

6. All names of specific places, nations, nationalities, geographical areas, street addresses, objects, and sacred names are capitalized.

   Taj Mahal

   500 East King Street

   Magna Charta

   Holy Koran

   Hope Diamond

   Kabul University

   Boone, NC, U.S.A.

Underscoring. Underscoring is the use of italics, a type style slanting upward to the right, used in the text to emphasize special meaning. Underscoring is used when foreign words are written. It is also employed to indicate foreign phrases or expressions that are not part of the native language. One should always underscore titles of books, bulletins, films, newspapers, magazines, pamphlets, and plays. Names of standard religious books such as the Bible, the Koran, and the Talmud are not underscored.

1. The greatest farce since Leninism is <u>Glasnost</u>.
2. <u>The Wall Street Journal</u> is published by the Dow Jones Company.

Apostrophe ('). An apostrophe is a superscript sign (') used in punctuation to show: (1) possessive forms of nouns and some pronouns, (2) contractions and omissions, and (3) plurals of letters, figures, and words. Some more special uses of apostrophes are:

1. The possessive form of singular nouns and some pronouns is formed by adding ('s) at the end of the word as in the following examples:

   baby's crib

   child's toy

   man's behavior

2. If the noun ends in *s*, the possessive is formed using ('s). Plural nouns ending in *s* need only the apostrophe. Words not ending in *s* that are plural need ('s) at the end.

   Charles's mother was at the church.

   The Rosses' car caught on fire at the school.

   men's dormitory

   children's toys

3. To form the possessive of indefinite pronouns, add ('s) at the end of the word.

   someone's

   everybody's

   whomever's

   one's

4. Apostrophes are not used for some possessive personal pronouns, such as:

   yours, ours, his, hers, theirs

5. The following examples indicate the use of apostrophes for missing letters and numbers in contractions:

   can't, wasn't, isn't, the roaring '20s, o'clock.

   Note: Care is needed in using the contractions *it's, let's, and who's.*

   1. "*It's*" is a contraction meaning it is.

      It's a nice day.

   2. "*Its*" is the possessive form without the apostrophe, meaning belonging to it.

      That car and its design are superb.

3. *"Let's"* means let us.

> *Let's go to the store.*
>
> He lets them go to the store.

4. *"Who's"* means who is.

> *Who's going to the store?*

5. *"Whose"* is the possessive form of the word who.

> *Whose turn is it to go to the store?*

6. Apostrophes are sometimes used to show plurals of letters, numbers, and words.

> There were 3 A's and only 2 F's in the whole class.
>
> There should be ten 20's and seven 100's in that wallet.
>
> There are too many *and's* in this paragraph.

7. The apostrophe is used to indicate slang conversation and idiomatic possessive forms.

> How 'bout it. (How about it.)
>
> Ya'll come. (You all come.)

SPELLING OR WRITING NUMBERS

Written numbers may either be spelled out or displayed in figures. Great variation exists in this practice among writers and publishers. Numbers through one hundred are spelled out for books, newspapers, and magazine articles, including larger numbers that can be written in two words. The numbers four hundred and four million are spelled out; these are only two words, but do not spell out 399, which is four words. The following guidelines should be used in writing numbers.

1. When a number starts a sentence, it is written out unless it is a date. When possible, rewrite a sentence to avoid starting with a number.

   Twelve students registered for the evening lab.

   1929 was the year America stood still.

2. Hours are written in figures before a.m. (ante meridiem, time from midnight to noon) and p.m. (post meridiem, time from noon to midnight). However, they are spelled out before "o'clock." Dates are written in numerical figures except in certain formal social correspondence such as wedding invitations. The abbreviations 1st, 2nd, 3rd, among others, can be used to write dates if the year is omitted.

   I will see you tomorrow at either 11:45 a.m. or 1:15 p.m.

   I leave for school at eight o'clock.

   John was born January 11, 1987.

   Have your application and resume to me by the 8th of May.

3. Page, chapter, measurements, statistical data, decimals, and stock and bond prices are written in figures.

   You will find that graph on page 19, chapter 5.

   Carlson played football in 1988, weighed 210 lbs., and was 6 feet 7 inches tall.

Productivity in the non-manufacturing sector decreased from 2.3 percent before 1967, to 0.9 percent to the period 1973, and to a disappointing 0.1 percent since then.

Crude oil sold at $29.15 a barrel. Texaco common stock sold at $58.50 per share. Benchmark U.S. Treasury bonds gained 7/8 of a point, or about $8.75 for each $1000 face amount.

4. When fraction numbers are used alone, they should be hyphenated and written out. If the number cannot be written in two words, use the hybrid form.

We were two-fifths through our journey before the car broke down.

In $13^1/_2$ years that tree grew two-tenths of a foot.

5. Ordinal numbers indicating order of rank are spelled out if they are one or two words. Write *st, nd, rd* with dates and other numbers.

Eighth Box

3rd floor

171st unit

twenty-first item

It was the one hundred forty-fifth anniversary event that was celebrated.

Summary

The above discussion is not intended to cover all aspects of punctuation. Writers should study the many aspects of punctuation, special marks, capitalization, and italics. Mastery of composition, grammar, and punctuation can be achieved through the study of recent handbooks on the use of the English language. Excellent sources of consultation for quick reference purposes include language dictionaries, encyclopedias, and this book. People interested in studying punctuation topics in greater detail will find the following books beneficial:

Kane, S. Thomas. *The New Oxford Guide to Writing*. New York: Oxford University Press, 1988.

Coe, M. Richard. *Toward a Grammar of Passages*. Carbondale, IL: Southern Illinois University Press, 1988.

The Great American English Handbook. Jacksonville, IL: Perma-Bound Books, 1987.

SPELLING RULES

One important key to professional quality work is good spelling. Accurate spelling should be observed during both the writing and proofreading stages. It is beneficial to memorize troublesome words and double-check for correct spelling. A dictionary should be consulted for the correct spelling and appropriate meaning of irksome words. Spell-checking capabilities are found on most word processors today and should be used when available. Although these checkers examine drafts quickly for misspellings, proofreading is still needed because the spell checker cannot spell most proper nouns or distinguish between similar words, such as *dyeing* and *dying*. The following are some helpful rules for spelling, but because there are many exceptions to these rules, a dictionary should be consulted for correct spelling when in doubt.

1. Whenever a suffix beginning with a vowel is added to a word, such as *ed, er, est, ing*, it is necessary to double the last consonant. This rule applies to short, single-stressed vowels.

   plan — planned, ship — shipped, stop — stopped

   red — redder, big — bigger, small — smaller, rob — robber

   thin — thinnest, big — biggest, fat — fattest

   begin — beginning, jog — jogging, swim — swimming

   No doubling:

   end — ended, boat — boating, hate — hating, sing — singing

2. When the last three letters of the word fall consonant-vowel-consonant (CVC), the final consonant is not doubled.

   pay — paying, convey — conveying, display — displaying

3. When adding a suffix to a word ending in *y*, which is preceded by a consonant, the *y* is changed to *i*, except the suffix *ing*. If the *y* is preceded by a vowel, the *y* stays. The *y* is changed to *ie* before *s*.

   i: happy — happier, try — tried, study — studied, copy — copied

   ing: study — studying, buy — buying, try — trying, copy — copying

   vowel: pay — pays, convey — conveyed, attorney — attorneys

   ie: fly — flies, family — families, study — studies

   When changing to past tense, if the letter before the *y* is a vowel, the *y* is kept.

   portray — portrayed, delay — delayed

   This rule does not apply to some one-syllable words and proper nouns.

   day — daily, lay — laid, pay — paid, say — said, Kelly — three Kellys

   Generally, the final silent *e* is dropped when a suffix is added that begins with a vowel, such as *ing* and *able*, or the *e* is preceded by a *u*. The *e* is kept if the suffix begins with a consonant. When the ending *e* makes the *c* or *g* sound like *s* or *j*, usually the *e* is retained.

   vowel: age — aging, come — coming, drive — driving, shave — shaving, drive — drivable

   e: before u   true — truly, argue — argument

   consonant: hope — hopeful, hate — hateful, like — likely, love — lovely, nine — ninety, awe — awesome

   ge, ce: manage — management, courage — courageous, change — changeable, notice — noticeable, enforce — enforceable

4. Whenever a word is accented on its final syllable with a short vowel sound, the final consonant is doubled before the suffix.

   omit — omitted, fog — foggy, permit — permitted, occur — occurring

   The final consonant is not doubled when the vowel sound in its syllable is long, or when the syllable is unaccented.

   eat — eaten, leer — leering, greet — greeting, rail — railing, counsel — counselor, question — questionable

5. Generally speaking, *i* must be written before *e*, except after *c*, or when an

ay sound is encountered, such as in *neighbor* and *weigh*. Most people remember the old jingle:

"Write i before e except after c, or when sounded as ay as in neighbor and weigh."

achieve, brief, field, hygiene

ceiling, deceive, receipt

reign, sleigh, freight

Among the exceptions are included words sounding with a *shen*, where *ie* is included in spellings such as *efficient, sufficient,* and *ancient.*

6. Adding *s* or *es* to make a singular word plural:

Add an *s* to the plural of most nouns, but add *es* if the plural is pronounced as another syllable. The plurals of nouns ending in *ch, sh, s, x,* and *z* require an *es*.

door — doors, key — keys, hat — hats

box — boxes, buzz — buzzes, guess — guesses

7. An *s* is added to nouns ending in *o*, preceded by a vowel. If the noun ends in *o* preceded by a consonant, *es* is generally added.

studio — studios, radio — radios, trio — trios, potato — potatoes, tomato — tomatoes, hero — heroes

PRINCIPAL GRAMMATICAL TERMS

In the English language, there are at least seven classifications of words based on their usage in a sentence. Each of these classifications poses a title, or grammatical term. Following are seven terms describing these classification and demonstrative examples.

Nouns. A noun is a person, a place, or an object and generally is the subject of a sentence.

1. Proper nouns identify specific people, places, things, and objects and are always capitalized.

   Dr. Brown, Paris, Coke, Islam, France

2. Common nouns identify people, things, objects in general and are not capitalized.

   physician, cities, religion, country

3. Group nouns cite groups of people, things, objects, and places and are not capitalized.

   audience, club, company, committee, flock, orchestra, team, herd

Verbs. Verbs describe an action, an occurrence, or the existence of an object, or express a feeling.

1. Action verbs describe what the subject does.

   The girl *danced* all night.

   Charles *climbed* the tree.

2. Linking verbs connect the subject to words that explain the action or distinguish it.

   The cat *was* soaked.

   Dr. Brown *is* our teacher.

3. Transitive verbs link with the object of the action.

   The boy *dragged* the cat.

   The pitcher *threw* the ball.

4. Intransitive verbs do not have an object to complete their meaning.

   The cat *scratched*.

   Their plot *failed*.

5. Verb phrases are made of more than one word.

   The well *has run* dry.

   The professor *will be* jogging.

6. Active voice verbs demonstrate the subject doing the action.

   The cat *scratched* the couch.

   A hornet *stung* Lori.

7. Passive voice verbs indicate the subject being acted upon.

   The couch *has been damaged* by the cat.

   The refund *was received* by Mr. Williams.

Adjectives. An adjective is a word that describes, qualifies, limits, or points out a noun or pronoun.

It is a *beautiful* day.

He is a *cheerful* individual.

Adverbs. These words describe verbs, adjectives, other adverbs, or entire clauses. An adverb is easily identified in a sentence, since all adverbs tell how, when, where, why, how often, or to what extent.

how   The water dripped *slowly*.

when   He ran slowly *recently*.

where   He walked *outside* the track.

Pronouns. A pronoun, meaning "for a noun," is a word that can be substituted for a noun.

1. Personal pronouns are used to refer to people or things and show their number and gender.

   I, me, you, yours, she, hers, it, its, they, we, us, my, mine, our, ours, he, him, her, them, his, their, theirs

2. Demonstrative pronouns point out particular persons, places, or objects. They are used in the third person, and can be singular, such as *this, that,* or plural, such as *these, those.*

   This is my book.

   These are my shoes.

Those are my books.

That is my car.

3. Indefinite pronouns point to a particular object or person in general terms such as *some, each, one, everyone, anyone, neither, everybody, no one,* and *nobody*.

Somebody sold me that book.

Each person must take one ticket.

4. Intensive pronouns give emphasis to nouns or pronouns that precede them in a sentence. Words that end in *self* or *selves* are examples of these.

I *myself* wrote this example.

We *ourselves* will pay the rent.

5. Relative pronouns introduce dependent clauses of adjectives or nouns. The words *who, whoever, whom, whomever, that, what, which, whose* are frequently used for this purpose.

The services were offered to *whomever* wanted them.

Over there is the cat *that* scratched you.

We invite *whoever* will come.

6. Words used in asking questions such as *who, whom, which, whose,* and *what* are called interrogative pronouns. They can also be combined with the word *ever,* such as *whoever* and *whomever*.

Who came to the party?

Whoever went to the party stand up.

7. Reflexive pronouns end in *self* or *selves,* showing that the subject acts upon itself.

I paid the bill *myself*.

I hurt *myself*.

The child rocked *herself* on the swing.

They went to the game by *themselves*.

Prepositions. Prepositions are words that indicate how a noun or a pronoun is related to some other word in the sentence. Examples include *to, for, of, in, with, below, through, up, upon,* etc. Groups of words like *according to, in spite of, in addition to,* and *prior to* may also be used as prepositions. Prepositions connect the object to the rest of the sentence.

They wandered *into* the canyon.

She walked *across* the tracks.

I climbed the staircase *in spite of* the doctor's advice.

Note: A sentence should not end with a preposition unless the construction makes the sentence extremely awkward if it does not do so.

Conjunctions. Conjunctions are connecting words that indicate a relationship between words, phrases, and clauses.

1. Coordinating conjunctions include *and, but, or, nor, for,* and *yet*. They join grammatically equal units such as two independent clauses.

John was very polite, *but* Charles was very rude.

She would not dance with David, *nor* would she sing with John.

2. Subordinating conjunctions join dependent or subordinate clauses to independent clauses. Examples of these words include *although, as, because, if, since, though, unless, moreover, nevertheless, when, where, while, finally, after, lest, so that*, and *than*.

   We *finally* went to a fast food restaurant because David wanted to go there.

   He acted *as if* he were sick.

3. Correlative conjunctions join clauses with a pair of words, such as *either-or, not only-but also, neither-nor*.

   He reads *not only* for information *but also* for pleasure.

4. Interjection conjunctions are words used to show feeling, surprise, emotion, or exclamations. They can be used to stand alone or be part of a sentence.

   Well, Lori, you finally got a job!

   Ouch! Get off my injured foot!

   Aha! Now you found it.

Documentation: Footnotes and Bibliographies

9

INTRODUCTION

According to Webster's Dictionary, the literal meaning of the word *documentation* is, "Leading readers to other sources." Scholarly work that is based on the knowledge of others must give the exact informational sources from which it was taken. This avoids suspicion of plagiarism and provides additional sources of information for the reader. Illustrating the sources also verifies thorough research and demonstrates the writer's intellectual honesty. Documentation that consists of footnotes and bibliographies provides this information and additional references on the topic. Reference notes such as explanatory notes, references, or comments about material in the text are most commonly found at the bottom of a page (footnotes) or separately at the end of a manuscript (endnotes). The bibliography represents a listing that includes complete information on the sources of all the cited information in the text. It is the final step in writing a document. This chapter details the importance of, as well as the proper format for, the use of footnotes and bibliographies.

FOOTNOTES

A footnote traditionally meant a note of comment, or a reference that was literally placed at the foot or bottom of the page. This was indicated by a numbered marker at the end of the cited statement. The broader term "reference notes" is more commonly used. This term means that the notes can be placed at the bottom of the page or elsewhere at the end of a chapter or book. The sources of statistical information, quoted material, facts, interviews, lectures, opinions, published information, acknowledgments, borrowed ideas, and other forms of expressions are footnoted. However, general sayings, common information, self-generated ideas, and conclusions do not require footnotes. For example, stating "Joseph Stalin was a dictator" does not require documentation. However, to write that Joseph Stalin ordered the killing of Bukharin requires a footnote. The author may also use footnotes for other purposes such as discussion notes, which are used to make a point or a comment that will not disrupt the reader's thoughts and flow of reading. Discussion notes assist readers through clarification and referrals to discussions elsewhere in the text.

There are several kinds of footnotes. These include those used for reference purposes, those use for cross reference purposes, and those that include content. The cross-reference footnotes are used for referrals within the text. Content footnotes include both discussions and clarifications. Writing this information in the text may either interrupt the line of thought, lessen or distract the reader's interest, or be of no interest to some readers. However, each of the following kinds of footnote serves important functions.

1. *Reference footnotes* lend authority and validity to the written material by presenting the sources of facts, opinions, and conclusions on which the

research is based. In the case of quotations and paraphrased material, the use of reference footnotes avoids any suspicion of plagiarism.

2. *Footnotes used as cross references* refer readers to other various parts of the text for additional facts and information. They clarify discussions in the text and assist the reader in comprehending the material.

3. *Content footnotes* clarify the text with supplementary information, when the inclusion of this material in the text may interfere with the thought process of the reader. They are also used to amplify or elaborate on what is discussed in the text. In addition, content footnotes are used by authors to acknowledge assistance or contributions to one's work.

Footnotes, in a convenient form, provide information on the sources of facts stated in the document. As the sources vary, such as books, magazines, speeches, articles, letters, and television programs, special conventions are developed to make footnotes easy to understand and consistent in presentation. These conventions consist of styles used, placement, and content.

Style Certain recognized styles are used when presenting documentation in various disciplines. The principles of documentation remain the same in all styles, requiring writing the sources of facts, opinions, and other details as to where information was found. Documentation consists of two parts — the citations in the text and the corresponding complete entries in the notes and the bibliography. Numerous style guides are published explaining the various conventions used in presenting this information. There are basically two documenting styles.

Traditional footnote-bibliography style. This format is used in writing graduate, undergraduate, and other papers in humanities and social sciences. This style calls for writing footnotes on the page where referrals are made. It also provides the convenience of looking for information at a glance at the bottom of the page. A drawback of this method is the problem associated with typing to accommodate the number of lines for the footnote on the page. Some readers feel it presents distraction and clutter on the page. A variation of this style, called *note-bibliography*, calls for presenting the footnotes separately at the end of the manuscript along with a bibliography. Authors of documents such as dissertations that are to be produced on microfilm should consider using footnotes at the bottom of the page. This will help eliminate the distraction of turning back and forth on the microfilm reader when looking for information.

Parenthetical-reference system. This format uses brief information in parentheses in the text, instead of the traditional superscript numbers. A list at the end of the document gives complete information on cited items in the text. There are variations within this style, which are explained in this chapter. The disadvantage of this style is that readers must turn back and forth to the end of the document for information.

Many other methods use modifications based on the above two styles. The final selection of which style to use depends on individual preferences, the nature of the research, and the institutional requirements.

Methods of Citation

The in-text parenthetical documentation style (Author-Page) of the Modern Language Association (MLA) is recommended by most language and literature teachers. The American Psychological Association (APA) in-text (Author-Date) style is used in the behavioral and social sciences. Most scientific disciplines use the in-text parenthetical (Numbers-Page) style that is recommended by the Council of Biology Editors in their publication, *CBE Style Manual*. The traditional *Chicago Manual* (Footnote-Endnote) style is widely used in the field of humanities. The following style guides represent the most frequently recommended manuals:

PARENTHETICAL MLA AUTHOR-
PAGE DOCUMENTATION

Modern Language Association of America. *MLA Handbook for Writers of Research Papers*, by Joseph Gibaldi and Walter S. Achtert. 3rd ed. New York: Modern Language Association, 1988.

PARENTHETICAL APA AUTHOR-
DATE DOCUMENTATION

American Psychological Association. *Publication Manual of the American Psychological Association*. 3rd ed. Washington: American Psychological Association, 1983.

PARENTHETICAL CBE
NUMBERS-PAGE

Council of Biology Editors. Style Manual Committee. *CBE Style Manual: A Guide for Authors, Editors, and Publishers in the Biological Sciences*. 5th ed. Bethesda, MD: Council of Biology Editors, 1983.

TRADITIONAL CHICAGO
(FOOTNOTE-ENDNOTE)

University of Chicago. *The Chicago Manual of Style*. 13th ed. Chicago: Univ. of Chicago Press, 1982.

Selecting a style before writing simplifies gathering correct information and preparing the citations and bibliography. Whichever style is selected, authors must observe appropriate margins, capitalizations, indentations, headings, punctuation, spacing, and other formats that are recommended for that style. Citations in the body of the text must be uniform in usage throughout. Corresponding footnotes should easily identify the source and relate correct information. Writers must become familiar with the style used in their discipline. It is recommended to ask publishers or instructors for whom a manuscript is prepared which documentation style to use. Then authors should become familiar with the style and be consistent in its usage.

Four documentation styles are widely used in the preparation and writing of most term papers, theses, dissertations, and other reports. The four styles are each suitable for a specific discipline. These four styles are: (1) Parenthetical MLA (Author-Page) Documentation Style, (2) Parenthetical APA (Author-Date) Documentation Style, (3) Parenthetical CBE (Numbers-Page) Documentation Style, and (4) Traditional Chicago (Footnote-Endnote) Documentation Style.

**Parenthetical MLA (Author-
Page) Documentation Style**

This is a popular style used for preparing papers in humanities and related fields such as languages, literature, music, and philosophy. It is based on the recommendations of the influential Modern Language Association, through the publication of their manual, *MLA Handbook for Writers of Research Papers*, 3rd ed. (New York: MLA, 1988). The revised version of the traditional MLA system of footnotes appearing at the bottom of the page has been replaced with in-text parenthetical citations. This revision eliminates the trial and error calculations of how many lines to type on a page in order to accommodate the corresponding footnotes. The citations on the page consist of the author's last name and the page number(s) where the information can be found. When a work cited has two or three authors, all names are written followed by the page number. For more than three authors, the phrase *et al.* or *and others* is indicated. This information is written within parentheses at the end, or where it will not impede the flow of the sentence in the text, for example, (Darwin 59). A semicolon separates the items in parentheses when two or more works are cited, as in (Faulkner 110-112; Lewis 220-222). If several works by the same author are cited, words from the title are included to identify the specific source, such as (Darwin, Origin, 84). If the author or the title of the source is mentioned in the text, only the page number(s) appears within the parentheses at the end of the sentence, such as, "Darwin found that the evolution of the species will continue (84)." If the work does not have an author, the title is treated as the author. Paraphrases and quotations are indicated by the inclusion of the author's last name and page number parenthetically at the end. For block quotations, the parenthetical author-number information is given at the end, outside the period. At the end of the manuscript in a list titled "Works Cited," complete information is provided for all sources cited in the text. This list is arranged alphabetically by the author's last name, or by the first word of the title of articles or books where author is not indicated, such as newspaper articles. A second list titled "Works Consulted" may also be included at the end after the "Works Cited" section. This list will include other significant works that were read in preparation for writing but were not cited in the text. The emphasis of the revised MLA system is on simplicity and the inclusion of needed information to identify the source with the least amount of confusion and clutter.

Content notes are treated as traditional footnotes or endnotes and listed at the bottom of the page or on a separate sheet at the end of the text. As with traditional footnotes, a superscript number is placed at the end of the sentence in the text, and then the related footnote is typed at the bottom of the page.

In the following samples and in the bibliography section, examples of most MLA styles in text citations and their corresponding entries in the "Works Cited" list are presented:

Sample of citations and corresponding entries in "Works Cited" list:

A book with one author, the author identified in the text, but not quoted:

In his important work in <u>The Affluent Society</u>, Galbraith points out that the elimination of depressions is the <u>sine qua non</u> of any viable economic system (94).

A book with one author, the author not identified in the text and quoted:

"The prevention of depressions remains the <u>sine qua non</u> for economic security" (Galbraith 94).

"Works Cited" entry:

Galbraith, John Kenneth. The Affluent Society. New York: Mentor, 1958.

A book with two authors, authors identified in the text:

In their text, Organizational Behavior, Roberts and Hunt observe that President Ronald Reagan was a young registered Democrat, then he was paid by General Electric to deliver conservative speeches, ultimately he became the president of the Republican party (264).

A book by two authors, authors not identified in the text:

"The simplest and most obvious way to get someone to accept a position contrary to one he now espouses is to ask him to make a public statement in favor of the contrary position" (Roberts and Hunt 265).

"Works Cited" entry:

Roberts, H. Karlene, and David M. Hunt. Organizational Behavior. Massachusetts: PWS-KENT Publishing, 1991.

Books by more than two authors, authors identified in the text:

As Filley et al. point out, "Clearly defined objectives let organization members know their responsibilities and the scope of their authority to initiate independent action" (141).

Books by more than two authors not identified in the text:

"Clearly defined objectives let organization members know their responsibilities and the scope of their authority to initiate independent action" (Filley et al. 141).

"Works Cited" entry:

Filley, C. Allen, Robert J. House, and Steven Kerr. Management Process and Organizational Behavior. Glenview, IL: Scott, 1976.

Journal article by one author, author identified and quoted in the text:

As Schwartz suggests, "Career interruptions, plateauing, and turnovers" are expensive to employers who have invested heavily in training and development (65).

Journal article by one author, author not identified in the text, but quoted:

"Career interruptions, plateauing, and turnovers are expensive. The money corporations invest in recruitment, training and development are less likely to produce top executives among women than among men, and the invaluable company experience that developing executives acquire at every level as they move up through management is often lost" (Schwartz 65).

"Works Cited" entry:

Schwartz, Felice N. "Management Women and the New Facts of Life." <u>Harvard Business Review</u> 89.1 (1989): 65.

Journal article by two authors identified in the text, but not quoted:

As Barsoux and Lawrence point out, France is closer than other nations to making management a separate profession, with its own standards and regulations for entry into the discipline (58).

Journal article by two authors, authors not identified in the text:

"France is one of the few countries where management is treated as a profession with its own entry qualifications" (Barsoux and Lawrence 58).

"Works Cited" entry:

Barsoux, Jean-Louis, and Peter Lawrence. "The Making of a French Manager." <u>Harvard Business Review</u> 69.4 (1991): 58.

A source with no author, title mentioned in the text:

"Buzzing into Summer" warns that a heavy invasion of insects is on the way for the U.S. (34).

A source with no author, title not mentioned in the text:

"The insect scourge arrives even as environmental concerns make the battle harder to fight" ("Buzzing into Summer" 34).

"Works Cited" entry:

"Buzzing Into Summer." <u>Newsweek</u>. 21 May 1990: 34.

A citation to a multi-volume source, author identified in the text:

Contrasted to quantity theorists, on the subject of the flexibility of labor, Keynes argues that international trade is a dire undertaking to market merchandise overseas in order to perpetuate employment at home (3: 382).

A citation to a multi-volume source, author not identified in the text:

"International trade would cease to be what it is, namely, a desperate expedient to maintain employment at home by forcing sales on foreign markets and restricting purchases, which, if successful, will merely shift the problem of unemployment to the neighbor which is worsted in the struggle, but a willing and unimpeded exchange of goods and services in conditions of mutual advantage" (Keynes 3: 382).

"Works Cited" entry:

Keynes, John Maynard. <u>The General Theory Employment Interest and Money</u>. 7 vols. New York: Macmillan, 1973.

A work in translation, author identified in the text:

Gabriel Garcia Marquez makes an interesting correlation between the scent of bitter almonds and the fate of unrequited love (3).

A work in translation, author not identified in the text:

"It was inevitable: the scent of bitter almonds always reminded him of the fate of unrequited love" (Marquez 3).

"Works Cited" entry:

Garcia Marquez, Gabriel. <u>Love in the Time of Cholera</u>. Trans. Edith Grossman. New York: Penguin, 1989.

A source in a collection, emphasis on the editor of the collection:

"The word 'theater' is derived from the Greek word meaning to see, and indicates that the basis of what goes on in a theater is spectacle, something to look at. The words in themselves often have a secondary function." (Frye, Baker, and Perkins 874).

"Works Cited" entry:

Frye, Northrop, et al., eds. <u>The Practical Imagination: Stories, Poems, Plays</u>. New York: Harper, 1980.

Note: If the source has more than three authors, one may cite only the first and add *et al.* (Frye et al. 874) or one may cite all authors' names as they appear on the title page.

Emphasis on the author in the collection:

Miller took full advantage of contemporary availability in stage lighting and sound reproduction techniques to add spectacle and realism to his plays (1249).

"Works Cited" entry:

Miller, Arthur. <u>Death of a Salesman</u>. <u>The Practical Imagination: Stories, Poems, Plays</u>. Eds. Northrop Frye, et al. New York: Harper, 1980. 1249-1316.

Poetry:

Whenever fewer than three lines of poetry are quoted, they are typed within the text. The lines are separated by a slash (/) with a space on each side. At the end of the quoted poems, the line information is given in parentheses. For a subsequent citation, only the line numbers are parenthetically given. When more than three lines of a poem are produced, they are separated from the body of the text, single-spaced, and typed without quotation marks.

In text:

The aged and confused Prufrock, weathered by time, staring into the future, bewilderedly asks: "Shall I part my hair? / Do I dare to eat a peach? / I shall wear white flannel trousers, and walk upon the beach." (Eliot, "The Love Song of J. Alfred Prufrock," 1249, lines 122-124).

"Works Cited" entry:

Eliot, T.S. "The Love Song of J. Alfred Prufrock." <u>The Practical Imagination: Stories, Poems, Plays</u>. Eds. Northrop Frye et al. New York: Harper, 1980.

A subsequent citation to the same source:

"I should have been a pair of ragged claws / Scuttling across the floor of silent seas" ("The Love Song," lines 73-74).

Association authorship:

Many private organizations contribute resources to educational institutions; for example, AT&T donated over $36.5 million in 1988 (AT&T, 25).

"Works Cited" list:

AT&T, <u>Annual Report</u>, 1988.

Unpublished speech:

... (Krump).

"Works Cited" entry:

Richard J. Krump, "Social Alienation of Employees at Work," speech presented to the regional meeting of American Psycho-Sociological Association. Moscow, TN, 13 Dec. 1981.

Personal interview:

...(Weinberger 29).

"Works Cited" entry:

Caspar Weinberger, interview, <u>U.S. News & World Report</u>, 9 July 1984, p. 29.

Personal letter:

...(Helms 1).

"Works Cited" entry:

Helms, Jesse. Letter to President Ronald Reagan. 14 Sept. 1984.

Government documents:

...(<u>Census Catalog 1984</u> 93).

"Works Cited" entry:

United States Department of Commerce, Bureau of the Census. <u>Census Catalog 1984</u>. Washington: GPO, 1984.

Encyclopedia article:

...("John Wilkes Booth" 19-21).

"Works Cited" entry:

"John Wilkes Booth," <u>Colliers Encyclopedia</u> 13th ed.

Legal cases:

...(General Electric Co. v. School 1984).

"Works Cited" entry:

General Electric Co. v. School, 623 S.W. 2nd 482 ref. nre. <u>West's General Digest</u>, pp. 817-821.

Parenthetical APA (Author-Date) Documentation Style

Disciplines such as psychology and other behavioral sciences use the popular APA documentation style, recommended by the American Psychological Association. This style is recommended in the preparation of dissertations, theses, and most research articles prepared for publication in business journals. The APA style is recommended for writing manuscripts in the following disciplines:

Agriculture	Geology
Anthropology	Home Economics
Archaeology	Linguistics
Astronomy	Physical Education
Biology	Political Education
Botany	Political Science
Business	Psychology
Education	Sociology

The APA (Author-Date) style is a parenthetical identification of the source of information in the text. The author's last name and the date of publication are enclosed in parentheses, such as (Cargil, 1961). In contrast, the MLA (Author-Page) style gives the author's last name and page number, such as (Cargil 59). This date feature of the APA style allows the reader to know how recent the work is. If the author's name is written in the sentence, the date of publication is placed in parentheses after the name such as, "Cargil (1961) wrote that additional research is needed on the subject." Some instructors or institutions may require the page number to be included as well, such as (Cargil, 1961, p. 36).

Quoted material of more than two lines is indented five spaces from the left margin. References for the quotation may appear at the beginning or the end of the quotations. Long quotations are double-spaced. The advantage of the APA style is the elimination of references at the bottom of the page in favor of a final "References" list that appears at the end of the manuscript. This alphabetized list includes information on all cited works and is equivalent to the traditional bibliography. It includes all references cited in the text with the addition of sources the author consulted or read for background information.

The content notes for this style are indicated as traditional footnotes and endnotes. The reference, as with a footnote, is indicated in the body of the paper at the end of a sentence with a superscript number. The corresponding number and its associated footnotes are typed at the end of the page. Start with number one for the first footnote with consecutive numbers throughout the document. The notes may be listed separately at the end of the manuscript after the "References" section and titled "Footnotes." The first line of each footnote is typed on the left margin, and the remaining lines are indented three spaces.

Double spacing is used between and within entries, according to the *APA Handbook*. Listing is by the author's last name, followed by the initials of the first and middle names. The following are examples of frequently used APA style entries:

A book with one author, the author not identified in the text but quoted:

In any economic system the elimination of depressions is the <u>sine qua non</u> of economic viability (Galbraith, 1958).

A book with one author, quoted directly:

"The prevention of depressions remains the <u>sine qua non</u> for economic security" (Galbraith, 1958, 94).

Note: When a direct quotation is used, the page number is always given, even in Author/Date style.

"References" entry:

Galbraith, J.K. (1958). <u>The affluent society</u>. New York: Mentor, 94.

A book with two authors, authors identified in the text:

In their text, <u>Organizational behavior</u>, Roberts and Hunt observe that President Ronald Reagan was a young registered Democrat, then he was paid by General Electric to deliver conservative speeches, ultimately he became the president of the Republican party (1991).

A book with two authors, authors not identified in the text:

"The simplest and most obvious way to get someone to accept a position contrary to one he now espouses is to ask him to make a public statement in favor of the contrary position" (Roberts and Hunt, 1991).

"References" entry:

Roberts, H.K. & Hunt, D.M. (1991). <u>Organizational behavior</u>. Massachusetts: PWS-KENT Publishing. 265.

A book with more than two authors, first time identification:

Filley, House, and Kerr suggest that clearly defined objectives are necessary for subordinates to function smoothly (1976).

A book with more than two authors, second identification:

Filley et al. suggest .... (1976)

"References" entry:

Filley, A.C., House, R., & Kerr, S. (1976). <u>Management process and organizational behavior</u>. Glenview, IL: Scott, Foresman.

Journal article, author identified in the text:

As Schwartz suggests, "career interruptions, plateauing and turnovers" are expensive to employers who have invested heavily in training development (1989).

"References" entry:

Schwartz, F.M. (1989). Management women and the new facts of life. <u>Harvard Business Review</u>, <u>65.1</u>, 65-76.

Journal article by two authors, authors identified in the text and quoted:

As Barsoux and Lawrence point out, France is closer than other nations to making management a separate profession, with its own standards and regulations for entry into the discipline (1991).

Journal article by two authors, authors not identified in the text:

"France is one of the few countries where management is treated as a profession with its own entry qualifications." (Barsoux and Lawrence, 1991).

"References" entry:

Barsoux, J.L. & Lawrence, P. (1991). The making of a French manager. <u>Harvard Business Review</u> <u>69.4</u>, 38-43.

A source with no author:

This summer the U.S. may suffer from one of its worst invasions of insects ("Buzzing into Summer," 1990).

A source with no author, title mentioned in the text:

"Buzzing into Summer" warns that a heavy invasion of insects is on the way for the U.S. (1990).

"References" entry:

Buzzing into summer. (1990, May 21). <u>Newsweek</u>, p. 34.

A citation to a multivolume source, author identified in the text:

Contrasted to quantity theorists, on the subject of the flexibility of labor, Keynes argues that international trade is a dire undertaking to market merchandise overseas in order to perpetuate employment at home. (1973).

A citation to a multivolume source, author not identified in the text:

"International trade would cease to be what it is, namely, a desperate expedient to maintain employment at home by forcing sales on foreign markets and restricting purchases, which, if successful, will merely shift the problem of unemployment to the neighbor which is worsted in the struggle, but a willing and unimpeded exchange of goods and services in conditions of mutual advantage." (Keynes, 1973).

"References" entry:

Keynes, J.M. (1973). <u>The general theory employment interest and money</u>. (Vol. 7). New York: Macmillan.

Note: If all the volumes of a multivolume source are used in the manuscript, the total number of volumes must be cited in the reference list rather than just the single volume used as above.

A work in translation:

Marquez makes an interesting correlation between the scent of bitter almonds and the fate of unrequited love (1989).

"References" entry:

Marquez, G.G. (1989). <u>Love in the time of cholera</u> (E. Grossman Trans.) New York: Penguin.

Work in an edited work or a collection:

Wilder suggests that the world is striving so hard to make something of itself that everybody needs to rest every 16 hours or so (1948).

"References" entry:

Wilder, T. (1948). <u>Our town</u>. In M.M. Nagelberg (Ed.), <u>Drama in our time</u>. New York: Harcourt.

Content notes are treated as traditional footnotes or endnotes and listed at the bottom of the page or on a separate sheet at the end of the text.

Parenthetical CBE (Numbers-Page) Documentation Style

This system is used in the related fields of applied and medical sciences and engineering. The following is a list of disciplines that use this parenthetical documentation style as described in the *CBE Style Manual*:

Biology	Health
Chemistry	Nursing
Computer Sciences	Mathematics
Engineering	Medicine

Parenthetic documentation (numbers) is recommended by the Council of Biology Editors in their publication, *CBE Style Manual*. The CBE format is based on numbers assigned to items that are listed in the bibliography. This style should be used only when the instructor or the publisher asks for it. Because of variations in the use of this style in a number of disciplines, it is recommended to ask for guidance from the instructor and to consult the *CBE Manual* itself. In the text where citations are required, numbers are typed in brackets or in parentheses, such as [5] or (5). The number may also be underlined inside the brackets such as (<u>5</u>), as long as the usage is consistent in the text. These numbers are assigned to individual items in a list at the end of the manuscript known as "Works Cited." This list, unlike the author-date style of citation, has numbers assigned to its references. References are begun by assigning the first reference with the number (1). The next succeeding number after that, such as (2), is given to any further reference. The "Works Cited" list is arranged alphabetically or by the order of appearance in the text. A clear disadvantage of this system of citation is that when a new source is inserted, all items in the text and the "Works Cited" list must be renumbered. If a reader finds the statement — "Brown's (5) research concluded that the Alaskan waters are polluted" — in the text, upon looking up the item number (5) in the "Works Cited" section at the end of the manuscript, complete information on Brown's work will be found. Whenever a reference to the same work is repeated in the text, it is given the same original number. If the text does not contain the author's name, then both the name and the citation number are included within parentheses, such as, "Alaskan waters (Brown 5) are ...." If two authors are cited, both authors are cited using a comma to separate their citation numbers, such as (5,7). If there are more than two authors cited in sequence from the "Works Cited" section, then the citation numbers are separated by a dash, such as (3-5), indicating three sources: 3, 4, and 5. When page numbers are given, they are separated from the source number by a colon, such as (5:59), where (5) stands for the fifth entry in the "Works Cited" list and (59) for the page number. When two authors and two page numbers are given for a citation, the citation would be typed as, "Conrad and Brown called for government water control in Alaska (4:75, 8:34)."

Content notes are treated as footnotes, and the reference is indicated in the sentence with the citation number in superscript. The associated footnote is separated from the text with a solid line and placed at the bottom of the page. If there are many content notes, they are placed at the end of the paper after the "Works Cited" section and labelled "Notes."

The Traditional Chicago (Footnote-Endnote) Style

This traditional method is popular in writing research papers in arts and languages. This system is used in the following fields:

Art	Philosophy
Dance	Religion
History	Theater
Music	

This older system of footnotes or endnotes is the one in which a superscript (raised) number at the end of a sentence refers the reader to the bottom of the page (footnotes) or to a separate list that is prepared at the end of the manuscript and is called "Endnotes." Footnote numbers are assigned progressively throughout a document. Book-length manuscripts may be separately numbered by chapters or sections. For endnotes, numbers are placed consecutively at the end of sentences throughout the document where citations are needed. At the end of the document, a list titled "Endnotes" is provided, with corresponding notes for each of the numbers in the text. The Chicago Style also calls for the preparation of a numbered bibliography at the end of the paper. This is an alphabetically arranged list of all cited sources and other sources that were read and consulted by the author during the preparation of the manuscript.

The presentation and content of footnotes include the following order: (1) author's name, (2) title of the work, (3) page(s) from which information was obtained, and (4) in the case of content footnotes, brief sentences or paragraphs to amplify, explain, or clarify discussions in the text. Footnotes may also be used as cross references.

Cross references are notes that refer the reader to appendices or discussions located elsewhere in the text for further information on the topic. They are placed on the page where they appeared, or they are treated as notes at the end of the page. *Content footnotes* are brief sentences or paragraphs used to amplify or explain any discussions in the text. These are typed single-spaced and entered as footnotes at the bottom of the page. The following is an example of information in the text and the corresponding footnote:

Text:

```
Theoreticians can ignore the ceteris paribus problem
or simply salute it with a wave of the hand.¹
```

Footnote:

```
1. Julian L. Simon, Basic Research Methods in Social
   Sciences: The Art of Empirical Investigation (New
   York: Random House, 1968), p. 47.
```

Whenever later references are made to sources already cited, Latin abbreviations *Ibid.*, "in the same place"; *Op. cit.*, "in the same work", and *Loc. cit.*, "in the place cited" are used. *Ibid.* is used to refer to the preceding footnote. The term *Op. cit.* is used to refer to a footnote previously cited, but not the preceding one. *Loc. cit.* refers to a previous footnote, when the page number for the second reference is the same as the first.

Footnote appearing for the first time (complete citation):

```
1. Julian L. Simon, Basic Research Methods in Social
   Sciences: The Art of Empirical Investigation (New
   York: Random House, 1968), p. 47.
```

Footnote appearing for the second time (complete detail not given):

```
2. Julian L. Simon, Basic Research Methods in Social
   Sciences: The Art of Empirical Investigation, p. 58.
```

Footnote to the same source, no intervening footnotes:

```
3. Ibid., p. 16. [Simon's book, but different page]
```

Footnotes to the same work following each other closely, but with other works listed between:

```
8. Simon, op. cit., p. 67. [Simon's book, but different page]
12. Simon, loc. cit. [Simon's book, same page as footnote #8]
```

Format. The footnote number is typed in the text in superscript Arabic numerals, without any intervening spaces, after all ending punctuation marks. This number is indicated at the end of the last sentence in a paragraph containing information for the cited reference. These numbers are entered consecutively through the document for each chapter or section, or for the entire manuscript. Some publishers or instructors may require beginning numbering afresh for each page. It is important to determine institutional preferences and to be consistent in usage. Type the number one-half space above the line. No period, bracket, or any other mark is typed after this number. A corresponding number referring to this footnote is then typed on the line, at the bottom of the page. All cited notes for the same page appear at the bottom of the page. The text is separated from the footnotes by a solid line typed from margin to margin. Alternatively, a 1½ inch line can be used beginning at the left margin. This line is typed one double space from the last line of the text.

The first line of the footnote, at the bottom of the page, is indented five spaces from the left margin. A corresponding Arabic number is typed on the line. A period is typed after this number, followed by a single space and the note. Since footnotes are considered a sentence or group of sentences, the first letter of the note is capitalized. When a footnote appears for the first time, it documents complete information on the source. This includes the author, title of the work, place of publication, date, and page(s). In later consecutive references to the same source, it is not necessary to repeat all this information. Instead, the word *Ibid.* (in the same place) is typed. This avoids repetition of information. The word *Ibid.* means that the citations are in the same footnote reference as the preceding one. The name of the author is given in its standard form, starting with the first name. For more than two authors, the first author's name is typed followed by "and others" or *et al*. This is then followed by the title of the publication. If the publication is a book, the title is underlined. When the publication is an article in a journal, the name of the journal is underlined, and the title of the article is enclosed in quotation marks.

Numbering. There are several ways to number footnotes. The *continuous method*, often used in short research papers, uses consecutive Arabic numbers throughout the document. For example, if the last number of the footnote on a page is (4), the number for the first footnote on the next page will be (5). In long reports and books, footnotes are numbered consecutively only in sections or chapters. If the last footnote of a page or chapter is numbered (4), the first footnote on the next page or chapter will begin with the number (1). This system makes it easy to add or delete a footnote without disturbing numbers on other pages. The following are illustrations of common note forms using the *Chicago Manual* style entries:

SAMPLE OF INDIVIDUAL FOOTNOTE ENTRIES

Book with one author:

Peter Ferdinand Drucker, <u>Management: Tasks, Responsibilities, Practices</u>, 1st ed. (New York: Harper, 1974), 40.

Charles Darwin, <u>The Expression of the Emotions in Man and Animal</u> (Chicago: Univ. of Chicago Press, 1965), 271.

Book with two authors:

Richard Barnet and Ronald E. Muller, <u>Global Reach</u> (New York: Simon, 1975), 300.

Edwin Eames and Judith Granich Goode, <u>Anthropology of Cities</u> (Englewood Cliffs, N.J.: Prentice, 1977), 205.

Book with three authors:

Robert J. Thierauf, Robert C. Klekamp, and Daniel W. Geeding, <u>Management Principles and Practices</u> (California: Wiley, 1977), 715.

Allen C. Filley, Robert J. House, and Steven Kerr, <u>Management Process and Organizational Behavior</u> (Glenview, Il.: Scott, Foresman, 1976), 212.

Book with more than three authors:

Ronald Stupak, et al., <u>Understand Political Science</u> (Sherman Oaks, Ca.: Knopf Publishing, 1977), 25.

Richard A. Johnson, et al., <u>Management, Systems and Society: An Introduction</u> (California: Goodyear, 1976), 78.

Edited book:

Alvin C. Eurich, ed. <u>Campus 1989: The Shape of the Future in American Higher Education</u> (New York: Delacorte, 1968), 153.

Steven L. Spiegeil, ed. <u>At Issue: Politics in the World Arena</u> (New York: St. Martin's, 1973), 162.

Book by one author, revised by another:

John B. Watson, rev., <u>Behaviorism</u> (New York: Norton, 1958), p. 78.

Alec Nove, rev., <u>The Soviet Economy</u> (New York: Praeger, 1969), p. 121.

Author(s) or editor(s) not named:

<u>Computer Documentation</u> (Boston: Little, Brown, 1983), 15.

<u>The Times Atlas of the World</u>, 5th ed. (New York: New Times, 1975), 27.

Book in a multivolume series:

W.H. Hazard, <u>The Art and Architecture of the Crusader States</u>, 4 vols. (Madison, Wi.: Univ. of Wisconsin Press, 1977), 2:25-28.

Jack M. Sasson. <u>Jonah</u>. The Anchor Bible, 24 vols. (New York: Doubleday, 1990), 24:23.

Richard Beale Davis. <u>Intellectual Life in the Colonial South, 1585-1763</u>. 3 vols. (Knoxville: Univ. of Tennessee Press, 1978). 2:45.

Translated book:

Vasilio O. Klyuchevsky. <u>Peter the Great</u>, trans. Archibald Liliana (New York: St. Martin's, 1958), 221.

Corporate authorship:

University of Chicago. <u>The Chicago Manual of Style</u>, 13th ed. (Chicago: Univ. of Chicago Press, 1982), 75.

The Presidential Task Force on Acid Rain. <u>Acid Rain and Corporate Profits</u> (Washington, GPO, 1984), 78.

Committee authorship:

Interagency Committee on Women's Business. <u>Annual Report to the President 1980</u>. United States Small Business Administration (Washington: GPO, 1981), 65.

Committee on Taxation, Resources, and Economic Development. <u>Land Value Taxation: The Progress and</u>

Poverty Centenary, eds. Richard W. Lindholm and Arthur
D. Lynn, Jr. (Madison, Wi.: Univ. of Wisconsin Press,
1982), 85.

Anonymous author:

Literary Market Place: The Directory of the American
Book Publishing Industry, 1984 ed. (New York: Bowker,
1983), 44.

Pseudonymous book:

Mark Twain [Samuel Clemens], Huckleberry Finn (Chicago: Scott, 1951), 25.

Dr. Seuss [Theodore Geisel], Horton Hatches the Egg
(New York: Random House, 1940), 34.

Book of the Bible:

St. Luke, The New Testament (New York: Collins Clear-
Type Press, 1969), 195.

St. Matthew, The New American Standard Bible (Philadelphia: A.J. Holman, 1976), 200.

Article in a newspaper:

(Signed article)

Jack F. Matlock, "The Politics of Russian Economic
Reform," Wall Street Journal, 5 Nov. 1991, A18.

Jack Scism, "Texas Company to Acquire Burlington Metal
Processor," Greensboro News and Record, 29 Oct. 1991, B5.

(Unsigned article)

"Alcohol Consumption Found to be Highest Among
Southerners," Wall Street Journal, 11 Aug. 1988, A5.

"CBS Hits Grand Slam With Series Ratings," Greensboro
News and Record, 29 Oct. 1991, A1.

Quotation in a newspaper:

President Ronald Reagan, quoted in The Charlotte
Observer, 12 Sept. 1984, A3.

Walter Mondale, quoted in The Washington Post, 11
Sept. 1984, A1.

Signed editorial:

Erik Brady, "Make Way For a New Woman," editorial, USA
Today, 8 Nov. 1991, A8.

Richard Oppel, "Vinroot For Mayor," editorial,
Charlotte Observer, 30 Oct. 1991: A12.

Unsigned editorial:

"No Double Standard," editorial, Greensboro News and
Record, 28 Oct. 1991, A8.

"The City Council Races," editorial, <u>The Charlotte Observer</u>, 30 Oct. 1991, A12.

Letter to the editor:

Shah Mahmoud, letter. "Helms: An American Hero," <u>Charlotte Observer</u>, 8 March, 1990, A18.

Thomas O'Brien, letter, "Would More Prisons Slow Crime?" <u>The Washington Post</u>, 12 Nov. 1991, A20.

Newsletter:

The Operations Management. <u>OMA News Letter</u>, Waco, TX, Summer 1990, Vol. 4, No. 2, 4.

A Special Message from Austin Kiplinger. <u>Kiplinger Washington Letter</u>, Washington, vol. 68, No. 68, p. 3.

China Project Celebrates 10th Anniversary. <u>Appalachian Focus</u>, (Boone, N.C.: Appalachian State Univ.), Winter, 1991 vol. 20, no. 4, 5.

Article from a magazine:

(Signed)

George L. Church, "Mission of Mercy," <u>Time</u> (29 April 1991): 40.

Rick Telander, "His Time is Passing," <u>Sports Illustrated</u> (4 Nov. 1991): 39.

(Unsigned)

"Slower Growth Will Keep the Recovery Rolling," <u>Fortune Magazine</u> (9 July 1984): 12.

"Cameras," <u>Consumers Digest</u> (November/December 1991): 91.

Editorial in a magazine:

Harold Evans, "Free Speech and Free Air," Editorial. <u>U.S. News & World Report</u> (May 11, 1987): 82.

Article in an anthology:

Elton Mayo, "The Seamy Side of Progress." <u>Readings in Management: Land Marks and New Frontiers</u>. ed. Ernest Dale (New York: McGraw-Hill, 1970), 131-134.

Eve Merriam, "Leavetaking." <u>Discoveries in Literature</u>. eds. Edmond Ferrell, Ruth Cohen, and Jane Christensen. Glenview, Il.: Scott Foresman, 1987. 33-34.

Article in a scholarly journal:

C.V. Prestowitz, A. Tonelson, and R. W. Jerome, "The Latest Gasp of Gaitism," <u>Harvard Business Review</u> (March-April 1991): 130-38.

Shah Mahmoud, "Where Do We Get our Future Managers?" <u>Marquette Business Review</u>, vol. 18, no. 4 (Winter, 1974): 189.

Article in a scholarly journal with continuous pagination:

Herschel I. Grossman, "A General Equilibrium Model of Insurrections" <u>American Economic Review</u>, 81.4 (September 1991): 912.

Ian M. McDonald, and Robert Solow, "Wage Bargaining and Employment," <u>American Economic Review</u>, 71 (1981): 896-908.

Dan W. Brock, "The Value of Prolonging Human Life," <u>Philosophical Studies</u> 50 (1986): 401-26.

Article from a journal with separate pagination:

Jeremy J. Siegel, "Does It Pay Stock Investors to Forecast the Business Cycles?" <u>Journal of Portfolio Management</u>, vol. 18, no. 1 (1991): 27-34.

Clive Morley, "Modeling International Tourism Demand: Model Specification and Structure," <u>Journal of Travel Research</u>, vol. 30, no. 1 (1991): 40-41.

Article from a journal with more than one series:

Carol Frost, "Modern History," <u>Kenyon Reviews</u> ns 13.2 (1991): 132.

Friederich Reinhard, "Fortune's Journeymen in the Abyss of Sleep," <u>Kenyon Reviews</u> ns 5.3 (1983) 8-22.

Two articles from journal(s) by same author(s):

C. George Alter, and E. William Becker, "Estimating Lost Future Earnings Using the New Worklife Tables," <u>Monthly Labor Review</u>, 108, no. 2 (1985) 39-42.

_____. and _____. "The Probability of Life and Work Force Status in the Calculation of Expected Earnings," <u>The Journal of Risk and Insurance</u> 14, no. 2 (1983) 364-75.

Article in a proceedings:

Marek Wermus, and James A. Pope, "Scheduling Harbor Pilots," <u>Proceedings of the 26th Annual Meeting Southeast AIDS</u>, Myrtle Beach, S.C. 1990. vol. 20. NC: Appalachian State Univ., 1990, 35.

Government document:

United States Department of Commerce: Bureau of the Census, <u>Census Catalog 1984</u> (Washington: GPO, 1984), 93.

United States Department of Education, <u>Annual Report, Fiscal Year, 1983</u> (Washington: GPO, 1984), 27.

Manuscript, unpublished dissertation, thesis:

Mark Twain, Notebook 32, ts. Mark Twain Papers. Univ. of California, Berkeley.

Lewis A. Randolph, "Development Policy of Four U.S. Cities" (Ph.D. diss., Ohio State Univ., 1990) 15.

Bill O. Bradley, "A Study of Systems Contracting" (Thesis, Appalachian State Univ. 1975), 22.

Law case:

General Electric Co. v. Schmal, 623 S.W. 2d 482, ref nre., <u>West's General Digest</u>, p. 1564.

Grasso v. U.S., 535 F.Sup 309, aff 716 F.2d 907., <u>West's General Digest</u>, p. 1564.

Lewis v. Exxon Corp., 417 S.O.2d 1292 rev 441 S.O.2d 192.

McNeil v. State., 642 S.W.2d 526.

Jane Roe et al., v. Henry Wade., 410 US 113, 35 L Ed 2d 147, 93 S Ct 705.

Encyclopedia:

(Unsigned article)

"Thomas Alva Edison," <u>Encyclopedia Britannica</u>. 1989 ed.

"Andrew Carnegie," <u>Academic American Encyclopedia</u>. 1980 ed.

(Signed article)

J. Lucille Williamson, "Household Appliances." <u>Collier's Encyclopedia</u>. 1989.

Nelson M. Blake, "John James Audubon." <u>Encyclopedia of Southern Culture</u>. 1989.

Pamphlet:

<u>Professional Scouting</u>. Irving, Tx.: Boy Scouts of America, 1990.

<u>Ski the Summit</u>. Denver: Colorado Dept. of Tourism, 1991.

Review:

Robert Craft, "The Maestro and the Market." Review of <u>Understanding Toscanini: How He Became an American Culture-God and Helped Create a New Audience for Old Music</u>, by Joseph Harowitz. <u>New York Review of Books</u> 9 April 1987, 20-27.

Bernard Gwertzman, "He'd Rather Be Right Than Foreign Minister." Review of <u>Future Belongs to Freedom</u>, by Edward Shevardnadze. <u>New York Times Book Review</u> 22 Sept. 1991, 7.

Speech:

Richard J. Krump, "Social Alienation of Employees at Work." American Psycho-Sociological Association of America, Moscow, Tennessee, 13 Dec. 1981.

Anton J. Campanella, "Business and Education: A Logical Partnership." Address delivered to the Symposia on the Role of Higher Education. Monmouth College, West Long Branch, New Jersey, 28 Oct. 1983.

Published speech:

Donald N. Frey, "Developing Corporate Classrooms," delivered to the American Society for Training and Development Annual Convention, <u>Vital Speeches</u>, Dallas, 23 May 1984, 637.

James E. Perrella, "Challenging the Hazards of International Business," <u>Vital Speeches of the Day</u>, delivered at the Annual Conference of the North Carolina World Trade Association, Charlotte, N.C., 26 April 1984, 553.

Lecture:

Shah Mahmoud, Class Lecture. "Exploring Dimensions of Planning." Management 4610. Appalachian State Univ., Boone, N.C., 27 Sept. 1990.

Personal interview:

Clarence Gray, personal interview, 11 Oct. 1991.

Published interview:

Caspar Weinberger, interview, <u>U.S. News & World Report</u>, 9 July 1984, p. 29.

William Winant, interview, <u>Financial World</u>, 8-12 Feb. 1984, p. 17.

Television program:

<u>Vietnam War Stories</u>. HBO, Prod. Stanley Karnow. Boston. 20 July 1988.

Film or motion picture:

<u>Gone With the Wind</u>. dir. Victor Fleming. prod. David O. Selznick. With Clark Gable, Leslie Howard, and Vivien Leigh. Metro-Goldwyn-Mayer, 1939.

<u>Terminator 2: Judgement Day</u>. dir. and prod. James Cameron. With Arnold Schwarzenegger and Linda Hamilton. TriStar, 1991.

<u>Management by Objectives</u>. (Motion Picture) Associated British-Pathe, London. In association with Time Business News and British Institute of Management. London, 1969. Released in the U.S. by BNA Communications.

Filmstrip, slide, transparency:

<u>Marketing and Distribution</u>. Filmstrip. Alphaventure Released by Xerox Films, 1975.

<u>The Management of Difficult Labor</u>. Slide Set MEDCOM, 1974.

Economics In Business. (Transparencies) Visual Products Division, 3M Company, 1969.

Computer database:

Gerald D. Bailey, and William F. Adams, "Leadership Strategies for Nonbureacratic Leadership." NASSP-Bulletin v74 nS24 March 1990 ERIC file 23, item 4.

B.K. Berger, Whirlpool declares quarterly dividend. PR Newswire, August 21, 1990. InfoTrac, 1991.

Computer software:

Personal Law. Computer software, version 1.1 (Coral Gables: BLOC Publishing Corp, 1991), disk.

Sideways. Computer software, version 3.2 (Cambridge: Funk Software, Inc., 1990), disk.

Unpublished raw data from study, untitled work:

Shah Mahmoud, [Common Stock Earning Prediction Based on Industry Sales]. Unpublished raw data. 1991.

C.A. Herbert, [Facilitating Learning Efficiency: Assessment Scores]. Unpublished raw data. 1983.

Unpublished manuscript:

P.K. Brown, Business Failures During Recessions. Unpublished manuscript, Ohio State Univ. Michigan. 1991.

Personal letter:

David Brown, letter to the author. 30 Oct. 1991.

Creighton G. Frampton, personal letter to the author, 5 Aug. 1984, p. 2.

SUBSEQUENT REFERENCES

Whenever additional referral is made to the same source(s), the following abbreviated format is used:

Book with one author:

Drucker 58.

Books with two authors:

Sidney and Burtle, The Great Wheel 67.

Books with more than three authors:

Stupak et al. 87.

Corporate authorship:

University of Chicago 58.

Unsigned article:

"Alcohol Consumption" 5.

Signed article:

Matlock 18.

Secondary Footnote Forms

<u>Ibid</u>. (<u>ibidem</u>). This footnote citation means "in the same place." It refers to the last preceding source cited; reference found on the same page as the previous source.

<u>Ibid</u>., p. 75. This footnote citation refers to the last preceding source, but to a different page.

<u>Loc. cit</u>. (<u>loco citato</u>). This footnote citation means "in the place cited." It indicates the reference is found on the same page as the previous source cited (used when there are other intervening footnotes in between).

<u>Op. cit</u>. (<u>Opere citato</u>). Footnote citation from nonconsecutive sources where other reference footnotes intervene. Author's last name and page number are required.

<u>Passim</u>. "Here and there," refers to inclusive pages covering considerable stretches of textual material or parts in a section or chapter from which the opinions or references are obtained.

<u>Supra</u>. "Above," is a cross reference to a previous page, section, or statement within the researched material itself, rather than an outside source.

<u>Infra</u>. "Below," is a cross reference similar to *Supra* but applies to a succeeding part of the research.

Examples:

`Ibid., p. 32.`

`Ibid.`

`Loc. cit.`

`Darwin, op. cit., p. 106.`

`Passim. Chapt. III.`

`Supra. p. 6.`

`Infra. p. 29.`

BIBLIOGRAPHIES

A bibliography is a list of sources, which are referred to, quoted in the text, or consulted by the author during research and writing. Scholarly writing requires a critical review and study of available information on the subject under investigation. Writers gather material from a variety of sources during research in order to gain knowledge about the subject. The amount of information and the number of references collected during this process depend upon the nature and comprehensiveness of research and writing. A bibliography is the final step in the writing process. The purpose of the bibliography, in contrast to footnotes, is to provide a complete listing and description of the works cited, consulted, and read. Items listed in the bibliography should be selective and should easily identify the source. Bibliographies also provide the interested reader a handy reference list of additional sources of information. Variations in the format of presenting bibliographies are minor among the different documentation styles. These variations are based on the traditional footnote-endnote (*Chicago Style*) and the in-text parenthetical (*APA-MLA*) documentation styles discussed at the beginning of this chapter. However, the overall method of presentation essentially involves the same purpose and content. The established conventions for the presentation of bibliographies include: classification, format, content, numbering, and style.

Classification of Bibliographies

Several types of bibliographies are prepared for different purposes and requirements. These depend on the documentation style selected, the discipline, the nature of the research, and the institutional requirements. For the preparation of brief reports, essays, and term papers, a list titled "Works Cited" is prepared that includes the actual references cited in the document. If needed, an additional bibliography may be typed separately that will include other references that were studied but not cited in the manuscript. A second type contains not only references cited but those that were used in the preparation of the document as well. This is commonly labeled "Works Consulted" or "Bibliography." A third type involves a comprehensive listing of references used and those read and noted by the author during research on the topic. This is also labeled "Bibliography." It may be necessary to prepare two separate lists, one for items cited in the text and another for notable items that were consulted.

Whenever extensive bibliographies are produced, it is best to classify or categorize them in some manner, such as by books, journal articles, and government publications, or by subject matter, for each chapter or section. This arrangement is preferred when more than forty entries are involved. Another arrangement is to prepare a separate bibliography for each section, such as at the end of each chapter in a book. A further arrangement is classification by primary and secondary sources. This method of grouping is popular in the preparation of detailed research manuscripts in the fields of humanities and social sciences. Another type of bibliography is the annotated bibliography. This includes a few brief sentences following the inclusion of a bibliography entry. This may be a description, a summary, or an observation of an entry. It is often a good source of additional information for the reader. Below is an example of an annotated bibliography.

Annotated bibliography:

Allen, F.R., et al. <u>Technology and Social Change</u>. New York: Appleton-Century-Crofts, 1957.

The first comprehensive and systematic treatment of the subject by sociologists.

Blau, Peter M. <u>Bureaucracy in Modern Society</u>. Random House Studies in Sociology, No. 12. New York: Random House, 1956.

Combines theoretical sophistication with skillful use of concrete materials.

Format

The bibliography heading is centered between the margins and typed without ending punctuation as Bibliography, Works Cited, or in capital letters BIBLIOGRAPHY, WORKS CITED on the fifth double-spaced line below the top of the page. The first entry of the bibliography is triple-spaced from the title.

According to the revised *MLA Handbook*, bibliography entries are double-spaced. However, unless recommended otherwise, one way is to single-space within entries and double-space between them. This is a common practice for the preparation of business reports and papers that are typed single-spaced. Each entry is typed flush with the left margin, and the ensuing lines, if any, are indented five spaces. If several works by the same author are cited consecutively, repetition of the name(s) is avoided by typing a line of three hyphens, flush with the left margin, followed by a period and two spaces. In the case of annotated bibliographies, the comments are single-spaced and placed one space below the last underhung line of the bibliography preceding it. The rest of the lines are arranged four spaces from the left margin. Examples of entries for a periodical and a book are:

Periodical:

```
Mahmoud, Shah. "Where Do We Get Our Future Managers?".
Marquette Business Review 10.4 (1974): 189-193.
```

Book:

```
Wren, A. Daniel. The Evolution of Management Thought.
New York: The Ronald Press Company, 1972.
```

There are some basic differences in form between a footnote and a bibliography citation for periodical articles and books. These are as follows:

Footnote entry:

```
1. Peter Ferdinand Drucker, "Business Objectives and
   Survival Needs: Notes on a Discipline of Business
   Enterprise," Journal of Business (April 1958): 81.
```

Bibliography entry:

```
Drucker, Peter Ferdinand. "Business Objectives and
Survival Needs: Notes on a Discipline of Business
Enterprise." Journal of Business April 1958: 81.
```

The forms for a book entry are:

Footnote entry:

```
1. Peter Ferdinand Drucker, Management: Tasks, Respon-
   sibilities, Practices, 1st ed. (New York: Harper,
   1974), 40.
```

Bibliography entry:

```
Drucker, Peter Ferdinand. Management: Tasks, Respon-
sibilities, Practices, 1st ed. New York: Harper, 1974.
```

Content The most important function of a bibliography is to identify and list all works cited and consulted. As such, it is essentially similar to a footnote. In a footnote, the name of the author is given in consecutive order, while in a bibliography, the surname is listed first. Other differences are the inclusion of the page(s), and the number of times a footnote is cited. In a bibliography, the work is cited once, and page references are omitted, except in the case of articles appearing in newspapers, magazines, or periodicals. There are some other differences in the format of presentation among the various styles used. Bibliography entries contain three categories of information. These include author, title, and facts of publication.

Author. This includes the names of any authors, editors, translators, and corporate or institution writers. The name of the author is typed as found in print, last name first. If there is more than one author, the names are typed in the order in which they appear in print. However, the name of the first author is inverted and used in the alphabetical listing of the bibliography. A comma is used to separate the first name of the first author from the others. If there are more than three authors, the name of the first author can be listed followed by *et al*. In the case of unknown or corporate authors, title and publication title are used. If multiple works by the same author(s) are listed, an unbroken line, three hyphens in length and flush with the left margin, is typed, followed by a period to indicate the omitted name.

Title. Titles of books are underlined (to be italicized in print) and typed as they appear in print. Subtitles are separated by a colon and one space. Except for prepositions, articles, and conjunctions, all first letters are capitalized. (This does not apply to an APA-style bibliography, where only the first word of the title is capitalized.) In the case of journal articles, the name of the article is enclosed in quotation marks, followed by a period. The name of the journal is then underlined and a comma is entered. Finally, volume number, month, year of publication, and page numbers are indicated.

Fact of Publication. This includes the place of publication, the publisher, and the date of publication. The place of publication may be given by only the name of the city if the city is well-known. If published in several cities, the name of the first city is indicated. This is followed by a colon and one space. Next the publisher's identity is given in abbreviated form in the MLA style, such as Houghton for Houghton Mifflin and Yale UP for Yale University Press. These abbreviations are used irregularly, but the use must be consistent throughout the document. (See Appendix E for MLA recommended abbreviated names of publishers.) Next, the edition or volume number of the book is indicated such as (Second Edition) or abbreviated as (2nd ed.). The place of publication, such as city and state, is typed and followed by a colon. This is followed by the name of the publisher and a comma. Some styles abbreviate words such as "Company" to "Co." and "Limited" to "Ltd.," and eliminate words such as "The." Finally, the date of publication is given, followed by a period. Facts of publication are given in order of the edition, place of publication, publisher, and date of publication. If any information such as place of publication, publisher, or date cannot be found, n.p., n.p., and n.d. are used accordingly.

Bibliographical entries are listed alphabetically by the author's last name. For a group or corporate author, the first word, excluding any articles such as A, An, and The, is used for the alphabetical arrangement. Whenever the author is unknown, such as in the case of newspaper articles, pamphlets, and encyclopedias, the first word of the title, excluding any articles, is used for the alphabetical arrangement. The alphabetical arrangement is letter by letter, rather than word by word.

The Revised MLA Style   The revised MLA style is popular in business, languages, history, philosophy, literature, and other humanities. It is based on the recommendations of the influential Modern Language Association, through their publication *MLA Handbook for Writers of Research Papers* (3rd ed., 1988). The revised format is a significant departure from the traditional methods of preparing footnotes and bibliographies.

The revised MLA style substitutes "Works Cited" for a bibliography that includes only sources cited in the text. Material read in the preparation of the manuscript but not cited is separately prepared and titled "Works Consulted." The MLA eliminated the traditional "Bibliography," which was literally a list of all sources consulted. Traditional discussion and clarification citations can still be footnoted at the bottom of the page, or alternatively they can be placed separately, under a "Notes" section placed before the "Works Cited" at the end of the manuscript. These notes are numbered to correspond with respective citation numbers in the text. This revised MLA style has eliminated the placement and squeezing of footnotes at the end of each page. It simplifies the presentation of information for the reader without confusion or clutter.

The following is the order of presentation of the elements of an entry in the "Works Cited" list, according to the revised MLA style: author, title, fact of publication, particulars of publication — place, publisher, and date.

Author. The last name of the first author is written first, followed by the full first name and any middle initial. Names of additional authors are given in the order in which they appear on the book. The word "and" is used before the last author. Individual names are separated by commas; periods are placed after initials. A period is also placed after the last author name. In the case of corporate authors, such as agencies, committees, and institutes, the name is spelled out. For a book of collections, the name of the editor(s) is used for the author, and the abbreviation (ed.) is written. If the author is not known, such as in the case of magazine and newspaper articles, the title is written first, placed in quotation marks, and followed by a period. This is used in place of the author.

Titles. Titles of books, including any subtitles, are typed in upper and lower case letters as they appear in print. This title is underlined, followed by a period. Article titles are typed with a period at the end and placed in quotation marks. This is followed by the journal or newspaper title, which is underlined. For an entry from an anthology or a collection, the title of the cited work and the collection name are written.

Particulars of Publication. This includes facts that extend, qualify, and interpret information in the identification of the proper source. It includes referral to the editor, translator, edition number, volume, and title in a series with its volume and number. The format for the abbreviation, punctuation, and presentation of these is given in the examples at the end of this discussion.

Facts of Publication. The name of the city is written and separated from the state name with a comma. Next, a colon is entered, followed by the name of the publisher in the abbreviated format recommended by the MLA. (A list of these abbreviations is included in Appendix E.) If a book has two publishers, as is the case with many paperback books, both publishers are indicated, with the paperback imprint publisher first (Anchor-Doubleday). Following the publisher and a period, the year of publication is written, also followed by a period. For a journal article, after the underlined title and one space, the volume number is entered in Arabic numerals. After a space, the month and the year are enclosed in parentheses, followed by a colon and the inclusive page numbers. This format varies for magazine and newspaper articles. The following are examples:

Journal:

```
Yukl, Gary. "Managerial Leadership: A Review of Theory
and Research." Journal of Management 15 (June 1989):
251-289.
```

Magazine:

```
Callahan, Tom. "Going for the Cup: Dennis Conner is
Racing to Come Back." Time 9 Feb. 1987: 42-45.
```

Newspaper:

```
Rosenthal, Andrew. "Sununu Resigns Under Fire as Chief
Aide to President; Cites Fear of Hurting Bush." The
New York Times 4 Dec. 1991: A1.
```

CORRECT PUNCTUATION AND MECHANICS WITHIN A BIBLIOGRAPHY

1. The "Works Cited" section is typed following the manuscript at the end on a separate page, and is numbered as a continuation of the text.

2. The title of the page "Works Cited" is typed one inch from the top, and two lines are left between the title and the first entry.

3. Every citation is typed on the margin; any additional lines are indented five spaces. Individual entries are double-spaced in between.

4. Entries are not numbered. Double spaces are used between individual entries throughout the "Works Cited" list.

5. Entries are listed in alphabetical order by the author's name. The author's last name is typed first. For second, third, or subsequent authors, the normal order of the name is typed after the first author is listed.

6. If several works by the same author are included in the "Works Cited" list, they are listed in alphabetical order. Second and subsequent entries by the same author are typed by a line of three hyphens, followed by a period. After two spaces, the full title of the work is typed. If an author is unknown, the first word of the title is used, ignoring A, An, or The, if these begin the title.

7. Arabic numerals are used throughout, except in the case of titles of persons (King George III), or preliminary pages of a work that are indicated in Roman numerals.

8. Lower case letters are used for all entries such as vol., ed., trans., col., and others, except when they follow a period.

9. The city of publication, if known, is indicated. The state names are generally omitted. Abbreviated publisher names are used, such as McGraw for McGraw-Hill Publishing Company. Abbreviations such as Inc., Co., and Ltd. are omitted. Emphasis is on identification and simplicity.

10. Commas are not used between the volume number and the title of journals.

11. The abbreviations "p." or "pp." (for "page" and "pages") are eliminated. Page numbers are not listed in these entries, except for newspapers, journals, and magazines, because page numbers were entered parenthetically in the manuscript.

12. Instead of Roman numerals, Arabic numerals are used for referring to volume number, even if the cited work uses Roman numerals. Roman numerals are used only for pages that are so numbered, such as in the case of prefaces.

13. Colons are used to separate volume numbers from page numbers: 3: 278-95. (indicates pages 278-95 in the volume number 3.)

14. For periodicals, the page numbers are separated from the date with a colon, not a comma. Also, the comma before the date or volume number is eliminated.

The following arrangement represents the order of information for entries:

The following are illustrations of commonly used citations and their corresponding arrangements of entries as they will appear in the works cited list, according to the revised MLA style:

BOOKS	ARTICLES
Author(s)	Author(s)
Editor(s)	Title of article (put in quotation marks)
Title (underscored)	Name of periodical (underlined)
Place of publication	Volume number (in Arabic numerals)
Edition (if more than one)	Date of publication
Publisher's name	Page number(s)
Date of publication	

BOOKS **Book with one author:**

Drucker, Peter Ferdinand. <u>Management: Tasks, Responsibilities, Practices</u>. 1st ed. New York: Harper, 1974.

Higgins, James M. <u>The Management Challenge</u>. New York: Macmillan, 1991.

Corwen, Leonard. <u>Your Resume: Key to a Better Job</u>. 3rd ed. Englewood Cliffs, NJ: Prentice, 1988.

Book with two authors:

Rolfe, E. Sidney, and James L. Burtle. <u>The Great Wheel: The World Monetary System</u>. New York: McGraw, 1953.

Hanke, E. John, and Arthur G. Reitsch. <u>Business Forecasting</u>. 3rd ed. Boston: Allyn, 1989.

Book with three authors:

Tate, E. Curtis, Marilyn L. Taylor, and Frank S. Hoy. <u>Business Policy: Administrative, Strategic, and Constituency Issues</u>. Plano, TX: Business Publications, 1987.

Campbell, P. John, Richard L. Daft, and Charles L. Hulin. <u>What to Study</u>. Newbury Park, CA: Sage, 1982.

Book with more than three authors:

Stupak, J. Ronald, et al. <u>Understanding Political Science: Arena of Power</u>. New York: Knopf, 1977.

Levin, I. Richard, et al. <u>Quantitative Approaches to Management</u>. 5th ed. New York: McGraw, 1983.

Multiple books by same author:

Heilbroner, Robert L. <u>The Limits of American Capitalism</u>. New York: Harper, 1966.

—. <u>The Making of Economic Society</u>. Englewood Cliffs, NJ: Prentice, 1962.

—. <u>The Worldly Philosophers: The Lives, Times, and Ideas of the Great Economic Thinkers</u>. New York: Simon, 1953.

Edited book:

Mendel, P. Arthur, ed. <u>Essential Works of Marxism</u>. New York: Bantam, 1961.

Kan, A.H., and G. Rinnooy, eds. <u>New Challenges for Management Research</u>. New York: Elsevier Science, 1985.

Book edition other than first:

Galbraith, John Kenneth. <u>The Affluent Society</u>. 3rd ed. Boston: Houghton, 1976.

Wren, Daniel. <u>The Evolution of Management Thought</u>. 3rd ed. Boston: Wiley, 1987.

Book by one author, revised by another:

Watson, John B., rev. <u>Behaviorism</u>. New York: Norton, 1958.

Nove, Alec, rev. <u>The Soviet Economy</u>. New York: Praeger, 1969.

Author(s) or editor(s) not named:

<u>Computer Documentation</u>. Boston: Little, 1983.

<u>The New Copyright Law</u>. Glenview, IL: Scott, 1979.

Book in a multivolume series:

Hazard, W.H. <u>The Art and Architecture of the Crusader States</u>. 4 vols. Madison: U of Wisconsin P, 1977.

Davis, Richard Beale. <u>Intellectual Life in the Colonial South, 1585-1763</u>. 3 vols. Knoxville: U of Tennessee P, 1978.

Translated book:

(Emphasis on the work)

<u>The Meaning of the Glorious Koran</u>. Trans. Pickthall, Mohammed Marmaduke. New York: NAL, 1953.

(Emphasis on the translator)

Schumpeter, Alois Joseph, trans. <u>The Theory of Economic Development</u>. By Redvers Opie. Cambridge: Harvard U P, 1934.

Corporate authorship:

University of Chicago. <u>The Chicago Manual of Style</u>. 13th ed. Chicago: U of Chicago P, 1982.

The Presidential Task Force on Acid Rain. <u>Acid Rain and Corporate Profits</u>. Washington: GPO, 1984.

Committee authorship:

Interagency Committee on Women's Business. <u>Annual Report to the President 1980</u>. United States Small Business Administration, Washington: GPO, 1981.

Pseudonymous book:

Twain, Mark [Samuel Clemens]. <u>Huckleberry Finn</u>. Chicago: Scott, 1951.

Dr. Seuss [Theodore Geisel]. <u>Horton Hatches the Egg</u>. New York: Random, 1940.

ARTICLES **Newspaper article:**

(Signed article)

Matlock, F. Jack Jr. "The Politics of Russian Economic Reform." <u>Wall Street Journal</u> 5 Nov. 1991: A18.

Scism, Jack. "Texas Company to Acquire Burlington Metal Processor." <u>Greensboro News and Record</u> 29 Oct. 1991: B5.

(Unsigned article)

"Alcohol Consumption Found to be Highest Among Southerners." <u>Wall Street Journal</u> 11 Aug. 1988: A5.

"CBS Hits Grand Slam With Series Ratings." <u>Greensboro News and Record</u> 29 Oct. 1991: A1.

(Signed editorial)

Brady, Erik. "Make Way for a New Woman." Editorial. <u>USA Today</u> 8 Nov. 1991: A8.

Oppel, Richard. "Vinroot for Mayor." Editorial. <u>Charlotte Observer</u> 30 Oct. 1991: A12.

(Unsigned editorial)

"No Double Standard." Editorial. <u>Greensboro News and Record</u> 28 Oct. 1991: A8.

"The City Council Races." Editorial. <u>Charlotte Observer</u> 30 Oct. 1991: A12.

Letter to the editor:

Mahmoud, Shah. Letter. "Helms: An American Hero." <u>Charlotte Observer</u> 8 March 1990: A18.

O'Brien, Thomas. Letter. "Would More Prisons Slow Crime?" <u>The Washington Post</u> 12 Nov. 1991: A20.

Newsletter:

The Operations Management. <u>OMA News Letter</u> Waco, TX. Summer 1990. 4-2, 4.

China Project Celebrates 10th Anniversary. <u>Appalachian Focus</u> NC: Appalachian State University. 20-4, 5.

Magazine article:

(Signed)

Church, George L. "Mission of Mercy." <u>Time</u> 29 April 1991: 40-41.

Telander, Rick. "His Time is Passing." <u>Sports Illustrated</u> 4 Nov. 1991: 39-43.

(Unsigned)

"Slower Growth Will Keep the Recovery Rolling." <u>Fortune Magazine</u> 9 July 1984: 12.

"Cameras." <u>Consumer's Digest</u> Nov./Dec. 1991: 91.

Article in an anthology:

Mayo, Elton. "The Seamy Side of Progress." <u>Readings in Management: Land Marks and New Frontiers</u>. Ed. Ernest Dale. New York: McGraw, 1970. 131-134.

Merriam, Eve. "Leavetaking." <u>Discoveries in Literature</u>. Eds. Edmond Ferrell, Ruth Cohen, and Jane Christensen. Glenview: Scott, 1987. 33-34.

Article in a scholarly journal with continuous pagination:

Grossman, Herschel I. "A General Equilibrium Model of Insurrections." <u>American Economic Review</u> 81.4 (September 1991): 912.

McDonald, M. Ian, and Robert Solow. "Wage Bargaining and Employment." <u>American Economic Review</u> 71 (1981): 896-908.

Article in a scholarly journal with separate pagination:

Siegel, J. Jeremy. "Does It Pay Stock Investors to Forecast the Business Cycles?" <u>Journal of Portfolio Management</u> 18.1 (1991): 27-34.

Morley, Clive. "Modeling International Tourism Demand: Model Specification and Structure." <u>Journal of Travel Research</u> 30.1 (1991): 40-41.

Article in a journal with more than one series:

Frost, Carol. "Modern History." <u>Kenyon Review</u> ns 13.2 (1991): 132.

Friederich, Reinhard. "Fortune's Journeymen in the Abyss of Sleep." <u>Kenyon Review</u> ns 5.3 (1983): 8-22.

Article in a journal with two or more authors:

Alter, C. George, and William E. Becker. "Estimating Lost Future Earnings Using the New Worklife Tables. <u>Monthly Labor Review</u> 108.2 (1985): 39-42.

Article in a proceedings:

Wermus, Marek, and James A. Pope. <u>Scheduling Harbor Pilots</u>. Proceedings of the 26th Annual Meeting Southeast AIDS, Myrtle Beach, SC. 1990. Vol. 20. Boone, NC: Appalachian State U, 1990.

OTHER SOURCES

Government document:

Department of Commerce, Bureau of the Census. <u>State and Metropolitan Area Data Book</u>. Washington: GPO, 1986.

U.S. Bureau of the Census. <u>County and City Data Book, 1988</u>. Washington: GPO, 1988.

Manuscript, unpublished dissertation, thesis:

Randolph, Lewis A. "Development Policy of Four U.S. Cities." Diss. Ohio State U, 1990.

Bradley, Bill O. "A Study of Systems Contracting." Thesis. Appalachian State U, 1975.

Law case:

Lewis v. Exxon Corp., 417 S.O.2d 1292 rev 441 S.O.2d 192.

McNeil v. State., 642 S.W.2d 526.

Encyclopedia:

(Signed article)

Williamson, J. Lucille. "Household Appliances." <u>Collier's Encyclopedia</u>. 1989.

Blake, Nelson M. "John James Audubon." <u>Encyclopedia of Southern Culture</u>. 1989.

(Unsigned article)

"Thomas Alva Edison." <u>Encyclopedia Britannica</u>. 1989 ed.

"Andrew Carnegie." <u>Academic American Encyclopedia</u>. 1980 ed.

Pamphlet:

<u>Professional Scouting</u>. Irving, TX: Boy Scouts of America, 1990.

<u>Ski The Summit</u>. Denver: Colorado Dept. of Tourism, 1991.

Review:

Gwertzman, Bernard. "He'd Rather Be Right Than Foreign Minister." Rev. of <u>Future Belongs to Freedom</u>, by Edward Shevardnadze. <u>New York Times Book Review</u> 22 Sept. 1991: 7.

Speech:

(Published)

Ruckelshaus, William D. "Solid Waste in America." Speech delivered to Cleveland City Club, 21 June 1991. <u>Vital Speeches of the Day</u> Vol. 57, No. 24, 1 Oct. 1991: 765.

(Unpublished)

Campanella, Anton J. "Business and Education: A Logical Partnership." Address delivered to Symposia on the Role of Higher Education. Monmouth College, West Long Branch, NJ: 28 Oct. 1983.

Published interview:

Ferraro, Geraldine. Interview. <u>U.S. News & World Report</u> 23 July 1984: 29.

Schwarzkopf, H. Norman. Interview. <u>U.S. News & World Report</u> 11 Feb. 1991: 36.

Lecture:

Mahmoud, Shah. Class lecture. "Exploring Dimensions of Planning." Management 4610. Appalachian State U, Boone, NC, 27 Sept. 1990.

Television program:

<u>Vietnam War Stories</u>. Prod. Stanley Karnow. HBO. Boston. 20 July 1988: 6

Film or motion picture:

<u>Gone With the Wind</u>. Dir. Victor Fleming. Prod. David O. Selznick. With Clark Gable, Leslie Howard, and Vivien Leigh. Metro-Goldwyn-Mayer, 1939.

<u>Terminator 2: Judgement Day</u>. Dir. and Prod. James Cameron. With Arnold Schwarzenegger and Linda Hamilton. TriStar, 1991.

<u>Management by Objectives</u>. (Motion Picture) Associated British-Pathe, London. In association with Time Business News and British Institute of Management. London, 1969. Released in the U.S. by BNA Communications.

Filmstrip, slide, transparency:

Marketing and Distribution. Filmstrip. Alphaventure Released by Xerox Films, 1975.

The Management of Difficult Labor. Slide set. MEDCOM, 1974.

Economics in Business. Transparencies. Visual Products Division, 3M Company, 1969.

Computer database:

Bailey, D. Gerald, and William F. Adams. "Leadership Strategies for Nonbureacratic Leadership." NASSP-Bulletin v74 nS24 March 1990 ERIC file 23, item 4.

Berger, B.K. Whirlpool declares quarterly dividend. PR Newswire, 21 Aug. 1990. InfoTrac, 1991.

Computer software:

Personal Law. Firm 1.1, Computer software. Coral Gables: BLOC Publishing Corp, 1991.

Sideways. Vers. 3.2, Computer software. Cambridge: Funk Software, Inc., 1990.

Personal letter:

Brown, David. Letter to the author. 30 Oct. 1991.

Personal interview:

Gray, Clarence. Personal interview. 11 Oct. 1991.

The APA Style

This style, developed by the American Psychological Association, is preferred in writing for the behavioral sciences. A list titled "References," including all cited sources, is prepared on a separate page and placed at the end of the manuscript. The list is arranged in alphabetical order according to the surnames of the cited authors. Authors of term papers, theses, and dissertations may single-space the reference entries and use double-spacing between individual entries. Documents submitted for publication to journals require double-spacing within entries. This allows space for copy editing and proofreader's marks. The first line of each entry is typed flush with the left margin, and all succeeding lines for the same entry are indented three spaces. Each entry should contain information about the author, date, title, and facts of publication in that order.

Punctuation and Capitalization. The main punctuation components used in a reference are periods, commas, parentheses, colons, and brackets. Periods are used to separate the main elements: author, date, title, and facts of publication. Commas are used within these divisions where appropriate. Colons are used after place of publication and before the publisher's name. Parentheses enclose additional information within each section such as date, volume number, and edition. Brackets [ ] are used to indicate that the material is a description of content, not a title. The first letter of the title and subtitle of a book and proper names is capitalized.

Author. Authors are presented by surname, alphabetically listed, followed by their initials. A period is used at the end of the author element with an ampersand (&) before the last author. For example: Strunk, W., Jr., & White, E.B. Commas separate authors' last names from their initials. For edited books, the abbreviation "Ed." or "Eds." is typed parenthetically after the last editor's name, followed by a period. The names of corporate authors are spelled out, such as American Psychological Association for APA. If the author's name is unknown, the title of the work is written in place of the author.

Date. A book's date of publication is written in parentheses after the author information. In the case of magazines and newspapers, the year, followed by a comma, and the month and date are all placed in parentheses, such as (1991, March 5). If the document is in press and not yet published, the words "in press" are written parenthetically.

Title. Titles of books are underlined, but titles of articles are not underlined or put in quotation marks. Titles of journals are underlined and typed in upper and lower case letters. The first word of the title and subtitle, proper nouns, and words after periods or colons is capitalized. Additional identifying information such as editions, volumes, and revisions is enclosed in parentheses and typed after the title, as (2nd ed.). No periods are used between the title and this information, unless the period is part of the title. If this information identifies the work, it is enclosed in brackets such as [Letter to the editor]. A period follows this element. The volume number is underlined, followed by a comma and the page numbers as, (<u>Harvard Business Review, 5</u>, 25-31.) The letters pp. are typed for magazine and newspaper articles, but not in reference to a journal article.

Facts of Publication. Facts of publication include the city and the publisher. Only the name of the city of publication is typed unless the city is not well-known or other cities have similar names. The state name is abbreviated according to the U.S. Postal Service format (see Appendix D). The state designation is followed by a colon. The name of the publisher can be indicated in shortened format as shown in Appendix E. Words such as "Company," "Co.," "Inc.," "Limited," "Ltd." are omitted. Names of association presses such as universities are spelled out. Following are examples of most common citations and their associated bibliographical entries.

Books

Book with one author:

Drucker, P.F. (1974). <u>Management: Tasks, responsibilities, practices</u> (1st ed.). New York: Harper.

Byers, L.L. (1984). <u>Strategic management</u>. New York: Harper.

Book with two authors:

Rolfe, E.S., & Burtle, J.L. (1953). <u>The great wheel: The world monetary system</u>. New York: McGraw.

Hanke, E.J., & Reitsch, G.A. (1989). <u>Business forecasting</u> (3rd ed.). Boston: Allyn and Bacon.

Glombiewski, T.R., & Munzenrider, F.R. (1988). <u>Phases of burnout</u>. New York: Praeger.

Book with three authors:

Tate, E.C., Taylor, L.M., & Hoy, S.F. (1987). <u>Business policy: Administrative, strategic, and constituency issues</u> (2nd ed.). Plano, TX: Business Publications.

Campbell, P.J., Daft, L.R., & Hulin, L.C. (1982). <u>What to study</u>. Newbury Park, CA: Sage.

Book with more than three authors:

Murphy, R.M., Fraser, K.S., & Haras, E. (1990). <u>Raising rabbits for pleasure and profit</u>. Charleston, WV: Biways.

Multiple books by same author:

Heilbroner, R.L. (1953). <u>The worldly philosophers: The lives, times, and ideas of the great economic thinkers</u>. New York: Simon.

Heilbroner, R.L. (1962). <u>The making of economic society</u>. Englewood Cliffs, NJ: Prentice.

Heilbroner, R.L. (1966). <u>The limits of American capitalism</u> (1st ed.). New York: Harper.

Edited book:

Mendel, P.A. (Ed.). (1961). <u>Essential works of Marxism</u>. New York: Bantam.

Kan, A.H. & Rinnooy, G. (Eds.). (1985). <u>New challenges for management research</u>. New York: Elsevier Science.

Book edition other than first:

Galbraith, J.K. (1976). <u>The affluent society</u> (3rd ed.). Boston: Houghton.

Wren, D. (1987). <u>The evolution of management thought</u>. (3rd ed.). Boston: Wiley.

Book by one author, revised by another:

Watson, J.B. (1958). <u>Behaviorism</u> (rev. ed.). New York: Norton.

Nove, A. (1969). <u>The soviet economy</u> (rev. ed.). New York: Praeger.

Author(s) or editor(s) not named:

<u>Computer documentation</u>. (1983). Boston: Little.

<u>The times atlas of the world</u>. (1975). (5th ed.). New York: New Times.

<u>The new copyright law</u>. (1979). Glenview, IL: Scott.

Book in a multi-volume series:

Hazard, W.H. (1977). <u>The art and architecture of the crusader states</u> (Vol. 4). Madison: University of Wisconsin Press.

Sasson, J.M. (1990). <u>Jonah</u>. The Anchor Bible (Vol. 24B). New York: Doubleday.

Davis, R.B. (1978). <u>Intellectual life in the colonial south, 1585-1763</u> (Vol. 4). Knoxville, TN: University of Tennessee Press.

Translated book:

Klyiuchevsky, V.O. (1958). Peter the great. (L. Archibald, Trans.). New York: St. Martin's.

Schumpeter, A.T. (1934). The theory of economic development. (R. Opie, Trans.). Cambridge: Harvard University Press.

Corporate authorship:

University of Chicago. (1982). <u>The Chicago manual of style</u> (13th ed.). Chicago: University of Chicago Press.

The Presidential Task Force on Acid Rain. (1984). <u>Acid rain and corporate profits</u>. Washington: GPO.

Committee authorship:

Annual report to the President 1980. (1981). By Interagency Committee on Women's Business. United States Small Business Administration, Washington: U.S. GPO.

Pseudonymous book:

Twain, M. [Samuel Clemens]. (1951). <u>Huckleberry Finn</u>. Chicago: Scott.

Seuss, Dr. [Theodore Geisel]. (1940). <u>Horton hatches the egg</u>. New York: Random.

ARTICLES **Article in a newspaper:**
(Signed article)

Matlock, F.J. Jr. (1991, November 5). The politics of Russian economic reform. <u>The Wall Street Journal</u>, sec. A, p. 18.

Scism, J. (1991, October). Texas company to acquire Burlington metal processor. <u>Greensboro News and Record</u>, sec. B, p. 5.

(Unsigned article)

Alcohol consumption found to be highest among southerners. (1988, August 11). <u>The Wall Street Journal</u>, sec. A, p. 5.

CBS hits grand slam with series ratings. (1991, October 11). <u>Greensboro News and Record</u>, sec. A, p. 1.

(Signed editorial)

Brady, E. (1991, November 8). Make way for a new woman of the year. [Editorial]. <u>USA Today</u>, sec. A, p. 8.

Oppel, R. (1991, October 30). Vinroot for mayor. [Editorial]. <u>The Charlotte Observer</u>, sec. A, p. 12.

(Unsigned editorial)

No double standard. (1991, October 28). [Editorial]. <u>Greensboro News and Record</u>, sec. A, p. 8.

The city council races. (1991, October 30). [Editorial]. <u>The Charlotte Observer</u>, sec. A, p. 12.

Letter to the editor:

Mahmoud, S. (1990, March 8). Helms: An American hero [Letter to the editor]. <u>The Charlotte Observer</u>, sec. A, p. 18.

O'Brien, T. (1990, November 12). Would more prisons slow crime? [Letter to the editor]. <u>The Washington Post</u>, sec. A, p. 20.

Newsletter:

The operations management (1990, Summer). <u>OMA News Letter</u> Waco, TX: Vol. 4, No. 2, p. 4.

China project celebrates 10th anniversary (1991, Winter). <u>Appalachian Focus</u> Boone, NC: Appalachian State University. Vol. 20, No. 4, p. 5.

Magazine article:

(Signed)

Church, L.G. (1991, April 29). Mission of mercy. <u>Time</u>, pp. 40-41.

Telander, R. (1991, Nov. 4). His time is passing. <u>Sports Illustrated</u>, pp. 39-43.

(Unsigned)

Slower growth will keep the recovery rolling. (1984, July 9). <u>Fortune Magazine</u>, p. 12.

Cameras. (1991, November/December). <u>Consumer Digest</u>, p. 91.

Article in an anthology:

Mayo, E. (1970). The seamy side of progress. In Ernest Dale (Ed.), <u>Readings in management: Land marks and new frontiers</u>. pp. 131-134. New York: McGraw.

Merriam, E. (1987). Leavetaking. In E. Ferrell, R. Cohen, & J. Christensen (Eds.), <u>Discoveries in literature</u>. pp. 33-34. Glenview: Scott.

Article in a scholarly journal with continuous pagination:

Herschel I.G. (1991 September). A general equilibrium model of insurrections. <u>American Economic Review</u>, <u>81</u>, 912.

McDonald, I.M., & Solow, R. (1981). Wage bargaining and employment. <u>American Economic Review</u>, <u>71</u>, 896-908.

Brock, D.W. (1986). The value of prolonging human life. <u>Philosophical Studies</u>, <u>50</u>, 401-26.

Article in a scholarly journal with separate pagination:

Siegel, J.J. (1991). Does it pay stock investors to forecast the business cycles? <u>Journal of Portfolio Management</u>, <u>18</u>(1), 27-34.

Morley, C. (1991). Modeling international tourism demand: Model specification and structure. <u>Journal of Travel Research</u>, <u>30</u>(1), 40-41.

Article in a journal with more than one series:

Frost, C. (1991). Modern history. <u>Kenyon Review</u>, ns <u>13.2</u>, 132.

Friederich, R. (1983). Fortune's journeymen in the abyss of sleep. <u>Kenyon Review</u>, ns <u>5.3</u>, 8-22.

Article in a journal with two or more authors:

Alter, C.G., & Becker, W.E. (1985). Estimating lost future earnings using the new worklife tables. <u>Monthly Labor Review</u> <u>108.2</u>, 39-42.

Article in a proceedings:

Wermus, M., & Pope, A.J. (1990). Scheduling harbor pilots. In K.E. Fitzpatrick, & J.R. Baker (Eds.), <u>Proceedings: The Institute of Management Sciences</u>. (pp. 312-313). Boone, NC: Appalachian State University.

Oᴛʜᴇʀ Sᴏᴜʀᴄᴇs

Government document:

Department of Commerce, Bureau of the Census. (1986). <u>State and metropolitan area data book</u>. Washington: U.S. Government Printing Office.

U.S. Bureau of the Census. (1988). <u>County and city data book, 1988</u>. Washington: U.S. Government Printing Office.

Manuscript, unpublished dissertation, thesis:

Bradley, O.B. (1975). <u>A study of systems contracting</u>. Unpublished master's thesis. Appalachian State University, Boone, NC.

Randolph, L.A. (1990). <u>Development policy of four U.S. cities</u>. Unpublished doctoral dissertation. Ohio State University, Cincinnati.

Law case:

<u>Pennzoil v. Texaco</u> (1987). S. W. 2d 768 (TX).

<u>Crane v. Consolidated Rail Corp</u>. (1984). 731 F. 2nd 1042 (2nd Cir.).

Encyclopedia:

(Signed article)

Williamson, J.L. (1989). Household appliances. <u>Collier's Encyclopedia</u>. pp. 305-309.

(Unsigned article)

<u>Encyclopedia Britannica</u>. (1989). Thomas Alva Edison. p. 370.

Pamphlet:

<u>Career as an aerospace-aircraft engineer</u>. (1981). Chicago: Institute for Research.

<u>Professional scouting</u>. (1990). Irving, TX: Boy Scouts of America.

<u>Ski the summit</u>. (1991). Denver: Colorado Department of Tourism.

Review:

Gwertzman, B. (1991, Sept. 22). He'd rather be right than foreign minister [Review of <u>Future belongs to freedom</u>]. New York Times Book Review, p. 7.

Speech:

Michelon, L.C. (1984, May 7). <u>Megatrends in management</u>. [A speech delivered to the Mahoning Valley Management Association.] Youngstown, Ohio.

Campanella, Anton J. (1983, October 28). <u>Business and education: A logical partnership</u>. [Address delivered to the Symposia on the Role of Higher Education.] Monmouth College, West Long Branch, NJ.

Published interview:

Ferraro, G. (1984, July 23). [Interview]. <u>U.S. News & World Report</u>. p. 29.

Schwarzkopf, H.N. (Gen.) (1991, Feb. 11). [Interview]. <u>U.S. News & World Report</u>, p. 36.

Lecture:

Mahmoud, S. (1990, Sept. 4). [Class lecture]. Exploring dimensions of planning. Management 4610, Appalachian State University, Boone, NC.

Television program:

Karrow, S. (Producer). (1988, July 20). <u>Vietnam war stories</u> [Television program]. HBO.

Film:

Fleming, V. (Director). (1939). <u>Gone with the wind</u> [Film]. Hollywood, CA: Metro-Goldwyn-Mayer.

<u>Management by objective</u>. (1979). [Film]. London: Associate British-Pathe.

Filmstrip, slide, transparency:

<u>Marketing and distribution</u>. (1975). [Filmstrip]. New York: Xerox Films.

<u>The management of difficult labor</u>. (1974). [Slide set]. MEDCOM.

<u>Economics in business</u>. (1969). [Transparencies]. Visual Products Division, 3M Company.

Computer database:

Bailey, D.G., & Adams, W.F. (1990). Leadership strategies for nonbureacratic leadership. <u>NASSP-Bulletin v74 nS24</u> March 1990 ERIC file 23, item 4.

Computer software:

<u>Personal law</u>, Firm 1.1. (1991). [Computer software]. Coral Gables, FL: BLOC Publishing Corp.

<u>Sideways</u>, Vers. 3.2. (1990). [Computer software]. Cambridge, MA: Funk Software, Inc.

Personal letter:

Brown, D. (1991, October 30). [Letter to the author].

Personal interview:

Gray, Clarence. (1991, Oct. 11). [Personal interview with the president of the Academy of Economic and Financial Experts].

The CBE Style

The CBE style is popular for writing research papers in natural sciences and for publishing in related academic fields. The guidelines of the Council of Biology Editors in their publication, *CBE Style Manual*, 5th ed. (1983), are followed for this format. The citations are prepared in a list titled "References" or "References and Notes" that is placed on a separate page at the end of the manuscript. This title is centered and typed one inch from the top of the paper. Some institutions may require using the words "Works Cited" for the title of the section. The first entry is typed one double space below this title. The entries are arranged alphabetically or sequentially according to their appearance in the text. The numbers for each entry may be typed with a period or in parentheses or in superscript format, such as 1. or (1) or [1]. Each of these numbers for the entries is typed on the margin, followed by two spaces and the capitalized initial letter of the first word. Additional lines are indented so they are typed below the initial letter of the first word of that entry. Double-spacing is used throughout the references section, and margins of one inch are maintained on all sides.

First, the last name of the author and the author's initials are typed. Additional authors' names, after initials, are separated by semicolons. Only the first letter of the first word of the title, subtitle, or any proper nouns or pronouns is capitalized. The titles of articles, books, and journals are not underlined. The volume and page numbers are indicated, followed by a semicolon, the year of publication, and a period.

There are variations in the use of this style. One should use this style upon the recommendation of an instructor or an institution. It is a good practice to ask for additional instructions. A sample of some common entries that are satisfactory for most college research and short papers is shown in this section. The reader may consult the *CBE Manual* for greater detail and other examples.

The following are illustrations of commonly used citations and their corresponding arrangements of entries as they will appear in the "Works Cited" list according to the CBE style:

BOOKS

Book with one author:

Markham, K.R. Techniques of flavonoid identification. London: Academic Press; 1982.

Zar, J.H. Biostatistical analysis. Englewood Cliffs, NJ: Prentice-Hall Inc.; 1984.

Book with two authors:

O'Keefe, J.; Nadel, L. The hippocampus as a cognitive map. Oxford: Clarendon Press; 1978.

Heston, L.; White, J. Dementia: A practical guide to Alzheimer's disease and related illness. Baltimore: Johns Hopkins Univ. Press; 1985.

Book with three authors:

Sambrook, J.; Fritch, E.F.; Maniatis, T. Molecular cloning: A laboratory manual. New York: Cold Spring Harbor; 1989.

Book with more than three authors:

Murphy, R.S.; Haras, E.; Fraser, K.S.; Lyons, H.W. The complete guide to raising rabbits. Charleston: FirstOut Press; 1991.

Multiple books by same author:

Woodson, R.D. Get the most for your remodeling dollar. White Hall, VA: Betterway Publications; 1991.

——. Rehab your way to riches. White Hall, VA: Betterway Publications, 1992.

Edited book:

Regan, J.D.; Parresh, J.A., editors. The science of photomedicine. New York: Plenum Press; 1982.

Book edition other than first:

March, J. Advanced organic chemistry. 3rd ed. New York: John Wiley & Sons; 1988.

Book by one author, revised by another:

Morris, S.C., Rat anatomy. Revised ed. Morris, D.A., editor. Washington: Harrison Press, 1992.

Author(s) or editor(s) not named:

Organoselenium chemistry. New York: John Wiley & Sons; 1987.

Book in a multivolume series:

Friedberg, E.C.; Hanawalt, P.C., editors. DNA repair: A laboratory manual of research procedures. New York: Marcel Dekker; Vol. 1, A and B (1981), Vol. 2. (1983), Vol. 3 (1988).

Translated book:

The meaning of the glorious Koran. Pickthall, M.M., translator. New York: New American Library; 1953.

Corporate authorship:

Food and Nutrition Board, National Research Council. Recommended dietary allowances. 10th ed. Washington: National Academy Press; 1989.

American Cancer Society. Cancer facts and figures — 1991, Atlanta: American Cancer Society; 1991.

Committee authorship:

Annual report to the president 1980. By Interagency Committee on Women's Business. United States Small Business Administration, Washington: U.S. GPO; 1981.

Pseudonymous book:

Twain, M. [Samuel Clemens]. Huckleberry Finn. Chicago: Scott; 1951.

Seuss, Dr. [Theodore Geisel]. Horton hatches the egg. New York: Random; 1940.

ARTICLES

Newspaper article:

(Signed)

Bishop, E.J. Arcane equations led Einstein and all of us into a relative world. The Wall Street Journal. 1991 Dec. 9:1 (col. 1), 8 (col. 1-5).

(Unsigned)

Alcohol consumption found to be highest among southerners. The Wall Street Journal. 1988 Aug. 11:Sec. A:5.

(Signed editorial)

Evans, H. Editorial. Free speech and free air. U.S. News & World Report. 1987 May 11:82 (col. 1).

Lolli, F. Editorial. How to avoid a wallet bender. Money. 1991 November:7 (col. 1).

(Unsigned editorial)

No double standard. Editorial. Greensboro News and Record. 1991 October 28: sec. A, p. 8.

The city council races. Editorial. The Charlotte Observer. 1991 October 30: sec. A, p. 12.

Newsletter:

The operations management. OMA News Letter. 1990 Summer, Waco, TX: Vol. 4, No. 2, p. 4.

China project celebrates 10th anniversary. Appalachian Focus. 1991 Winter. Boone, NC: Appalachian State University. Vol. 20, No. 4, p. 5.

Magazine article:

(Signed)

Church, G.L. Mission of mercy. Time. 1991 April:40-41.

(Unsigned)

Anonymous. Neurochemical control of productive behavior Physiol. Behav. 21:873-875; 1978.

Article in an anthology:

Gotlib. I.H.; Caine, D.B. Self-report assessment of depression and anxiety. In: Kendall, P.C., editor. Anxiety and depression, distinctive and overlapping features. San Diego, CA: Academic Press; 1989:131-169.

Article in a scholarly journal with continuous pagination:

Sporn, M.B.; Roberts A.B. Role of retinoids in differentiation and carcinogenesis. Cancer Research. 43:3034-3040; 1983.

Brock, D.W. The value of prolonging human life. Philosophical Studies. 50:401-26; 1983.

Article in a scholarly journal with separate pagination:

Eisenstein, A.A.; Stark, I. A nonsuppressible increase of glucagon secretion by isolated islets of high-protein-fed rats. Diabetes 25(1):52-55; 1976.

Giguere, V.; Ong, E.S.; Segui, P.; Evans, R.M. Identification of a receptor for morphogen retinoic acid. Nature. 330:624-629; 1987.

Article in a journal with more than one series:

Frost, C. Modern history. Kenyon Review. ns 13.2, 132; 1991.

Friederich, R. Fortune's journeymen in the abyss of sleep. Kenyon Review. ns 5.3, 8-22; 1991.

Article in a journal with two or more authors:

Alter, C.G.; Becker, W.E. Estimating lost future earnings using the new worklife tables. Monthly Labor Review. 108.2, 39-42; 1985.

Article in a proceedings:

Wermus, M.; Pope, A.J. Scheduling harbor pilots. Proceedings of the 26th Annual Meeting; Southeast AIDS, SC; Myrtle Beach, SC, 1990. Vol. 20. Boone, NC: Appalachian State Univ.; 1990.

OTHER SOURCES

Government document:

Department of Commerce, Bureau of the Census. State and metropolitan area data book. Washington: U.S. Government Printing Office; 1986.

U.S. Bureau of the Census. County and city data book, 1988. Washington: U.S. Government Printing Office; 1988.

Manuscript, unpublished dissertation, thesis:

Mador, J.C. Synthesis of a series of 4-anilino-7-nitrobenzrofurazans for the photochemical production of singlet oxygen. Boone, NC: Appalachian State Univ.; 1985. Thesis.

Lewis, A. Development policy of four U.S. cities. Maumee, OH: Ohio State Univ.; 1990. Dissertation.

Law case:

Pennzoil v. Texaco. S. W. 2d 768 (TX); 1987.

Crane v. Consolidated Rail Corp. 731 F. 2nd 1042 (2nd Cir.); 1984.

Encyclopedia:

(Signed article)

Williamson, J.L. Household appliances. Collier's Encyclopedia. 305-309; 1988.

(Unsigned article)

Encyclopedia Britannica. Thomas Alva Edison. 370; 1989.

Pamphlet:

Career as an aerospace-aircraft engineer. Chicago: Institute for Research.

American Cancer Society. Cancer Facts and Figures—1991, Atlanta, GA: American Cancer Society; 1991.

Review:

Gwertzman, B. He'd rather be right than foreign minister. Rev. of Future belongs to freedom, by Edward Shevardnadze. New York Times Book Review (22 Sept. 1991): 7.

Speech:

Michelon, L.C. Megatrends in management. A speech delivered to the Mahoning Valley Management Association. Youngstown, OH:7 May 1984.

Campanella, A.J. Business and education: a logical partnership. Address delivered to the Symposia on the Role of Higher Education. West Long Branch, NJ: Monmouth College; 28 Oct. 1983.

Published interview:

Ferraro, Geraldine. [Interview]. U.S. News & World Report; 23 July 1984.

Nixon, Richard. [Interview]. U.S. News & World Report; 23 July 1984.

Lecture:

Mahmoud, S. [Class lecture]. Exploring dimensions of planning. Management 4610, Boone, NC: Appalachian State Univ.; 27 Sept. 1990.

Television program:

Vietnam war stories. [Television program]. Prod. Stanley Karrow. HBO; Boston. 20 July 1988.

Film or motion picture:

Gone with the Wind [Motion picture]. Dir. Victor Fleming. Prod. David O. Selznick. Metro-Goldwyn-Mayer; 1939.

Terminator 2: Judgement Day [Motion picture]. Dir. and Prod. James Cameron. TriStar; 1991.

Management by Objectives [Motion picture]. Associated British-Pathe, London, in association with Time Business News and British Institute of Management, London; 1969. Released in the U.S. by BNA Communications.

Filmstrip, slide, transparency:

Marketing and distribution [Filmstrip]. Alphaventure. Released by Xerox Films; 1975.

The management of difficult labor. [Slide set]. MEDCOM; 1974.

Economics in business [Transparencies]. Visual Products Division, 3M Company; 1969.

Computer database:

Bailey, G.D.; Adams, W.F. Leadership strategies for nonbureacratic leadership. NASSP-Bulletin v74 nS24 Mar. 1990 ERIC file 23, item 4.

Computer software:

Personal law, Firm 1.1. Coral Gables, FL: BLOC Publishing Corp.; 1991.

Personal letter:

Brown, D. [Letter to the author]. Boone, NC: 30 October 1991.

Personal interview:

Gray, C. [Interview]. President's academy of economic and financial experts. 11 October 1991.

Manuscript Divisions and Headings

10

INTRODUCTION

Lengthy written material must be presented in a format that is appealing to the viewer, easy to read, and appropriate for the subject matter. Such organization will lend harmony to the presentation of the chapter titles, divisions, headings, subheadings, and other related sections, as well as to the entire manuscript. In presenting these sections, it is important to provide readable and attractive headings and pagination. Chapters, divisions, and subdivisions of equivalent headings call for uniform treatment. Established guidelines presented in the preparation of headings, page number positions, and styles will make the typed material attractive and easier to read. Documents such as articles, books, reports, and term papers generally contain three primary divisions: preliminaries, text, and reference matter.

PAGINATION AND FORMAT

The preliminaries (also known as front matter) supply background information and give guidance to the reader. The preliminaries may include the half-title, title page, copyright page, preface, dedication, table of contents, list of illustrations, list of tables, introduction, foreword, and acknowledgments. All preliminary pages, some of which are optional, must have some similarity in their composition and appearance. For example, the table of contents and list of illustrations should match in presentation. Preliminary pages are normally numbered with small Roman numerals such as i, ii, iii, etc., which may not be printed on the display pages. They are, however, counted as numbered pages. Page numbers are placed at the top center, at the top right, or at the bottom center of each page. The selected placement must be used consistently throughout the document.

The title page may consist of only the title of the work, yet it can also include the name of the author and the publisher. The copyright page is located on the back of the title page and indicates the publisher, the date, and the copyright notice. The dedication page follows the copyright notice. The preface page contains the purpose, importance, and nature of information presented in the text, along with any acknowledgments. It is presented after the copyright notice. The table of contents, which is labeled Contents or Table of Contents (typed in capital letters), usually follows the preface. The table of contents is important since readers frequently form their initial opinions about the material based on the organization of this table. Finally, the introduction presents an overview and an arrangement of the entire material.

THE TEXT — SHORT DOCUMENTS

The text of the document is presented in chapters, sections, divisions, and subdivisions. They can be presented chronologically, least to most important, or in any other logical arrangement. Headings of the chapters in the table of contents are designed to inform the reader about the included content of the material. All headings should provide information in a logical progression from one section to the next. In the presentation of limited manuscripts, only the introduction, major chapters, bibliography, and appendix are presented. However, longer documents may present comprehensive divisions, subdivisions, and other associated parts.

Styles used in typing the headings for sections, chapters, and other parts should enhance the presentation of the text and the order of importance of the headings. Although styles of typing headings vary in capitalization, underlining, bold-facing, and spacing, the writer should follow a consistent pattern in their usage throughout the manuscript. Four commonly used heading levels are sufficient for the preparation of most documents such as term papers and reports. These four levels are: (1) center of the page or main heading, (2) center of the page subheading, (3) flush or side subheading, and (4) indented paragraph subheading.

The center of the page or main heading is reserved for major sections and divisions. This heading is typed one and one-half to two inches from the top of the paper, centered, and written in capital letters. If there is more than one line, the lower lines are single spaced, centered, and capitalized. If possible, divide the lower lines so they are shorter than the preceding typed lines. Periods are not typed at the end, and the text usually follows this level title on the third line. These headings may be underlined and/or boldfaced. The following is an example of a main heading:

```
MANAGING CHANGE IN THE USSR
```

The center of the page subheading is centered and typed on the third line following a preceding text. The first letter of the first word, last word, words of five or more letters, all proper nouns, and adjectives is capitalized. Periods are not typed at the end, and the text is typed two lines below the title. The following is an example of how the center of the page subheading should appear:

```
The Politico-Legal Role of the Soviet Jurist
```

The third level heading is the flush or side subheading. This level heading is underlined and typed three lines below the text in the left margin. The first letter of the first word, last word, words of five or more letters, and all proper nouns and adjectives is capitalized. This level heading is underlined. The text follows this level title on the second line. The following is an example of a flush or side heading:

```
The Sovietsky Lectures
```

The fourth level headings are indented paragraph subheadings. These indented headings run into the paragraph and are typed two lines below the preceding text. The entire heading is underlined, followed by a period, two spaces, and the text on the same line. An example of an indented paragraph subheading is shown below:

```
Promises and Problems.
```

THE TEXT — LONG DOCUMENTS

For longer documents, it is common to use six levels or categories of headings. Each level of presentation should reflect the corresponding importance of that level in the text. At least six categories of headings can be used for longer documents. In order of their descending rank, they indicate the importance of that heading in the document. The following are these six categories:

1. Category one headings, reserved for major sections and divisions, are centered and typed in all capital letters. These headings may be underlined and/or boldface typed.

   <u>MANAGING CHANGE IN THE USSR</u>

   or

   MANAGING CHANGE IN THE USSR

   or

   <u>MANAGING CHANGE IN THE USSR</u>

2. The second category headings are typed three lines from the preceding paragraph. They are centered and not underlined or boldfaced. The first letter of the first word, last word, words of five or more letters, and all proper nouns and adjectives is capitalized.

   The Politico-Legal Role of the Soviet Jurist

3. The third category headings are typed three lines below the preceding paragraph and are placed at the left margin, underlined, and/or typed in boldface.

   <u>Problems and Promises</u>

   or

   Problems and Promises

4. The fourth category headings are placed at the left margin without being underlined.

The Soviet Agriculture

5. The fifth category headings are used for paragraph headings. These headings run into the paragraph, are indented more spaces, and are underlined or typed in boldface letters. Paragraph headings are followed by a period and a dash or two spaces and the text.

   <u>Ideology and Expansion</u>.—

   or

   Ideology and Expansion.—

6. The final category is used for paragraph headings that are not underlined or boldfaced. These are also followed by a period and a dash.

   Innovation and property concepts.—

Guidelines for Properly Presenting Headings

The following are some guidelines to follow in the proper presentation of headings and their styles:

1. The heading for the table of contents is centered and typed in capital letters one and one-half to two inches from the top edge of the paper. A triple space is left between this heading and the next entry.

2. In the table of contents, headings for chapters are typed at the left margin over the chapter heading columns that are to follow them. If a chapter heading is not used in the text, it is omitted. Second category headings are reserved for chapter headings. Each chapter number is typed in the left margin followed by a period and three spaces. These numbers may be either Arabic or Roman numerals. The chapter heading is then typed in capital letters followed by period leaders and the page number in the right margin.

3. Subheadings representing the third category are indented three spaces from the major heading. It is optional either to indicate page numbers following these headings or to type period leaders and indicate the page numbers in the right margin. All subheadings are typed in capital and lower case letters. (Capital letters are used for the first letter of the first word and all other important words in the title.)

4. If more than the three category headings are used, each subsequent level is indented three spaces from the preceding higher level headings. Only the first letter of the first word needs to be capitalized. It is important to be consistent throughout the text in the format, arrangement, and typing style used for all headings.

5. The period leaders, if used, are typed to the right margin and end at least three spaces from the longest page number on the page. The page numbers must align with the right margin.

6. When major divisions such as Part 1 and Part 2 are used, they are typed in capital letters and centered over chapter headings. All subheadings are typed under the chapter heading. Page numbers may or may not be typed for these headings, but if used, they are typed directly after them. This method is frequently used when there are many subheadings, usually of equal ranking.

In the reference section, materials such as bibliographies, glossaries, appendices, and indexes are presented. The *bibliography* serves as a handy reference demonstrating the inclusiveness of the research list, while also serving as an additional aid for further study on the topic. The *glossary* is a dictionary of specialized terminology used as an aid for the reader's quick review. The glossary helps the reader find definitions quickly without having to fumble through the text. The *appendix* presents supplementary material that may be of importance to some readers but can be distracting by inclusion in the text. Appendices are often a welcome source to the reader for additional information and explanation. Examples include letters, maps, copies of documents, statistical and mathematical tables, illustrative aids, and other related material. It is important that appendices represent relevant matter and not be a collection of afterthoughts. If appendices are included, they should be placed at the end of the paper and numbered in accordance with the text. If there is more than one appendix, it may be numbered in Arabic or Roman numerals or assigned capital letters. The *index* is an alphabetical listing of names, subjects, topics, and concepts. Corresponding page numbers are assigned so they can be found in the text. The index is a key to the book or manuscript. It provides a very convenient reference for the reader. A book's usefulness is enhanced by it, and readers continually refer to it. With this in mind, it is the writer's responsibility to determine the development and placement of an attractive, consistent, and acceptable format for the presentation of the references in the final copy.

Numbering of the Three Major Parts of the Paper

The following guidelines provide a key to numbering the major sections of lengthy manuscripts such as books, dissertations, and other documents. The following lists are in order of page numbers from the first page to the beginning of the text:

I.

Blank page

Book half-title page

Series page (if the book is one of a series)

Title page

Approval page (optional)

Copyright page (see discussion on copyrights in text)

Dedication page (optional)

Excluding the blank page, the above pages are usually assigned numbers. These numbers are not typed on the pages themselves.

II.

Table of contents

List of illustrations (optional)

List of tables (optional)

Foreword (optional)

Preface (including acknowledgments)

Introduction (if not part of the text)

Pages specified for the above are assigned small Roman numerals (i, ii, iii, iv, etc.). These numerals are typed at the bottom of the page.

III.

Text

Glossary (optional)

Bibliography

Appendix or appendices (optional)

Notes (optional)

Blank, separation, or half-title pages if used for sections, bibliographies, and appendix or appendices

Author index (optional)

Subject index (optional)

Vita (published works of the author, optional)

Blank page

Pages for the above are typed in Arabic numerals (1, 2, 3, 4, etc.). Page numbers may be placed at the top center, top right, or bottom center. Whichever method is selected, it must be used consistently throughout the document. The blank pages and the vita, if included, are not numbered. If half-title pages are used to divide sections or the reference material, such as bibliographies, appendices, and indexes, they are assigned numbers, which are not typed on the page. The titles of these pages are typed in capital letters. They are centered slightly above the middle of the page.

GUIDELINES FOR TYPING THE PAPER

The appearance of a manuscript is important. Correct typing, placement, type style, and paper used contribute a great deal to a document's profile. The manuscript should be as easy to read and as pleasing to the eye as possible. A neat, well-constructed appearance may be a deciding factor in attracting a reader. Too often, readers are prejudiced by careless typing and sloppy final work. Proper presentation makes a document attractive and easy to understand. Text, diagrams, illustrations, graphics, and other parts of a document should be formatted suitably and harmonize in appearance. Word processors are ideal instruments for this purpose. Writers at any level will benefit by learning word processing. The formatting features of such word processors will display on the screen redesigned appearances before the document is typed or printed out. The design and layout of title pages, tables of contents, bibliographies, and other parts can be very conveniently manipulated in order to produce professional results. Unless one is skilled in the use of word processors and similar electronic typewriters, it is best that the final manuscript be typed by a qualified typist. Writers should follow the recommendations of publishers or instructors for the document's format and other mechanical details. Handwritten manuscripts should never be submitted. The following list presents some guidelines for the presentation of the final copy.

1. If a word processor or other modern electronic typewriter is used, select a clear and readable typeface for typing the final copy. It is worthwhile to become aware of the vast variety of fonts, pitch, proportional spacing, and other capabilities of these machines. Great care should be used in mixing or using unpopular formats for term papers and other short manuscripts. Avoid mixing type sizes and styles; special fonts and styles are appropriate for use in specialized and scientific work. Dot matrix style, in which printers type letters and other characters using dots, should not be used for final copies. For longer manuscripts such as books, it is best to leave these decisions to the publisher.

2. Type only on one side of good quality, white $8\frac{1}{2}$ by 11-inch bond paper with a rag content of 25 percent or more. The legibility of the typewritten material will be enhanced with a fresh ribbon or printer cartridge. Several copies may be desired in the case of theses, dissertations, and other reports. These can be photocopied or produced on carbon or other lower quality paper.

3. Elite type (12 characters per inch) is becoming increasingly popular and is commonly recommended. Pica type (10 characters per inch) may also be used. On the average, there are ten words to the line and 250 words to the page.

4. All typed material should be centered with margins of one and one-half inches from the top, bottom, and lefthand side of the paper. Type the first line nine lines from the top. Set margins at 15 and 75 for pica type or 18 and 90 for elite type. The center of the page will be 45 or 54, respectively.

Typed print should not extend beyond these margins. Computerized printers are flexible and vary greatly for these dimensions.

5. Paragraphs should be uniformly indented five spaces from the lefthand margin. The last line on the page should not be left partially blank unless it is the end of a paragraph. All quoted matter over five lines is indented ten spaces from the left margin. It may be single spaced with triple spacing before and after the quotation.

6. Double spacing should be used throughout the entire manuscript, making the paper more readable and attractive. Single spacing is used only for quotations, footnotes, bibliographies, and itemized data tables. Items such as table of contents, bibliography, indexes, and appendices may be typed nine lines from the top to improve their appearance.

7. Page numbers are typed one inch from the top or on the sixth line. Do not type numbers with hyphens, periods, or parentheses. The most common practice is to type page numbers for section headings, such as preface or chapters, centered at the bottom margin.

8. Illustrations, charts, tables, etc., must conform to the prescribed margins. In cases where these graphics are large, place them broadside on the page or reduce their size.

9. The first line of each individual footnote should begin on the sixth space from the lefthand margin. The next line of the same footnote is single spaced and should begin at the lefthand margin. This gives each footnote citation the look of an indented paragraph. Each individual footnote is separated by a double space. Number footnotes consecutively throughout the paper, except in the case of large manuscripts, in which each section may be treated separately.

10. If the written material includes subdivisions with subtitles, they should be aligned with the left margin. They should be underlined but not capitalized (underlined material indicates italics in printing).

11. The author should always proofread the final material very carefully. The manuscript should be appropriately styled, typed, and corrected before submission. Included material, facts, quotations, and references should be verified for accuracy. The author alone is responsible for all errors in the final draft.

12. It is recommended to place the final paper in an appropriate, attractive cover. One may select from spiral binders, riveted binders, three-hole folders, or an array of other attractive plastic covers that are sold in a myriad of colors and styles.

There are variations regarding margins, pagination, and format among styles, publishers, and institutions. The writer should be aware of institutional requirements concerning the form and style of manuscript presentation. Scientific papers require different formats than do business or journalistic papers. The author should be familiar with the conventional form and style and follow it throughout the manuscript. In addition, the use of word processors has provided the capability to experiment with many fonts, styles, and character reproductions to produce a desirable final product.

ILLUSTRATION AND TABLE CONSTRUCTION

Proper presentation of statistical analysis, facts, and other findings, through exhibits such as illustrations and tables, makes for a convincing and effective report. Illustrations or figures are visual matter that includes graphs, charts, pictures, maps, drawings, and cartoons. Tables are orderly displays of numbers and other data exhibited in parallel columns and rows. Tables may support text discussions and explain or clarify significant findings, data, and other facts.

Place tables and illustrations within the text or separately in an appendix. If the table is supporting specific information in the text and is about half a page in length, place it in the body of the paper after referring to it. Separate this table from the text by three spaces both above and below, unless it is at the top or the bottom of the page. Place tables and illustrations that are large or a page in length on a separate page following referral to them in the text. Mention the table or illustration and page number in the text, such as "See Table 5, page 15." Whenever there are many tables or illustrations, or they interfere with the flow of reading, or referral to them is casual, place them in a separate appendix at the end of the manuscript.

The margins for the table should not be smaller than the margins for the text. It is preferred to type large tables horizontally with the top of the table at the right binding. All tables should have at least six parts: (1) number, (2) title, (3) captions, (4) stubs, (5) body, (6) footnotes and source.

Table number. Type and center table numbers in capital Arabic or Roman numerals consecutively throughout the paper or for individual chapters and sections. Type table numbers as "TABLE 5."

Title of tables. Select an appropriate descriptive title for the table. Write the time period covered by the data in the table. Capitalize all words or first, last, and main words of the title. Center the title below the table number and separate it from the body by a single or double line typed margin to margin.

Captions. Captions are headings for main columns and subdivisions of main columns. They suggest the nature of information in their respective columns.

Stubs. A stub is the heading of the left column, explaining the nature of data across the table to the left row. Stub titles should be selected suitably and should be parallel in structure. Type the first word of each entry in capital letters.

Body. The body of the table must present information in a logical, chronological, or some other flowing order. The table material is either single- or double-spaced. Use period leaders instead of lines to guide the reader from the stub entry to the first column of figures. Use commas to separate millions from thousands, and thousands from hundreds. For larger tables, arrange items in groups of five with double spacing between groups. Type three hyphens, periods, or n.a. where information is not available.

Footnotes and sources. Align footnotes to the table at the bottom. Type footnotes for the tables and illustrations in lower-case letters, using asterisks or other marks. This type of marking will reduce confusion with other footnotes and endnotes used throughout the text. The source of the table or the information from which the table is derived is typed at the bottom of the table.

Seriation

Seriation in writing is the listing of items in a sequential fashion. Items in a series are enumerated to lessen ambiguity, to clarify, and to emphasize context.

Individual words, phrases, sentences, or sections can be seriated. Units within a sentence, individual sentences, items, or paragraph items are identified with parenthetical numbers or letters. The usage of the numbers and letters and their inclusion in parentheses should be consistent throughout the document. Items are listed within the text when there are few and they do not interfere with the flow of reading. However, if the list is long or obstructs the flow of reading, it is set off from the text. In a series of paragraphs, the paragraphs are identified with Arabic numbers and are written at the beginning of each unit. The following guidelines are used in seriation:

1. When the number of items are limited in a paragraph or a sentence, the items are listed parenthetically with conventional punctuation marks. The use of the colon to introduce the items is optional. However, the items are not capitalized.

   ```
   The traditional managerial functions are (a)
   planning, (b) organizing, (c) commanding, and (d)
   controlling.
   ```

2. Whenever three or more items in a series have internal punctuation, a semicolon is used to separate the units.

   ```
   The chief operating officers of this company are:
   (1) Mr. Kevin Barnhill, head of finance department;
   (2) Miss Ashly Miller, head of marketing department;
   and (3) Mr. Brad Miller, head of production
   department.
   ```

3. If items in a series are compound sentences and are introduced with a colon, only the first letter of the first item is capitalized and a period is placed after the last item.

   ```
   Frederick W. Taylor in his original research
   observed the following: (a) Workers were generally
   lazy, and soldiered all day, (b) they had no interest
   in production or the overall purpose of the firm,
   and (c) they were selfish, interested only in
   economic incentives.
   ```

4. Whenever sentences or paragraphs are set off from the text in a series, the enumerations are indented five spaces. Arabic numerals are used, which may be enclosed in parentheses or followed by a period, and then followed by a single space. When the items are phrases or words and part of the lead sentence, they are treated as a series with a period placed at the end of the last item.

(Sentences)

```
Documentation of sources of information is not neces-
sary in the following circumstances:
1. facts are common knowledge,
2. the information is that of the author, and
3. most people believe in the validity of the
   information.
```

(Paragraphs)

Documentation of sources of information is not necessary in the following circumstances:

1. It is not necessary to give documentation whenever the information is common knowledge, as in stating: Stalin was a dictator. Russians revered Stalin and built monuments in his honor.

2. Documentation is not necessary when the information is that of the author as: When I was in the Soviet Union, I observed that people had no concern for political structure, organization, or human rights.

3. Documentation is not necessary when the information is known by a well-read person. For instance: Russian people are used to being ruled by dictators. It will be very difficult to implement democracy in that nation. The very nature of the Russian society is based on subservience.

5. **Bullets** may be used whenever sequential ranking is not desired or numbering is overused. The following is an example of the use of bullets:

    Some efficient ways to present discussions in a written report are:
    - Chronological
    - Spatial
    - Specific to general
    - General to specific
    - Increasing order of importance
    - Decreasing order of importance

In summary, when listing items underneath each other, the second and subsequent lines are written on the left margin, or placed under the indented first line. It is important to be consistent in usage throughout the document. If additional numbered listings are to be created under existing serialized items, the outline numbering rules discussed in Chapter 5 are used for this propose. Seriation should not be used to circumvent writing sentences and paragraph discussions.

Business, Inter-Office, and Employment Related Correspondence

11

INTRODUCTION

This section explains some aspects of writing letters, résumés, and communication within businesses. The extensive time spent in writing business letters affects professional life, making it necessary to learn how to write business correspondence correctly and type them in an appropriate format. Business correspondence represents a writer's attitudes and leaves a lasting impression on the reader. Employers frequently make judgments on the basis of the style and content of these correspondence.

STYLES OF BUSINESS LETTERS

Three popular styles have become standard in the presentation of business letters. These styles are: block/open punctuation style, modified block style, and simplified block style. The popularity of these styles was influenced by speed and efficiency on the older mechanical typewriters. Yet the proliferation and use of modern computers and word processors have allowed for greater flexibility. As a result there are greater individual choices and preferences in the selection of style, format, and presentation of business letters.

Block/Open Punctuation Style

Block and open punctuation style became popular because it required the least amount of manipulation on old typewriters. Using the block style permits one to type a letter faster than using other styles. In this style individual lines are typed on the left margin with no indentations, including the address and the signature block.

In open punctuation, no marks are placed after the salutation or complimentary close. Phrases within the body of the memo are punctuated in accordance with grammatical rules. Although this is an easy style to use, the block style is not liked by some people due to its unbalanced appearance (Figure 11-1).

Modified Block Style

The modified block style layout (Figure 11-2) resembles the block/open punctuation style with one notable difference. This difference is that the date and closing signature are typed on the righthand side, five spaces from the center line. In using this style, the date and signature may be typed on the right margin. A variation of this style is called the *modified semiblock*, in which the first line of each paragraph in the body of the letter is indented from the left margin.

Figure 11-1
Block/Open Punctuation Style

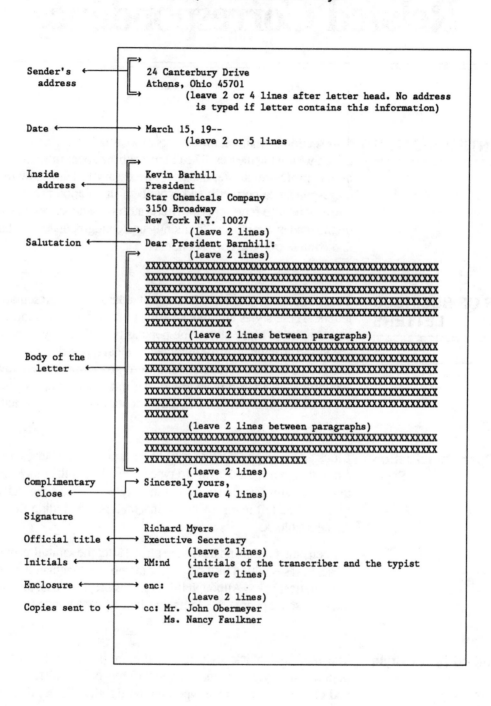

Sender's address

```
24 Canterbury Drive
Athens, Ohio 45701
        (leave 2 or 4 lines after letter head. No address
         is typed if letter contains this information)
```

Date

```
March 15, 19--
        (leave 2 or 5 lines
```

Inside address

```
Kevin Barhill
President
Star Chemicals Company
3150 Broadway
New York N.Y. 10027
        (leave 2 lines)
```

Salutation

```
Dear President Barnhill:
        (leave 2 lines)
XXXXXXXXXXXXXXXXXXXXXXXXXXXXXXXXXXXXXXXXXXXXXXXXXXXX
XXXXXXXXXXXXXXXXXXXXXXXXXXXXXXXXXXXXXXXXXXXXXXXXXX
XXXXXXXXXXXXXXXXXXXXXXXXXXXXXXXXXXXXXXXXXXXXXXXXXX
XXXXXXXXXXXXXXXXXXXXXXXXXXXXXXXXXXXXXXXXXXXXXXXXXX
XXXXXXXXXXXXXXXXXXXXXXXXXXXXXXXXXXXXXXXXXXXXXXXXXX
XXXXXXXXXXXXXXX
        (leave 2 lines between paragraphs)
```

Body of the letter

```
XXXXXXXXXXXXXXXXXXXXXXXXXXXXXXXXXXXXXXXXXXXXXXXXXX
XXXXXXXXXXXXXXXXXXXXXXXXXXXXXXXXXXXXXXXXXXXXXXXXXX
XXXXXXXXXXXXXXXXXXXXXXXXXXXXXXXXXXXXXXXXXXXXXXXXXX
XXXXXXXXXXXXXXXXXXXXXXXXXXXXXXXXXXXXXXXXXXXXXXXXXX
XXXXXXXXXXXXXXXXXXXXXXXXXXXXXXXXXXXXXXXXXXXXXXXXXX
XXXXXXXX
        (leave 2 lines between paragraphs)
XXXXXXXXXXXXXXXXXXXXXXXXXXXXXXXXXXXXXXXXXXXXXXXXXX
XXXXXXXXXXXXXXXXXXXXXXXXXXXXXXXXXXXXXXXXXXXXXXXXXX
XXXXXXXXXXXXXXXXXXXXXXXXXXXXX
        (leave 2 lines)
```

Complimentary close

```
Sincerely yours,
        (leave 4 lines)
```

Signature

Official title

```
Richard Myers
Executive Secretary
        (leave 2 lines)
```

Initials

```
RM:nd   (initials of the transcriber and the typist
        (leave 2 lines)
```

Enclosure

```
enc:
        (leave 2 lines)
```

Copies sent to

```
cc: Mr. John Obermeyer
    Ms. Nancy Faulkner
```

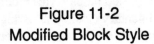

Figure 11-2
Modified Block Style

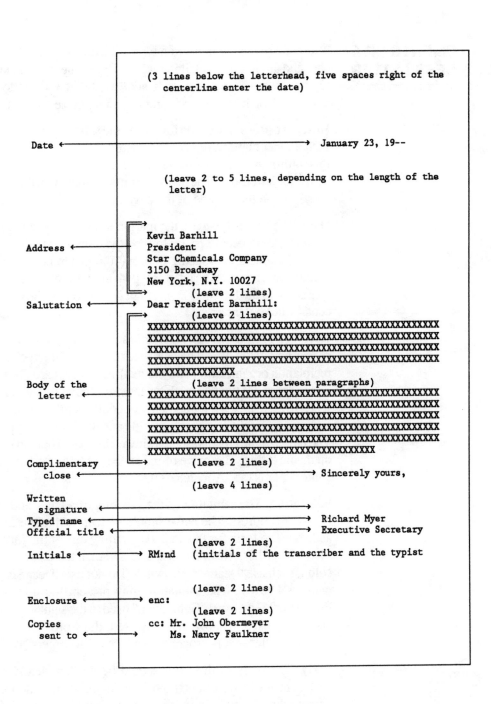

(3 lines below the letterhead, five spaces right of the centerline enter the date)

Date ← → January 23, 19--

(leave 2 to 5 lines, depending on the length of the letter)

Address ← → Kevin Barhill
President
Star Chemicals Company
3150 Broadway
New York, N.Y. 10027
(leave 2 lines)

Salutation ← → Dear President Barnhill:
(leave 2 lines)

Body of the letter ←
XXXXXXXXXXXXXXXXXXXXXXXXXXXXXXXXXXXXXXXXXXXXXXXXXX
XXXXXXXXXXXXXXXXXXXXXXXXXXXXXXXXXXXXXXXXXXXXXXXXXX
XXXXXXXXXXXXXXXXXXXXXXXXXXXXXXXXXXXXXXXXXXXXXXXXXX
XXXXXXXXXXXXXXXXXXXXXXXXXXXXXXXXXXXXXXXXXXXXXXXXXX
XXXXXXXXXXXXXXXX
(leave 2 lines between paragraphs)
XXXXXXXXXXXXXXXXXXXXXXXXXXXXXXXXXXXXXXXXXXXXXXXXXX
XXXXXXXXXXXXXXXXXXXXXXXXXXXXXXXXXXXXXXXXXXXXXXXXXX
XXXXXXXXXXXXXXXXXXXXXXXXXXXXXXXXXXXXXXXXXXXXXXXXXX
XXXXXXXXXXXXXXXXXXXXXXXXXXXXXXXXXXXXXXXXXXXXXXXXXX
XXXXXXXXXXXXXXXXXXXXXXXXXXXXXXXXXXXXXXXXXXXXXXXXXX
XXXXXXXXXXXXXXXXXXXXXXXXXXXXXXXXXXXXXXXXXX

Complimentary close ← (leave 2 lines)
→ Sincerely yours,
(leave 4 lines)

Written signature ←

Typed name ← → Richard Myer
Official title ← → Executive Secretary
(leave 2 lines)

Initials ← → RM:nd (initials of the transcriber and the typist

(leave 2 lines)

Enclosure ← → enc:
(leave 2 lines)

Copies sent to ← → cc: Mr. John Obermeyer
Ms. Nancy Faulkner

Simplified Block Style

The simplified block style (Figure 11-3) eliminates typing the salutation and complimentary closing, allowing the correspondence to be typed faster. It is also appropriate for use in impersonal situations or when the identity of the recipient is unknown.

ELEMENTS OF A BUSINESS LETTER

There are seven elements to a typical business letter. These elements require care and attention to detail in typing. The elements are: (1) the inside address, (2) the date, (3) the receiver's address, (4) the salutation, (5) the body, or content of the letter, (6) the complimentary close, and (7) the signature block.

Inside Address. This calls for typing the sender's mailing address line by line, with no indentations or ending punctuation. If a letterhead is used containing this information, the inside address is not typed; however, the date is included below the letterhead. The inside address is typed with the same information that is written on the outside of the envelope.

Date. The date is typed on the margin as part of the address with no period at the end. Some people prefer to type the date one double space below the address. Judgment on spacing between the different elements depends on the length of the letter. If the letter is typed on a letterhead, the date is typed double-spaced from the left margin, or if not typed on letterhead, five spaces from the center line of the paper.

Receiver's Address. The receiver's address is typed on the margin two to three spaces below the date. The name and the title of the recipient, the name of the recipient's organization, and the mailing address are all included on separate lines. These are typed exactly as they are found on the letterhead of the firm. It is critical to type the reader's name, courtesy title, and business title correctly and appropriately. It is best if the title and the name are typed on separate lines. The name of the city and state followed by the postal zip code are then entered on the next line. The name of the state is abbreviated using U.S. government abbreviations (see Appendix D).

Salutation. The salutation is the greeting of a letter and is typed two spaces below the address. The name should be identical to the first line of the inside address. The form for this includes writing one of the following: "Dear" Mr., Ms., Mrs., Miss., Rev., Dr., a space, and then the name is typed followed by a colon, such as, "Dear Mr. Brown:". (Do not use "Dear Sir" or "Madam" if the name is known.) The salutation may present the title, such as, "Dear Mr. President:". The word "Gentlemen" used in the salutation is considered biased and rarely used. If, however, it is used, the word "Dear" is not typed. For a broader audience it is proper to use "Dear Customers" or "Dear Colleagues."

Body. The body of the letter should be written clearly and concisely. It is written in one or more paragraphs, single-spaced with double-spacing between paragraphs. The first line of the paragraph may be indented, depending on the style. If possible, the letter should be narrowed to one page. If it is a two-page letter, one should avoid leaving only two or three lines for the next page. Additional pages are not typed on letterhead sheets of paper. These pages are given headings that include the recipient's name, the page number, and the date. Following are examples for the format of additional pages (Figure 11-4).

Figure 11-3
Simplified Block Style

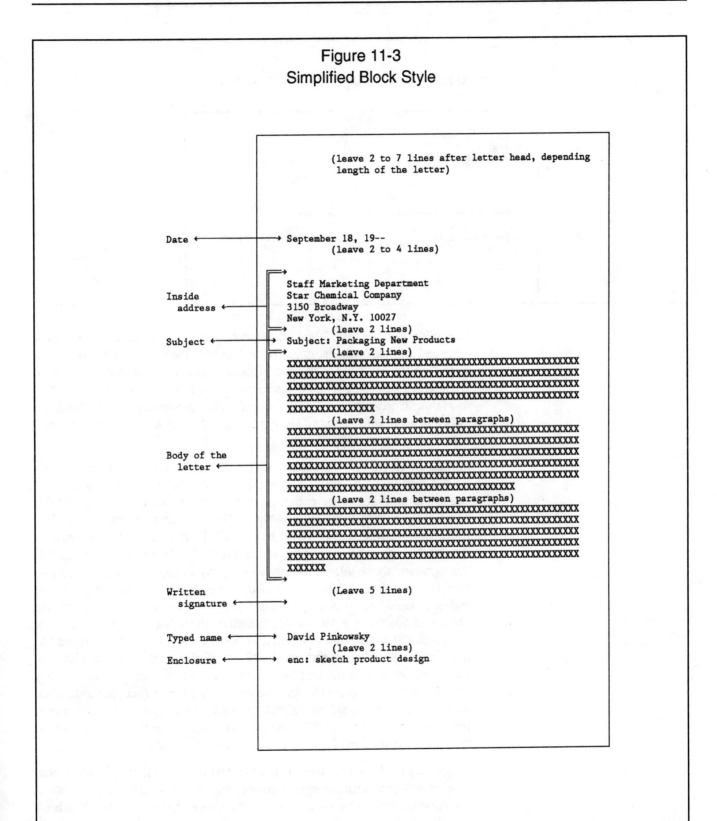

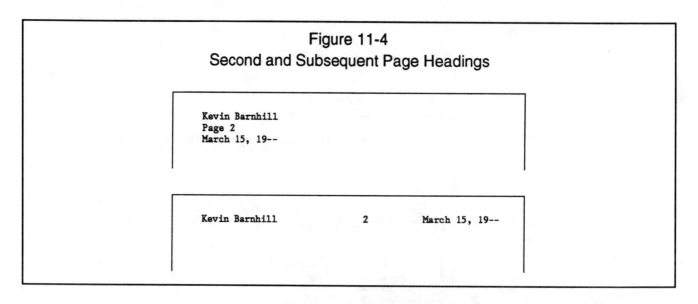

Figure 11-4
Second and Subsequent Page Headings

```
Kevin Barnhill
Page 2
March 15, 19--
```

```
Kevin Barnhill                2              March 15, 19--
```

Complimentary Close. The complimentary close is the termination of the letter and is typed on the margin. The first letter of the first word is capitalized, and a comma is placed at the end. This includes words or phrases such as: "Sincerely," "Cordially," and "Respectfully." The word "Sincerely" is a formal term; "Cordially" is used for professional acquaintances, while "Respectfully" is used with reports. They may be followed by the word "yours," depending on personal preferences.

Signature Block. The signature block includes the name, the title, the typist's initials, where or how many copies are sent, and the enclosure. The name is typed four lines below the complimentary close on the left margin. The full name of the author of the letter is typed. The appropriate word, such as Dr., Mrs., Miss, or Ms., can be typed in front of the name. The typed signature ensures the correct spelling of the author's name for the reader. The handwritten signature above this constitutes the legality of the letter. Following two lines below, initials of the author of the letter are indicated. Following the author's initials are a colon and the typist's initials. Examples of this are SM:BD or SM:bd. It is permissible to include the typist's initials only. If any other material accompanies the letter, the word enclosure (or [en]) is typed one line below the initials on the margin. If copies of the letter are sent to others, this is indicated by typing (cc) for carbon copy, (xc) for Xerox copy, or (copy to). This is always done in lower case letters. The letters (bcc) are used when the names of other recipients are not disclosed to the addressee. The name of the individual(s) is typed followed by two spaces. The names of additional recipients are also typed line by line below the first name.

In studying further on business writing and styles, the reader may select from a variety of books written for this purpose, such as a popular book that contains 100 typical everyday business letters, memos, and other discussions. This book is written by Russell J. Stephen and is titled *Writing at Work* (New York: Holt, Rinehart and Winston, 1985). Another comprehensive book on this subject is by Jeanne W. Halpern and is called *Business Writing Strategies and Samples* (New York: Macmillan, 1988).

Envelopes   Business correspondence is mailed in business envelopes (No. 10, [9 $\frac{1}{2}$ by 4 $\frac{1}{8}$ inches]), contrasted with small envelopes (No. 6 $\frac{3}{4}$,[6 $\frac{3}{4}$ by 4 $\frac{1}{8}$ inches]). The post office requests the receiver's address contain no commas or periods, be typed in capital letters, single-spaced, and include postal zip code. Whenever upper- and lower-case letters are written, they include periods and commas. On large envelopes (No. 10) the return address is typed $\frac{1}{2}$ inch from the left top edge. The receiver's address is typed $4\frac{1}{2}$ to 5 inches from the left edge, and $4\frac{1}{2}$ inches from the top edge of the envelope. For small envelopes (No. 6 $\frac{3}{4}$), the sender's address is typed $\frac{1}{2}$ inch from the left top edge. The receiver's address is typed 2 inches from the top and left edge. Directions for the post office, such as Special Delivery, are typed on the right side over the recipient's address. Instructions for the recipient, such as Personal, Confidential, or Open on a Certain Date are typed two spaces below the sender's address.

MEMOS (MEMORANDA)

The operation of most organizations depends on writing and circulating memos. Memos are widely used for inter-office communication of rules, policies, procedures, announcements, and other information. In contrast, business letters are principally used for external communication to stockholders, the business community, and the public. Memos are impersonal in tone and are one to two pages in length. The content of a memo should be brief and communicate the intent clearly. The design of the memo calls for quickness and simplicity in writing. Salutations, complimentary closes, signatures, and titles such as "Mr." and "Mrs." in the heading are eliminated. A standard memo has five parts: (1) "To:", (2) "From:", (3) "Date:", (4) "Subject:", and (5) the content of the memo. The typist's initials, enclosures, and copies sent to, are optionally typed at the end of the memo. Following are typical examples of three widely used formats for memos (Figures 11-7, 11-8, and 11-9).

RÉSUMÉS

When seeking employment locally at a fast-food restaurant, at a grocery store, or with an important regional firm, personal appearance is an important consideration. However, when searching for a professional position in a broader market, time and resources will not allow for too many personal appearances. Thus a personal résumé and a persuasive letter of application are appropriate for this purpose. The résumé is an instrument that needs critical preparation and presentation in order to produce desired results, as most professional positions are filled through receiving and evaluating them.

Before writing a résumé it is beneficial to evaluate one's aspirations, market opportunities, prevailing salaries, employer needs, and desired geographical locations. It is critical to search for a job that will match one's personal talents and aspirations with employer needs. A great deal of information needed for résumés is acquired through systematic contacts with other individuals, college placement bureaus, specialized employment agencies, related professional organizations, governmental sources, and employment-related publications.

Individuals can prepare two types of résumés. These are classified as the general-purpose *prospecting* résumé and the *specialized* résumé. The general prospecting résumé is appropriate when applying to more than one firm for diverse positions in one's field of interest. A number of these prospecting résumés are printed and sent to a large number of potential employers. This type

Figure 11-7

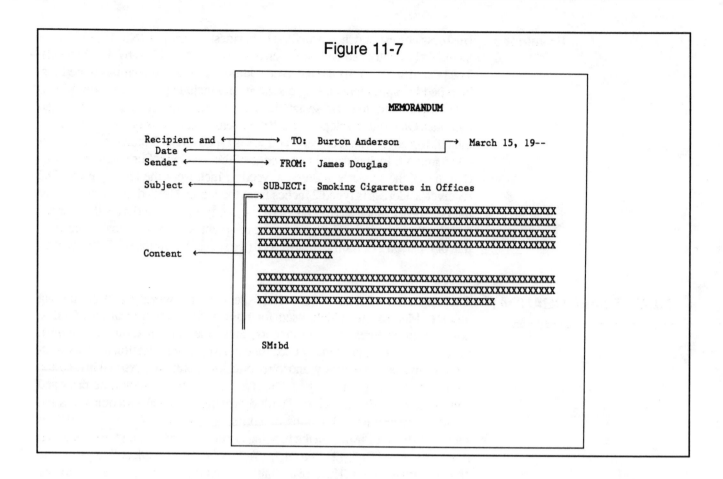

of résumé lists significant achievements, education, and experiences. The purpose is to bring to the attention of an employer a prospective candidate for an entry-level position. The goal of the candidate is to acquire a personal interview with a potential employer through this résumé. At the same time, employers use these résumés as a screening device.

The second type, the specialized résumé, gives detailed information related to the requirements of a specific position. If one wanted a position with a firm in corporate finance, the résumé should focus on related academic and work experiences in corporate finance. Listing courses taken in the discipline or listing corporate finance assignments with the bank where an applicant had worked would be two of many examples. This résumé should be critically prepared and sent to specific individuals and department heads who are responsible for actually hiring employees. Only a few of these résumés are prepared and sent to individuals in the targeted organization. In preparing this type of résumé some information should be obtained about the industry or company so that it may be used in the correspondence and interview session with the company's officials. This information is obtained by calling the company, receiving the annual reports, and reading financial newspapers and other material, such as *Peterson's Annual Guide/Careers*, and *Standard and Poor's Register*. Other similar helpful sources can be found in the library.

ADDITIONAL JOB SEARCH CORRESPONDENCE

A résumé should be accompanied by a carefully written cover letter introducing the applicant and arousing the reader's interest. If possible, one should include the specific position applied for and explain how one learned of the opportunity. The accompanying résumé should highlight the applicant's strengths for this position.

It is important to learn how to write other employment-related letters, as many types of letter are received and sent to the business world. Examples of résumés, cover letters, job acceptance letters, courtesy letters, and letters of recommendation are included at the end of this discussion.

Employment-Related Publications. Libraries provide a wealth of information about career opportunities, résumé preparation, job sources, and interview techniques. Most of this kind of information is listed in the library under *careers, jobs,* or *résumés.* Specialized books that give practical advice include *The Most Comprehensive Guide for Job Hunters and Career Switchers,* by Kathryn and Ross Petras (Las Cruces, NM: Poseidon Press, 1989) and *The Complete Résumé and Job Getter's Guide,* by Juvenal Angel (New York: Pocket Books, 1980), which includes four hundred sample résumés for a variety of jobs. Some detailed general-purpose, employment-related information may be found in these two books by the U.S. Department of Labor: the *Occupational Outlook Handbook* and the *Dictionary of Occupational Titles.* These volumes list job descriptions, requirements, opportunities, needed skills, and prospects. They also include discussions of salaries, required skills, promotions, working conditions, and geographical availability. The information found in them is used in the preparation of specialized résumés for potential employers.

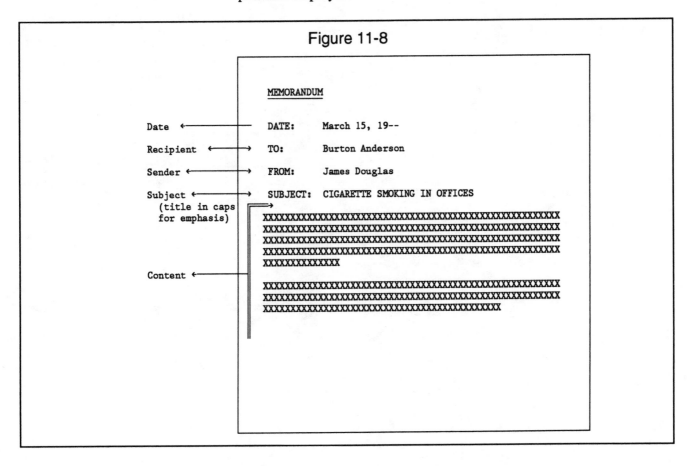

Figure 11-8

Figure 11-9

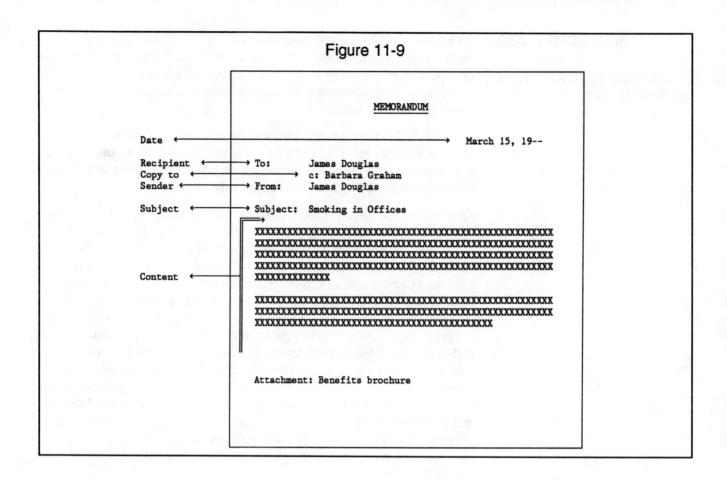

Figure 11-10

<u>JOHN T. WILLIAMS</u>
13 Riverside Road
Charlotte, NC 38739
Phone (704) 555-4534

<u>OBJECTIVE</u>
An entry-level management trainee position in marketing or in finance.

<u>EDUCATION</u>
University of Toledo, Toledo, Ohio
Received Bachelor of Business Administration, June 1984
Majored in Management with Minor in Banking
Dean's List, Grade Point Average: Major 3.6/4.0 Overall 3.4/4.0
Westside High School, Athens, Ohio
Graduated in the top quarter of the class of 125 students.
Took upper-level courses in English and mathematics.

<u>EXPERIENCE</u>
Linhill Industries (May-Aug. 1983)
Assistant to the Production Manager. Position: Trainee, learned computer
  word processing and work scheduling.

Eastside Bank (May-June 1982)
Assistant trainee to the Production Manager. Position: Assistant cashier,
  customer and computer operations.

Camp Farside (May-Aug. 1981)
Assistant outdoor Supervisor. Position: Trainee, learned payroll, camp
  operations, scheduling and construction supervision.

<u>HONORS AND AWARDS</u>
Outstanding young symphonist, Westside High School, 1973, 1974
Class Representative on Student Council Westside High School, 1973
Member Advisory Council Board, College Gazette, Toledo University

<u>COMMUNITY SERVICES</u>
Treasurer, Young Democrats, Maumee, Ohio, 1973-1975
Volunteered with Hunger Coalition and Hospitality House, 1973-75
Assisted Chamber of Commerce with community beautification drive, 1975

<u>HOBBIES</u>
Amateur saxophonist, photography, and cross-country jogging

<u>REFERENCES</u>
References will be furnished on request.

Figure 11-11

Mr. Jack Reagan
Micro Atlantic Company
600 West 113 Street
New York, NY 10025

Dear Mr. Reagan:

I am writing to support the application of Miss Ashland Miller for an administrative position with your firm.

I have observed Miss Miller's administrative capabilities for the last three years as coordinator of the marketing department. She has tremendous energy and enthusiasm, which she translates into the motivation of people working for her. She is both efficient and extremely competent in the performance of her duties.

Her personal integrity and commitment to work are without question. In her dealings with both members of her department and her superiors I have always observed both firmness and fairness.

One of her outstanding personal qualifications is her toughness of mind. She has the ability to seek consensus and then implement resulting policy evenly and fairly.

It is a pleasure to recommend Miss Miller and I hope that you will act favorably on her application. Her loss here will be a personal one for me and the department, but I know she has both the qualifications and the desire to succeed in a more senior administrative position.

If I can be of any further help, do not hesitate to contact me at the above address or by telephone (office: 734-263-6221; residence: 734-268-2631).

Sincerely yours,

Russel Jones
Director
Marketing Systems Group

Figure 11-12

2134 College Avenue
Mars Hill, North Carolina 78010

March 15, 19—

Mr. Kevin Barnhill
Sales Department
Star Chemical Company
Raleigh, NC 27615

Dear Mr. Barnhill:

Thank you for the opportunity of giving me time to discuss my qualifications for the position of management trainee with your firm.

I would like to take this occasion to express my sincere thanks for the courtesies that you and your staff provided me during my visit.

I was impressed by the resources of your firm and the unique opportunities and challenges that it provides for a young man.

Thanks again for your hospitality and a pleasant visit.

Sincerely yours,

Paul Evans

Figure 11-13

2314 College Avenue
Mars Hill, North Carolina 76801

March 14, 19—

Mr. Kevin Barnhill
Sales Department
Star Chemical Company
2400 Ninth Street
Flagstaff, AZ 86001

Dear Mr. Barnhill:

It gives me great pleasure to accept your offer, and I am looking forward
to the challenges and opportunities this position offers.

Please accept my thanks for the consideration and warm hospitality you have
shown me. I plan to move to Flagstaff, and will report to work on April
18, 19-, and am confident that my association with you will be pleasant,
rich, and productive.

Thanks again,

James Fulton

Figure 11-14

Mr. Jack Reagan
Micro Atlantic Company
800 Riverside Drive
Raleigh, NC 27615

Dear Mr. Reagan:

Mr. Timothy Harrison has asked me to write to you concerning his recent application for employment with your firm.

Mr. Harrison was a student of mine in the College of Business Administration, at Mars State University. As a student his performance was very satisfactory, he took his lessons well and I found him to be industrious in the performance of assignments.

It is a pleasure to recommend Mr. Harrison as one whom I believe has real possibilities. I will be glad to answer any questions you may have pertaining to his character and abilities.

Sincerely,

Richard Davidson
Professor

Figure 11-15

2045 Jordan Road
Las Cruces, New Mexico 80001

March 24, 19—

Mr. Harry Sturm
Director
Personnel Department
Foxboro Foods Company
600 Solano Drive
Las Cruces, New Mexico 88001

Dear Mr. Sturm:

Please consider this letter my application for the position of Management Trainee in the related areas of business administration advertised by your company in the Sunday, March 25, 1991 issue of the Las Cruces Sun News. I will be available for assignments May 1, 1991.

I received a Bachelor of Arts degree in Economics and European History from the University of North Carolina, Chapel Hill, in June 1989. I will be awarded a Master of Business Administration Degree from Toledo University in May 1991. My major areas of specialization included management and behavioral communication.

The skills I acquired in Supervisory Management during my work at Star Telephone and Telegraph Company and the academic preparations at the University of Toledo qualify me for an entry-level position with your firm.

Enclosed is a recent resume of my educational and administrative experiences. For additional information, you may contact me by letter or telephone at the office (704) 555-6594, or residence (704) 555-2984. I look forward to hearing from you.

Thank you for your consideration.

Sincerely yours,

Kevin Barnhill
Graduate Assistant

Enclosure

Appendices

Manuals and Other References for Writers

A number of manuals are available as guides for writing in specific disciplines. The Modern Language Association (MLA), the American Psychological Association (APA), the traditional *Chicago Manual of Style*, and the Council of Biology Editors' *CBE Style Manual* explained in this book are satisfactory for use in most disciplines, including the humanities, the social sciences, and the sciences and technologies. The details of style and format vary among different scientific and technical fields and often among publishers and publications within a discipline. The writer should consult manuals for a specific field or those assigned by an instructor or a publisher.

The list given below provides a second collection of references, indexes, computer databases, and other books used in the library for finding information. These books contain titles of articles, books, statistics, and other published material. For this purpose the reader may also consult references listed elsewhere in this manuscript. Finally, a select list of books on English composition, the publishing industry, copyright regulations, and current style manuals available is included for the convenience of the reader.

Style Manuals / Handbooks in Various Disciplines

AGRONOMY
Handbook & Style for ASA, CSSA, & SSSA Publications. 6th ed. Madison, WI: American Society of Agronomy. 1984.

ASTRONOMY
Style Manual for Guidance in the Preparation of Papers for Journals Published by the American Institute of Physics. 3rd ed. New York: American Institute of Physics, 1978.

BIOCHEMISTRY
Fasman, Gerald D. *Practical Handbook of Biochemistry & Molecular Biology.* Boca Raton, FL: CRS Press, 1989.

BIOLOGY
Style Manual Committee. *CBE Style Manual: A Guide for Authors, Editors, and Publishers in the Biological Sciences.* 5th ed. Bethesda, MD: Council of Biology Editors, 1983.

BIOMEDICINE
International Steering Committee of Medical Editors. "Uniform Requirements for Manuscripts Submitted to Biomedical Journals." *Annals of Internal Medicine.* 90 (Jan. 1979): 95-99.

BUSINESS   Campbell, William G., Stephen V. Ballou, and Carole Slade. *Form and Style: Theses, Reports, Term Papers*. 8th ed. Boston: Houghton Mifflin, 1990.

The Chicago Manual of Style. 13th ed. Chicago: University of Chicago Press, 1982.

Daw, Jessamon. *Writing Business and Economics Papers, Theses and Dissertations*. Totawa, NJ: Littlefield Adams, 1978.

Smith, Charles B. *A Guide to Business Research: Developing, Conducting, and Writing Research Projects*. Chicago: Nelson Hall, 1990.

CHEMISTRY   Fieser, Louis F., and Mary Fieser. *Style Guide for Chemists*. New York: Reinhold, 1972.

Handbook for ADAC Members. Washington: Association of Official Analytical Chemists, 1982.

Handbook for Authors of Papers in American Chemistry Society Publications. Washington: American Chemical Society, 1978.

COMPUTERS   Daiute, Collette. *Writing and Computers*. Reading, MA: Addison-Wesley, 1985.

Howie, Sherry Hill. *Reading, Writing and Computers*. Needham Heights, MA: Allyn & Bacon, 1989.

Wresh, William, ed. *The Computer in Composition Instruction: A Writer's Tool*. Urbana, IL: National Council of Teachers of English, 1984.

EARTH SCIENCE   Cochran, Wendell. *Geowriting: A Guide to Writing, Editing, and Printing in Earth Science*. 4th ed. Washington: American Geological Institute, 1984.

Style Manual for Biological Journals. 2nd ed. Washington: American Institute of Biological Sciences, 1964.

ECONOMICS   Officertal, Lawrence H. *So You Have to Write an Economics Term Paper*. East Lansing, MI: Michigan State Univ. Press, 1990.

EDUCATION   Katz, Sidney B., Jerome T. Kapes, and Percy A. Zirkel. *Resources for Writing for Publication in Education*. New York: Columbia Univ. Teachers College Press, 1980.

Turabian, Kate. Revised and expanded by Bonnie Birtwistle Honigsblum. *A Manual for Writers of Term Papers, Theses, and Dissertations*. 5th ed. Chicago: Univ. of Chicago Press, 1987.

ENGINEERING   Michaelson, Herbert B. *How to Write and Publish Engineering Papers and Reports*. 2nd ed. Philadelphia: Institute for Scientific Information, ISI Press, 1986.

Rathbone, Robert R., and James B. Stone. *A Writer's Guide for Engineers and Scientists*. Englewood Cliffs, NJ: Prentice-Hall, 1962.

FINANCE AND STOCKS   *Moody's Handbook of Common Stocks.* New York: Moody's Investors Service Inc., 1965-date.

Standard and Poor's Stock Reports. New York: Standard and Poor's Corp., 1971-date.

GEOGRAPHY   Haring, L. Lloyd, and John F. Lounsbury. *Introduction to Scientific Geographic Research.* 3rd ed. Dubuque, IA: W.C. Brown, 1982.

GEOLOGY   *Information for Contributors to Publications of the Geological Society of America.* Boulder, CO: Geological Society of America, 1979.

Suggestions to Authors of Reports of the United States Geological Survey. 6th ed. Washington: GPO, U.S. Geological Survey, 1978.

HISTORY   Kent, Sherman. *Writing History.* Rev. James T. Scheifer, 2nd ed. New York: Appleton-Century-Crofts, 1967.

McCoy, Florence N. *Researching and Writing in History: A Practical Handbook for Students.* Berkeley: Univ. of California Press, 1974.

Steiner, Dale R. *Historical Journals: A Handbook for Writers and Reviewers.* Santa Barbara, CA: ABC-Clio, 1981.

Stoffle, Carla, and Simon Karter. *Materials and Methods for History Research.* New York: Neal-Schuman, 1979.

LAW   The Columbia Law Reviews. *A Uniform System of Citation.* 13th ed. Cambridge, MA: Harvard Law Review Association, 1981.

Garner, Diane L., and Diane H. Smith. *The Complete Guide to Citing Government Documents: A Manual for Writers and Librarians.* Bethesda, MD: Congressional Information Service, 1984.

LIBRARY SCIENCE   Manheimer, Martha L. *Style Manual: A Guide for Preparation of Reports and Dissertations.* Vol. 5. New York: Marcel Dekker, 1990.

LINGUISTICS   *LSA Style Sheet: LSA Bulletin.* Washington: Linguistic Society of America, December 1986. Annual.

LITERATURE   Gibaldi, Joseph, and Walter S. Archtert. *MLA Handbook for Writers of Research Papers.* 3rd ed. New York: Modern Language Association, 1988.

MATHEMATICS   American Mathematical Society. *A Manual for Authors of Mathematical Papers.* 8th ed. Providence, RI: American Mathematics Society, 1984.

Swanson, Ellen. *Mathematics into Type.* Providence, RI: American Mathematics Society, 1990.

MEDICINE Barclay, William R. *Manual for Authors and Editors: Editorial Style and Manuscript Preparation.* 7th ed. Los Angeles: Appleton & Lange, 1981.

Huth, Edward J. *How to Write and Publish Papers in the Medical Sciences.* Philadelphia: Institute for Scientific Information, 1982.

Roberts, Efrangcon. *Good English for Medical Writers.* Springfield, IL: Charles C. Thomas, 1960.

MUSIC Helm, Eugene, and Albert T. Luper. *Words and Music: Form and Procedure in Theses, Dissertations, Research Papers, Book Reports, Programs, and Theses in Composition.* Totwa, NJ: European American Music Corp., 1982.

Irvine, Demar, ed. *Writing about Music: A Style Book for Reports and Theses.* 2nd ed. Seattle: Univ. of Washington Press, 1968.

NON-PRINT SOURCES Fleisher, Eugene B. *A Style Manual for Citing Microform and Nonprint Media.* Chicago: American Library Association, 1990.

PHYSICAL THERAPY *Style Manual: Physical Therapy.* 5th ed. Washington: Journal of the American Physical Therapy Association, 1985.

PHYSICS *Style Manual for Guidance in the Preparation of Papers.* 3rd ed. New York: American Institute of Physics, 1990.

POLITICAL SCIENCE Goehlert, Robert U. *Political Science Research Guide.* Monticello, IL: Vance Bibliographies, 1982.

Stoffle, Carla J., Simon Karter, and Samuel Pernacciaro. *Materials and Methods for Political Science Research.* New York: Neal-Schuman, 1979.

PSYCHOLOGY *Publication Manual of the American Psychological Association.* 3rd ed. Washington: American Psychological Association, 1983.

Sternberg, Robert J. *Writing the Psychology Paper.* Woodbury, NJ: Barron, 1977.

RELIGION Sayre, John L. *A Manual of Forms for Research Papers and D. Min. Field Project Reports.* Enid, OK: Seminary Press, 1988.

SCIENCE *American National Standard for Preparation of Scientific Papers for Written or Oral Presentation.* New York: American National Standards Institute, 1979.

Barrass, Robert. *Scientists Must Write: A Guide to Better Writing for Scientists, Engineers and Students.* London: Chapman and Hall, 1978.

Day, Robert A. *How to Write and Publish a Scientific Paper.* 3rd ed. Philadelphia: Oryx Press, 1988.

Scientific Writing for Graduate Students: A Manual on the Teaching of Scientific Writing. Edited by Peter F. Woodard. New York: Rockefeller University Press, 1990.

SOCIAL WORK   *Information for Authors About NASW Publications.* Silver Spring, MD: NASW, 1985.

SOCIOLOGY   Golden, M. Paticial. *The Research Experience.* Itasca, IL: Peacock, 1976.

Gruber, James, and Judith Pryor. *Materials and Methods for Sociology Research.* New York: Neal-Schuman, 1990.

A Guide to Writing Sociology Papers. New York: St. Martin's, 1986.

Mullins, Carolyn J. *A Guide to Writing and Publishing in the Social and Behavioral Sciences.* New York: Krieger, 1990.

STATISTICS   Conway, Frieda. *Descriptive Statistics.* Leicester, England: Leicester University Press, 1968.

Croxton, Frederick E. Mory, and D.J. Cowden. *Applied General Statistics.* 2nd ed. New York: Prentice-Hall, 1967.

Myers, John H. *Statistical Presentation.* Ames, IA: Littlefield, Adams, 1956.

REFERENCE BOOKS

Bell, Marion V., and Eleanor A. Swidan. *Reference Books: A Brief Guide.* Chicago: Association of College and Reference Libraries, 1986.

Borgman, Christine L., Dineh Moghdam, and Patti K. Corbett. *Effective Online Searching.* New York: Marcel Dekker, 1984.

Katz, William. *Introduction to Reference Work.* 4th ed., 2 vols. New York: McGraw-Hill, 1982.

——. *Your Library: A Reference Guide.* 2nd ed. New York: Holt, Rinehart and Winston, 1984.

Murphy, Robert W. *How and Where to Look it Up.* New York: Dutton, 1958.

Sheehy, Eugene P. *Guide to Reference Books.* 9th ed. Chicago: American Library Association, 1986.

Shores, Louis. *Basic Reference Sources: An Introduction to Materials and Methods.* Chicago: American Library Association, 1954.

Walford, Arthur J. *Walford's Guide to Reference Material.* 4th ed. London: The Library Association, 1980-date.

BIBLIOGRAPHIES

Amers, G. John. *The Comprehensive Index to the Publications of the United States 1881-1894.* Washington: GPO, 1905.

Besterman, Theodore. *A World Bibliography of Bibliographies.* 4th ed. 5 vols. Lausanne: Societas Bibliographica, 1965-1966.

Bibliographic Index: A Cumulative Bibliography of Bibliographies. New York: H.W. Wilson, 1938-date.

Cumulative Book Index. New York: H.W. Wilson, 1907-date.

Goff, Frederick R. *Incunabula in American Libraries: A Third Census of*

Fifteenth-Century Books Recorded in North American Collections. New York: Bibliographical Society of America, 1972.

National Union Catalog: Pre-1956. Chicago: American Library Association, 1968.

Poor, B. Perley. *The Descriptive Catalogue of Government Publications of the United States 1774-1881.* Washington: GPO, 1885.

DICTIONARIES

The American Heritage Dictionary. 2nd college ed. Boston: Houghton Mifflin, 1982.

The American Heritage Dictionary of the English Language. Boston: Houghton Mifflin, 1970.

The American Heritage Illustrated Encyclopedic Dictionary. Boston: Houghton Mifflin, 1990.

The Oxford English Dictionary. 19 vols. Oxford: Clarendon Press, 1986. (Also available on CD-ROM disk.)

The Oxford English Dictionary. 2nd ed. 20 vols. New York: Oxford Univ. Press, 1989.

The Random House Dictionary of the English Language. 2nd ed. unabridged. New York: Random House, 1987.

Webster's New World Dictionary of the English Language. New York: Simon and Schuster, 1988.

Webster's Ninth New Collegiate Dictionary. Springfield, IL: Merriam-Webster, 1988.

Webster's II New Riverside University Dictionary. Boston: Houghton Mifflin, 1990.

Webster's Third New International Dictionary, Unabridged: The Great Library of the English Language. Springfield, IL: Merriam-Webster, 1990.

PERIODICALS

Ayer's Directory of Newspapers and Periodicals. Philadelphia: Ayers, 1880-date.

Editor and Publisher International Year Book. New York: Editor and Publisher, 1920-date.

Katz, Bill. *Magazines for Libraries.* 4th ed. New York: R.R. Bowker, 1986.

Standard Periodical Directory. New York: Oxbridge, 1982.

Ulrich's International Periodicals Directory. New York: R.R. Bowker, 1932-date.

Union List of Serials in Libraries of the United States and Canada. 3rd ed. 5 vols. New York: R.R. Bowker, 1965.

INDEXES

AFRO-AMERICAN STUDIES

Gardener, George L. *Index to Periodical Articles by and about Negroes.* Champaign, IL: University of Illinois, Graduate School of Library Science, 1975.

/

Newman, Richard. *Black Index: Afro-Americans in Selected Periodicals 1907-1949*. New York: Garland, 1981.

ANTHROPOLOGY   *Anthropology Index*. New York: Garland, 1988

APPLIED SCIENCE   *Applied Science and Technology Index*. New York: H.W. Wilson. 1958-date.

ARCHITECTURE   *The Architectural Index*. Boulder, CO: Architectural Index, 1951-date.

BIOGRAPHY   *Biography Index*. New York: H.W. Wilson, 1946-date.

BOOKS   *The Bibliographic Index*. New York: H.W. Wilson, 1938-date.
Book Review Digest. New York: H.W. Wilson, 1905-date.
Book Review Index. Detroit: Gale, 1983.
Cumulative Book Index. New York: H.W. Wilson, 1946-date.
Paperbound Books in Print. New York: R.R. Bowker Company, 1971-date.
Subject Guide to Books in Print. New York: R.R. Bowker Company, 1957-date.

CLASSICS   *Essay and General Literature Index*. New York: H.W. Wilson, 1953.

COMPUTERS   *Computer Literature Index*. Phoenix: Applied Computer Research, 1971-date.
CIS Annual. Washington: Congressional Information Service, 1970-date.

DISSERTATIONS   *Dissertation Abstracts International*. Ann Arbor, MI: University Microfilms International, 1938-date.

EDUCATION   *Education Index*. New York: H.W. Wilson, 1929-date.

ENGINEERING   *Engineering Index*. New York: CCM Information Corp., 1972.

ENVIRONMENT   *Environment Index*. New York: Environment Information Center, 1971-date.

FINANCE   *F & S Index of Corporations and Industries*. Cleveland: Predicosts Inc., 1980-date.

GEOLOGY   *Bibliography and Index of Geology*. Boulder, CO: Geological Society of America, 1969.

HEALTH SCIENCE   *Completed Research in Health, Physical Education and Recreation, Including International Sources.* Reston, VA: American Alliance for Health, Physical Education, Recreation and Dance, 1981.

HISTORY   *America: History and Life.* Santa Barbara, CA: American Bibliographical Center, Clio Press, 1979.

ILLUSTRATION   Appel, Marsh C. *Illustration Index.* 4th ed. Metuchen, NJ: Scarecrow Press Inc., 1980.

LIBRARY SCIENCE   *Library of Congress Catalog. Books: Subjects.* Washington: Library of Congress, 1950.

LITERATURE   *Essay and General Literature Index.* New York: H.W. Wilson, 1990.

MEDICAL SCIENCE   *Scientific, Medical, and Technical Books Published in America.* Washington: National Academy of Sciences, 1946.

MUSIC   *Music Index.* Detroit: Information Service, 1949-date.

NEWS   *News Bank, Inc.* New Canaan, CT: News Bank, Inc., 1982-date.

NEWSPAPERS   *The National Newspaper Index.* Belmont, CA: Information Access, 1979-date (monthly).

PAMPHLETS   *Vertical File Index.* New York: H.W. Wilson, 1935-date (monthly).

PERFORMING ARTS   *Cumulative Dramatic Index.* Accumulation of F.W. Faxon Dramatic Index. Eds. F.W. Faxon, M.E. Bates, and N.C. Southerland. 2 vols. Boston: G.K. Hall, 1965.

   Play Index. New York: H.W. Wilson, 1949-date.

PERIODICALS   *A Cumulative Author and Subject Index to a Selected List of Periodicals.* New York: H.W. Wilson, 1929-date.

   Magazine Index. Belmont, CA: Information Access, 1959-date.

   Poole's Index to Periodical Literature. Boston: Houghton Mifflin, 1971.

   Readers' Guide to Periodical Literature. New York: H.W. Wilson, 1900-date.

PHILOSOPHY   *The Philosopher's Index.* Bowling Green, OH: Philosophy Documentation Center, 1982.

Philosophers Index: An International Index to Philosophical Periodicals. Bowling Green, OH: Bowling Green University, 1967-date.

POETRY | Granger, Edith. *Granger's Index to Poetry.* 8th ed. New York: Columbia University Press, 1986.

PSYCHOLOGY | *Index of Psychoanalytic Writings.* Boston: International University Press, 1971.

RELIGION | *Religion Index One: Periodicals.* Chicago: American Theological Library Association, 1949-date.

SCIENCE | *General Science Index.* New York: H.W. Wilson, 1978-date.

SOCIAL SCIENCES | *Social Sciences and Humanities Index.* New York: H.W. Wilson, 1965-date.
Social Sciences Index. New York: H.W. Wilson, 1974-date.

SONGS | Sears, Minnie E., and Phyllis Crawford. *Song Index.* Reprint of 1926 ed. Reprint Services, 1990.

SPEECH | Carity, Mitchel. *Speech Index.* 4th ed. Metuchen, NJ: Scarecrow Press Inc., 1966-80.

STATISTICS | *American Statistical Index.* Washington: Congressional Information Service, 1972-date.

U.S. GOVERNMENT | *Monthly Catalog of United States Government Publications.* Washington: United States Superintendent of Documents. 1895-date (monthly).

BIOGRAPHICAL REFERENCE SOURCES

Biography and Genealogy Master Index. Eds. Miranda C. Herbert and Barbara McNeil. 2nd ed. Detroit: Gale, 1990.

Biography Index: A Cumulative Index to Biographical Material in Books and Magazines. New York: H.W. Wilson, 1949.

Current Biography. New York: H.W. Wilson, 1940-date.

Dictionary of American Biography. 11 vols. New York: Scribner's, 1928-77.

McGraw-Hill Encyclopedia of World Biography. 12 vols. New York: McGraw-Hill, 1973.

Notable American Women, 1607-1950: A Biographical Dictionary. 3 vols. Cambridge, MA: Belknap Press of Harvard University Press, 1980.

Who's Who in America. Chicago: Marquis, 1899-date.

Who's Who in the World. Chicago: Marquis, 1972.

BOOK REVIEWS

Book Review Digest. New York: H.W. Wilson, 1905-date.

Book Review Index. Detroit: Gale, 1983.

Index to Book Reviews in the Humanities. Williamston, MI: Thomson, 1963-date.

NEWSPAPERS

Facts on File. New York: Facts on File, Inc., 1940-date.

Index of Times. London: The Times, 1907-date.

Index of U.S. Government Publications. Chicago: Infodata International, 1973-date.

Magazine Index. Menlo Park: Information Access Co., 1979-date.

National Newspaper Index. Menlo Park: Information Access Co., 1979-date.

News Bank. New Canaan, CT: News Bank, Inc., 1982-date.

Newspaper Index. Wooster, OH: Newspaper Indexing Center, Bell & Howell, 1972-date.

New York Times Index. New York: The Times, 1913-date.

Online Access to Wilson Indexes. New York: H.W. Wilson, 1985.

Poole's Index to Periodical Literature, 1802-1907. Ann Arbor, MI: Pierian Press, 1971.

Readers' Guide to Periodical Literature. New York: H.W. Wilson, 1900-date.

Wall Street Journal Index. New York: Dow Jones and Company, 1958-date.

STATISTICS

Dow Jones-Irwin Business Almanac. Homewood, IL: Dow Jones-Irwin, 1982.

Gallup, George Horace. *Gallup Poll: Public Opinion*. New York: Random House, 1972.

Information Please Almanac. New York: Simon and Schuster, 1947-83.

National Basic Intelligence Factbook. Washington: Central Intelligence Agency; Supt. of Docs., GPO. 1981-date.

The Statesman's Yearbook. New York: St. Martin's, 1939-date.

Statistical Abstract of the United States. Washington: U.S. Department of Commerce, Bureau of the Census, 1980-date.

Survey of Current Business. Washington: The Bureau of Economic Analysis, 1951-date.

United Nations Statistical Yearbook. New York: United Nations, 1988.

World Almanac and Book of Facts. New York: Press Pub. Co., 1923-date.

THESAURUSES

The Random House Thesaurus: College Edition. New York: Random House, 1990.

Roget's International Thesaurus. 4th ed. New York: Crowell, 1977.

Roget's Thesaurus of English Words and Phrases. London: Longman, 1990.

Roget's II: The New Thesaurus. Expanded ed. Boston: Houghton Mifflin, 1988.

Webster's Collegiate Thesaurus. Springfield, IL: Merriam-Webster, 1976.

Webster's New Dictionary of Synonyms. Springfield, IL: Merriam-Webster, 1984.

GRAMMAR

Fowler, H. Ramsey, and Jane E. Aaron. *The Little, Brown Handbook.* 4th ed. Glenview, IL: Scott, Foresman, 1989.

Hacker, Diana. *Rules for Writers: A Concise Handbook.* 2nd ed. New York: St. Martin's, 1988.

Kirszner, Laurie G., and Stephen R. Mandell. *The Holt Handbook.* 2nd ed. Fort Worth: Holt, 1989.

Lunsford, Andrea, and Robert Connors. *The St. Martin's Handbook.* New York: St. Martin's, 1989.

Watkins, Floyd C., and William B. Dillingham. *Practical English Handbook.* 8th ed. Boston: Houghton Mifflin, 1989.

COMPUTER DATABASES

Dialog

Dialog catalogs over 300 databases on a wide array of subjects, with more than 150 million entries. Its coverage includes government, health, education, social and physical sciences, humanities, and business. Some of the databases include AGRICOLA for agriculture and food sciences, MEDLINE for medicine, and ABI/INFORM for business. Its Electronic Yellow Pages list commercial and professional organizations, products, and services.

OCLC 1968-date

Online Computer Library Center, one of the largest online databases, lists the collection of 1,000 member libraries. Member libraries can arrange to borrow books through interlibrary loan arrangements from member libraries, or make photocopies of materials. It lists all the Library of Congress materials in English cataloged since 1968.

American Statistics Index (ASI) 1974-date

Annual, with monthly supplements. Indexes as many statistics as can be found that are published by any agency of the U.S. government. Includes extensive bibliographic information, Sudoc numbers, and lengthy abstracts and is organized by government department, agency, and subagency.

Bibliographic Retrieval Service (BRS)

Provides access to over 150 databases on a wide variety of subjects ranging from government agencies to professional organizations and the publishing industry. Among other topics it covers health, sports, sciences, computers, mathematics, robotics, and education.

Comprehensive Dissertation Index (CDI) 1861-date

This is the most complete subject and author index to doctoral dissertations written in the United States since 1861.

Business Currents Index

Annotated index of thousands of articles from over fifty business, academic, and finance publications. Publications covered include: *Business Week, Forbes, Inc., U.S. News & World Report, Harvard Business Review, Business Month, D&B Reports, Across the Board, Management Review, Nation's Business*, and *Venture*. Full text of most articles available.

Computerized Engineering Index (COMPENDEX) 1970-date

A most comprehensive collection of time-saving abstracts on worldwide developments in all related disciplines. COMPENDEX is the computerized version of Engineering Index.

Congressional Information Service (CIS) 1970-date

Comprehensive abstracts and indexes of current congressional documents. Arrangement of the material is by government committee, subdivided by the type of publication (documents, hearings, prints, reports, etc.).

Current Index to Journals in Education (CIJE) 1969-date

A comprehensive index to the educational periodical literature, covering more than 17,000 articles a year from over 750 journals in education and education-related disciplines.

Dow Jones News/Retrieval 1979-date

This database provides news related to corporations listed on the New York Stock Exchange, the American Stock Exchange, and the National Association of Securities Dealers. Includes automated quotations of stock on the Over-the-Counter market.

Educational Services Research Center (ERIC) 1966-date

The is the on-line version of *Resources in Education*. It includes a national information system for providing ready access to literature on education. It covers exemplary programs, research and development efforts, and related information that can be used in developing effective educational programs.

F & S Index of Corporations and Industries

Covers company, product, and industry information from over 750 financial publications, business-oriented newspapers, trade magazines, and special reports. Geographic coverage includes U.S., European, and other international corporations and industries.

Historical Abstracts (HA) 1973-date

Coverage begins with 1973 and includes articles and essays dealing with world history since 1450, excluding North America.

Index to Scientific Reviews (ISR)

Identifies and indexes over 20,000 reviews and articles from more than 2,700 of the world's most important scientific journals.

The Information Bank (The New York Times Information Service) 1969-date

Abstracts more than twenty news services, and also includes many special and general interest publications.

LEXIS and NEXIS 1821-date

Lexis provides a comprehensive library of legal research and information for law schools, firms, and courts. It includes millions of court opinions and federal and state statutes. Nexis provides full-text newspapers, journals, and references.

Machine Readable Cataloging (MARC)

Lists all English books of the Library of Congress cataloged since 1968.

MEDLARS/MEDLINE 1966-date

Medlars provides the material indexed by the National Library of Medicine.

Medline is the on-line version of *Index Medicus*. It covers broad areas of biomedicine. It indexes over 3,000 journals nationally and internationally.

Philosopher's Index Data Base 1940-date

Indexes books on philosophy and related fields. Includes extensive book reviews and author and subject indexes.

Science Citation Index (ISI) 1961-date

An international, interdisciplinary index to the literature of science, medicine, technology, and the behavioral sciences.

Smithsonian Science Information Exchange (SSIE)

Presents data on 179 existing and emerging information centers in fifty-three countries.

PUBLISHERS

Books in Print. New York: R.R. Bowker, 1948-date.

Cumulative Book Index. New York: H.W. Wilson, 1907-date.

Gill, Robert J. *Author-Publisher-Printer Complex*. 3rd ed. Baltimore: Williams & Wilkins, 1960.

Handbook for Authors. Washington: American Chemical Society, 1978.

Literary Market Place: The Directory of the American Book Publishing Industry. New York: R.R. Bowker, 1964-date.

Paperbound Books in Print. New York: R.R. Bowker, 1955-date.

Publishers' Trade List Annual. New York: R.R. Bowker, 1873-date.

Subject Guide to Books in Print. New York: R.R. Bowker, 1948-date.

COPYRIGHT PRACTICE

Nicholson, Margaret. *A Manual of Copyright Practice for Writers, Publishers, and Agents*. New York: Oxford University Press, 1956.

Pilpel, Harriet F., and Theodora S. Zavin. *Rights and Writers: A Handbook of Literary and Entertainment Law*. New York: E.P. Dutton, 1960.

Pilpel, Harriet F., and Morton David Goldberg, in cooperation with the Copyright Society of the U.S.A. *A Copyright Guide*. 4th ed. New York: R.R. Bowker, 1969.

Writers, Publishers, and Agents. 2nd ed. New York: Oxford University Press, 1956.

COMPOSITION

Axelrod, Rise B., and Charles R. Cooper. *The St. Martin's Guide to Writing*. 2nd ed. New York: St. Martin's, 1988.

Baker, Sheridan, and Robert E. Yarber. *The Practical Stylist with Readings*. 4th ed. New York: Harper and Row, 1986.

Bazerman, Charles. *The Informed Writer: Using Sources in the Disciplines*. 3rd ed. Boston: Houghton Mifflin, 1988.

Cook, Claire Kehrwald. *Line by Line: How to Improve Your Own Writing*. Boston: Houghton Mifflin, 1989.

Corder, W. Jim, and John J. Ruszkiewicz. *Handbook of Current English*. 7th ed. Glenview, IL: Scott, Foresman, 1987.

Elbow, Peter. *Writing with Power: Techniques for Mastering the Writing Process*. New York: Oxford Univ. Press, 1981.

Gorrel, L. Robert, and Charton Laird. *Modern English Handbook*. 6th ed. Englewood Cliffs, NJ: Prentice-Hall, Inc., 1976.

Hodges, John C. and Mary Whitten. *Harbrace College Handbook*. 8th ed. New York: Harcourt Brace Jovanovich, Inc., 1977.

Horner, Winifre Bryan. *Composition and Literature*. Chicago: University of Chicago Press, 1983.

Kennedy, Z.J., and Dorothy M. Kennedy. *The Bedford Guide for College Writers*. New York: St. Martin's, 1989.

Kuriloff, Peshe. *Rethinking Writing*. New York: St. Martin's, 1989.

Phelps, Louise Wetherbee. *Composition as Human Science*. New York: Oxford Univ. Press, 1988.

Ross-Larson, B. *Edit Yourself: A Manual for Everyone who Works with Words*. New York: Norton, 1982.

Trimmer, Joseph F., and James M. McCrimmon. *Writing with a Purpose*. 9th ed. Boston: Houghton Mifflin, 1988.

Strunk, William, Jr., and E.B. White. *The Elements of Style*. 3rd ed. New York: Macmillan, 1979.

Warriner, John E. *English Composition & Literature*. Chicago: University of Chicago Press, 1983.

Williams, Joseph M. *Style: Ten Lessons in Clarity and Grace*. 3rd ed. Glenview, IL: Scott, Foresman, 1989.

Yates, B.T. *Doing the Dissertation: The Nuts and Bolts of Psychological Research*. Chicago: Charles C. Thomas, 1982.

Vocabulary List

accede	yield, allow	comprehensive	all inclusive
acolytes	attendants	conceivably	possibly
acumen	insight, wit	condone	forgive, pardon
adamantly	unyieldingly	conjecture	forecast
admonition	advice, counsel	consternation	dismay
advert	turn to	consummate	complete
aesthetic	appreciation of beauty	contemptuously	scornfully
amalgams	mixtures, blends	conviction	belief
ambivalence	indecision	convoke	call together
ameliorate	relieve, improve	curriculum	course of study
amiable	friendly	dame	woman of high rank
amorphous	without shape	debauch	corrupt, pervert
ample	adequate	disparage	belittle
analogous	similar	disposition	makeup, nature
antecedent	preceding	dissonant	inharmonious
anthropomorphic	in human form	distort	twist
antipathy	feeling against	dogmatic	opinionated, stubborn
arbiter	judge	dynamic	powerful
ardent	enthusiastic	eccentric	odd
arduous	laborious	effervescent	lively, full of life
assiduously	persistently	elicit	draw, invoke
astutely	shrewdly	emasculate	to take away
augment	increase	embellish	decorate
baleful	threatening, evil	endure	bear under hardship
benign	kind, tender	enervating	weakening
bibliophile	lover of books	enigmatic	puzzling
bizarre	fantastic	entity	actual being, object
capricious	unpredictable	equanimity	composure, calmness
catapult	hurl, propel	exorbitant	too much
cede	yield	exploitation	taking full advantage of
circumvent	bypass, avoid	extoll	praise
colloquy	speaking together	exuberance	high spirits
commodiously	spaciously	fiasco	disaster
complacent	self-satisfied	flaunt	show off

forlorn .... unhappy, lonely
futility .... uselessness
gelt .... money
genesis .... origin
genial .... pleasant, agreeable
gist .... main idea
grandiose .... imposing
gregarious .... sociable
gullible .... easily deceived
hedonism .... belief that pleasure is the only good
humanism .... philanthropy
hybrid .... mixed
impelling .... motivating
impetuous .... hasty, rash
impose .... inflict
impunity .... freedom from harm
incentive .... stimulus
incredible .... unbelievable
indicative .... suggestive
inevitably .... certainly
inhibition .... constraint
innocuous .... harmless
insatiable .... unsatisfiable
instill .... inspire
institute .... set up or establish
insuperable .... cannot be overcome
intelligible .... understandable
intrigue .... interest, plot
introspection .... self-examination
invincible .... unconquerable
kilometer .... equivalent to .621 mile
laconic .... brief, blunt
lamenting .... grieving
legible .... neat, plain
lexical .... pertaining to words
limpid .... clear
magnanimous .... noble, lofty
malevolent .... wishing evil to
manifest .... illustrate, reveal
maudlin .... weakly, sentimental
meticulous .... careful

millennia .... thousands of years
misanthropic .... self-sacrificing
momentous .... important
mortal .... deadly
nongeneric .... not standard
nullify .... destroy
obsess .... preoccupy
octogenarian .... eighty year old
odious .... repugnant
omniscient .... all-knowing
optimum .... best
panacea .... remedy for all
panoramic .... wide, extensive
paradoxical .... contradictory
pathos .... feeling
pejorative .... disparaging, derogatory
per se .... by itself
percipience .... keen perception
perspective .... viewpoint
perverse .... corrupt
philanthropist .... humanitarian
phonetic .... concerning sound
plebiscite .... vote by the whole people
precarious .... risky
precursor .... predecessor
preposterous .... absurd
pretentious .... pompous, showy
probe .... investigate
procrastinate .... put off
proponent .... one who argues
provincial .... rural, bucolic
pseudo .... fake
purporting .... alleging, claiming
recalcitrant .... stubborn
recrimination .... accusation
refute .... prove wrong
remediation .... cure
retrograde .... going backward
retrospective .... looking at the past
satire .... ridicule
schism .... division
secede .... go away

sedulously .... industriously

seminar .... small, informal discussion group

sinister .... evil

smug .... self-satisfied

sonic .... pertaining to sound

stereotype .... typical of a group

stolid .... dull, not easily excited

stringent .... strict

subsequent .... following

surmise .... guess

surreptitious .... secret

sustain .... endure

sustaining .... maintaining

symbiosis .... living together

tenacity .... persistence

tertiary .... third

tortuous .... twisting

translucent .... letting light through

trivial .... not very important

unabridged .... not condensed

unequivocal .... clear

urban .... within a city

vacillate .... hesitate

vestige .... trace

vivacious .... lively, effervescent

Words Often Misspelled

absence	bookkeeper	courageous	embarrass
accessible	Britain	currency	embodying
accidentally	bureaucracy	dealt	eminent
accommodation	cafeteria	deceive	encouragement
achievement	calculator	deciphered	encumbrances
acknowledgment	calendar	decision	enforceable
acquaintance	cancellation	deferred	entitled
advantageous	canvasser	definite	equipment
advisable	capricious	definitely	equipped
aggravate	casualties	descend	especially
aggregate	ceiling	description	everything
alcohol	census	desperate	evidently
all right	changeable	dilapidated	exaggerate
allotment	characteristic	dimensions	excelled
amateur	collateral	disappearance	excellent
annihilate	colonel	disappointment	except
apparatus	commission	disapprove	exercised
apparent	commitment	disastrous	exhaust
appropriate	committee	disbursements	exhilarating
approximately	commodities	discipline	existence
arithmetic	comparatively	discrepancy	exorbitant
ascertain	compelled	discretion	experience
assiduously	conceivable	discussion	explanation
associate	concentrate	disseminate	extraordinarily
athletics	concession	distinct	facetious
attacked	confectionery	distributor	facilities
attendance	conferred	disturb	facsimile
attorneys	conscience	divine	familiar
authentic	consensus	dormitory	fascinate
authoritative	conspicuous	duly	fascinating
auxiliary	continually	ecstasy	favorite
basically	continuous	efficiently	February
beneficiaries	controversial	elaborately	forcibly
benefitted	correspondent	elementary	foreclosure

foreign	leisure	physical	seize
foretell	length	picnicking	sergeant
foundries	lenient	platoon	several
freight	liable	possession	severely
generally	license	practically	siege
grammar	likelihood	precede	similar
grateful	likely	precedence	sophomore
grievance	listening	preferable	souvenir
guaranteed	liveliest	preferred	specialty
harass	lose	prejudice	specifically
height	luxury	preparatory	specimen
hindrance	magazine	privilege	strategy
humorous	magnificent	professional	strenuous
hurriedly	maintenance	professor	strictly
hypocrisy	management	proffered	substantially
identify	maneuver	pronunciation	succeed
idiosyncrasy	merchandise	propaganda	successful
imitation	mileage	prophecy	superintendent
incidentally	miniature	psychology	supersede
incredible	miscellaneous	publicly	susceptible
indebtedness	mischievous	purpose	suspicious
indemnity	mislaid	pursue	symmetrical
independent	misstatement	pursuing	syndicate
indispensable	morale	quantity	technical
influential	mortgagor	questionnaire	technique
integrate	necessarily	quizzes	temperament
intelligent	noticeable	really	temperature
intention	nowadays	receive	thorough
interest	occasionally	recommend	traceable
interference	occurred	referring	unanimous
interfering	occurrence	rehearsal	unconscious
irrelevant	omission	relief	underlying
irresistible	ordinarily	religious	undoubtedly
irritated	outrageous	remembrance	unforeseen
itinerary	pamphlet	reminisce	unnecessarily
jealousy	paralleled	repetition	until
jewelry	particularly	representative	vacuum
judgment	partner	restaurant	warrant
knowledge	permanently	rhythm	weight
laboratories	personnel	ridiculous	wholesaler
laid	pertain	schedule	wholly
led	phenomenal	secretary	yield

Standard United States Postal Abbreviations

U.S. States	Abbreviations (Postal, MLA, and APA)	Abbreviations (Chicago Manual)
Alabama	AL	Ala.
Alaska	AK	Alaska
Arizona	AZ	Ariz.
Arkansas	AR	Ark.
California	CA	Calif.
Colorado	CO	Colo.
Connecticut	CT	Conn.
Delaware	DE	Del.
District of Columbia	DC	D.C.
Florida	FL	Fla.
Georgia	GA	Ga.
Hawaii	HI	Hawaii
Idaho	ID	Idaho
Illinois	IL	Ill.
Indiana	IN	Ind.
Iowa	IA	Iowa
Kansas	KS	Kans.
Kentucky	KY	Ky.
Louisiana	LA	La.
Maine	ME	Maine
Maryland	MD	Md.
Massachusetts	MA	Mass.
Michigan	MI	Mich.
Minnesota	MN	Minn.
Mississippi	MS	Miss.
Missouri	MO	Mo.
Montana	MT	Mont.
Nebraska	NE	Nebr.
Nevada	NV	Nev.
New Hampshire	NH	N.H.
New Jersey	NJ	N.J.
New Mexico	NM	N.Mex.

New York	NY	N.Y.
North Carolina	NC	N.C.
North Dakota	ND	N.Dak.
Ohio	OH	Ohio
Oklahoma	OK	Okla.
Oregon	OR	Oreg.
Pennsylvania	PA	Pa.
Puerto Rico	PR	P.R.
Rhode Island	RI	R.I.
South Carolina	SC	S.C.
South Dakota	SD	S.Dak.
Tennessee	TN	Tenn.
Texas	TX	Tex.
Utah	UT	Utah
Vermont	VT	Vt.
Virginia	VA	Va.
Washington	WA	Wash.
West Virginia	WV	W.Va.
Wisconsin	WI	Wis.
Wyoming	WY	Wyo.

Shortened MLA-Style Publisher Names

In documentation using the MLA style, the names of publishers are shortened. This style calls for shortening the words "University" and "Press" to "U" and "P", respectively. Where the name of the publisher is that of a person, only the last name is used. If the name has more than a single name, then only the first name is used. For example, "Holt" is written for "Holt, Rinehart and Winston, Inc."

Complete Name	MLA Shortened Name
Alfred A. Knopf, Inc.	Knopf
Allyn and Bacon, Inc.	Allyn
American Library Association	ALA
Appleton-Century-Crofts	Appleton
Ballantine Books, Inc.	Ballantine
Bantam Book	Bantam
Beacon Press, Inc.	Beacon
The Bobbs-Merrill Co., Inc.	Bobbs
Cambridge University Press	Cambridge UP
Charles Scribner's Sons	Scribner's
Clarendon Press	Clarendon
Columbia University Press	Columbia UP
D.C. Heath and Co.	Heath
Dell Publishing Co., Inc.	Dell
Dodd, Mead, and Co.	Dodd
Doubleday and Co., Inc.	Doubleday
Dover Publications, Inc.	Dover
E.P. Dutton, Inc.	Dutton
Ernest Benn, Ltd.	Benn
G.P. Putnam's Sons	Putnam's
Gale Research Co.	Gale
George Allen and Unwin Publishers, Inc.	Allen
Government Printing Office	GPO
Harcourt Brace Jovanovich, Inc.	Harcourt
Harper and Row Publishers, Inc.	Harper
Harry N. Abrams, Inc.	Abrams
Harvard University Press	Harvard UP
Holt, Rinehart and Winston, Inc.	Holt
Houghton Mifflin Co.	Houghton
Humanities Press, Inc.	Humanities
Indiana University Press	Indiana UP
J.B. Lippincott Co.	Lippincott
The Johns Hopkins University Press	Johns Hopkins UP
Little, Brown and Co.	Little
Macmillan Publishing Co., Inc.	Macmillan
McGraw-Hill, Inc.	McGraw
The MIT Press	MIT P
The Modern Language Association of America	MLA
The National Education Association	NEA
The New American Library, Inc.	NAL
Oxford University Press	Oxford UP
Penguin Books, Inc.	Penguin

Pocket Books ....Pocket

The Popular Press ....Popular

Prentice-Hall, Inc. ....Prentice

Princeton University Press ....Princeton UP

R.R. Bowker Co. ....Bowker

Rand McNally and Co. ....Rand

Random House, Inc. ....Random

St. Martin's Press, Inc. ....St. Martin's

Scott, Foresman and Co. ....Scott

Simon and Schuster, Inc. ....Simon

University Microfilms International ...UMI

University of Chicago Press ....U of Chicago P

University of Toronto Press ....U of Toronto P

The University Presses of Florida ......UP of Florida

The Viking Press, Inc. ....Viking

W.W. Norton and Co., Inc. ....Norton

Yale University Press ....Yale UP

Correction Symbols
for Proofreading

Symbols	Explanation	Mistake in text	Corrected text
‖	Align	‖ This is incorrect.	This is correct.
BF	Bold face	this is incorrect.	**This** is correct.
ctr	Center	⊐ This is incorrect.⊏	This is correct.
⌒⌄	Close up space	T his is incorrect.	This is correct.
ℓ	Delete	T his is the incorrect.	This is correct.
ℓ⌒	Delete and close space	This is incorrect.	This is correct.
∜	Insert apostrophe	Im wrong.	I'm right.
⦂	Insert colon	Following is correct∧	Following is correct:
⌃	Insert comma	See∧this is correct.	See, this is correct.
⫣	Insert em dash	See∧correct all.	See—correct all.
=	Insert hyphen	Correction∧free page	Correction-free page
(/)	Insert parentheses	Mistake∧page 3∧	Mistake (page 3)
⊙	Insert period	This is incorrect∧	This is correct.
?	Insert question mark	Is this correct∧	Is this correct?

;	Insert semicolon	Find all mistakes∧
		   correct all mistakes
			Find all mistakes;
			   correct all mistakes

#	Insert space	This is incorrect.	This is correct.
∧is	Insert indicated material.	This∧incorrect.	This is correct.
ital	Italics	This is incorrect.	This is *correct*.
STET	Let it stand	This is correct.	This is correct.
lc	Make lower case	This is Incorrect.	This is correct.
⊏	Move to left	⊏ This is incorrect.	This is correct.
⊐	Move to right	⊐This is incorrect.	This is correct.
sp	Spell out or correctly	This is icorrect,	This is correct.
tr	Transpose	This incorrect is	This is correct.

Frequently Used Abbreviations

The following list presents some common abbreviations. Most are of Latin origin and are traditionally used for brevity in scholarly research and writing. These abbreviations are used in footnotes, parenthetical literary references, bibliographies, and texts. A dictionary may be consulted for the meaning and standard usage of other abbreviations not included in this list.

A.D. ....*anno Domini* (in the year of our Lord)

a.k.a. ....also known as

a.m. ....*ante meridiem* (before noon)

abbr. ....abbreviation

anon. ....anonymous (unknown author)

ante ....before

art., arts. ....article(s)

bk., bks. ....book(s)

ca. or c. ....*circa* (about; used with approximate dates)

c.o.d. ....cash on delivery

ch. ....chapter

col., cols. ....column(s)

copr. ....copyright

CST ....Central Standard Time

diss. ....dissertation

div., divs. ....division(s)

e.g. ....*exemplia gratia* (for example)

ed., eds. ....editor(s)

EDT ....Eastern Daylight Time

EST ....Eastern Standard Time

et al. ....*et alii* (and others)

et seq. ....*et sequens* (and the following)

et passim ....and here and there

etc. ....*et cetera* (and so forth)

ex., exs. ....example(s)

f., ff. ....and following page(s)

f.o.b. ....free on board

fig., figs............figure(s)

i.e. ....*id est* (that is)

ibid. ....*ibidem* (in the same place, from the same work)

id. ....*idem* (the same)

Inc. ....Incorporated

infra ....below

loc. cit. ....*loco citato* (in the place cited; nonconsecutive footnote, same page)

Ltd. ....Limited

m. ....*meridiem* (noon)

MDT ....Mountain Daylight Time

ms., mss. ....manuscript(s)

MST ....Mountain Standard Time

n.b. ....*nota bene* (note well)

n.d. ....no date

n.n. ....no name

no., nos. ....number(s)

op. cit. ....*opere citato* (in the work cited; nonconsecutive footnote, new page)

p., pp. ....page(s)

p.m. ....*post meridiem* (after noon)

par., pars. ....paragraph(s)

pass. ....*passim* (throughout; here and there)

PDT ....Pacific Daylight Time

proc. ....proceedings

pseud. ....pseudonym

PST ....Pacific Standard Time

pt., pts. ....part(s)

rev. ....revised

sec., secs. ....section(s)

ser. ....series

sic .... thus

supra .... above, earlier in the text

univ. .... university

v., vv. or
   vs., vss. .... verse(s)

viz. .... *videlicet* (namely)

vol., vols. .... volume(s)

vs. .... versus (against)

Zip Code .... Zoning Improvement Program Code

APA Guidelines and Sample Pages

Divisions of the Manuscript. The American Psychological Association's (APA) author/date format is a comprehensive style used in the preparation of term papers, dissertations, theses, and articles intended for publication in academic journals. This format replaces the traditional footnotes. When a reference is made to an article, a book, or any other source, special information is placed in parentheses informing the reader where to locate the source of original information at the end of the manuscript. A list titled "Works Cited" is prepared and placed at the end of the paper that provides this information for the reader. This practice reduces distractions in reading the text and simplifies typing by eliminating footnotes at the end of the page. This style is used in the behavioral sciences and other disciplines, such as agriculture, biology, and physical education. Papers prepared for publication in scholarly business journals are also written according to the suggested guidelines explained in the *Publication Manual of the American Psychological Association*, 3rd ed. (Washington: APA, 1983). The principles of this author/date style are discussed in Chapter 9. The following paragraphs present a review of the suggested guidelines and illustrate the composition of the title pages, abstracts, references, and other pages.

Margins, Spacing, and Page Numbering. One-and-a-half-inch margins are kept on all sides, including the top and bottom of the paper. The first line of each paragraph is indented five spaces from the left margin, and the typed lines are not justified, meaning the ends of lines are not exactly the same. Quoted material of more than four typed lines is indented ten spaces from the left margin. The entire manuscript is typed double-spaced, except for long quotations, titles of tables, and footnotes, which may be single-spaced. Pages are numbered in Arabic numerals consecutively, starting with the first page of the text and including the last "Works Cited" section. Small Roman numerals (i, ii) are used for any preliminary pages.

A running head, which is an abbreviated part of the title of the paper, is typed on the title page and all other pages throughout the paper. This running head is used so that the manuscript's author is not identified when the article is submitted for blind review by the journal. The running head is typed ½ inch from the top and 1½ inches from the left margin. The page numbers beginning with the Arabic numeral (1) are typed one double space below the running head.

Title Pages. Margins of 1½ inches are kept at the top and bottom of each page and on the left- and righthand sides of the paper. The title of the manuscript is centered on the page. The initial letters of the first, last, and all other major words of the title are capitalized. Articles submitted to journals should include the names of the author and other principal investigators, the name of the association or the university where the author works, and the submission date (month, day, year). Each of these items is double-spaced and centered. None of these entries is boldfaced, underlined, or enclosed in quotation marks.

Term papers written for college courses require the student's name, the course designation, the instructor's name, and the submission date. Each of these items is typed on a separate line. Student papers do not need a page number for the title page, except when it is part of the preliminary pages. In this case, it is assigned the Roman numeral (i), but the number is not typed. The title page of an article prepared for publication in a journal requires the Arabic numeral (1), which is typed in the right margin. The following is an example of a title page:

Figure AP-1

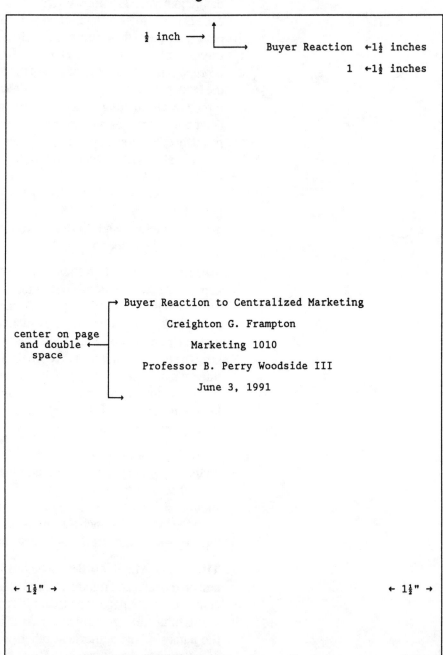

Abstracts. The abstract (a summary of the paper) may not be required for papers written in college, although its addition may enhance its submission. The running head title identifying the manuscript is typed $1/2$ inch from the top right of the paper on the margin. The page number is typed one double space below the running head on the right margin. When an abstract is included, it is assigned the small Roman numeral (ii) and then the separate title page is assigned the numeral (i), but this number is not typed on the page. The title "Abstract" is centered and typed $1^1/2$ inches from the top of the paper. The first line of the text is typed on the margin and double-spaced below the "Abstract" title. The entire abstract is typed in block form. This means that paragraphs are not indented. The following is an example of the format of an abstract.

Figure AP-2

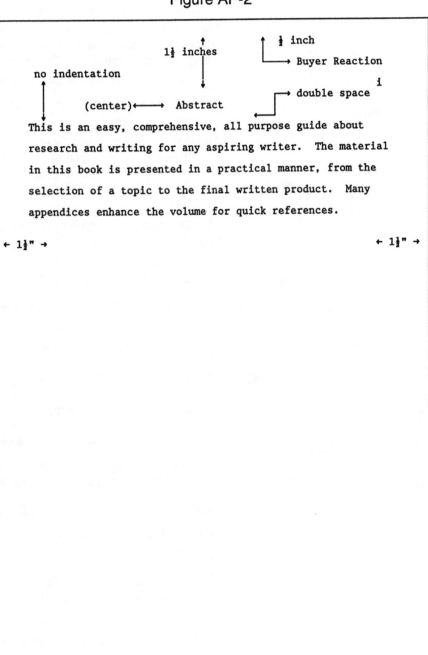

Text. The first page of the text is numbered page (1), if preliminary matter such as an abstract or outline is included. When preliminary matter is not included, and a title page is included, then the title page is assigned the number (1) and the text page number (2). The title of the manuscript is centered on the line and typed $1\frac{1}{2}$ inches from the top of the paper. The initial letters of the first, last, and all other major words of the title are capitalized. The title is not underlined, boldfaced, or enclosed in quotation marks. The first line of the text is typed a double space from the title and indented five spaces. The text is typed double-spaced. Right and left, top and bottom margins of $1\frac{1}{2}$ inches are maintained throughout the manuscript. Words are not hyphenated at the ends of lines. New headings continue the text and are not typed on separate pages, but included in the flow of the pages. Short quotations (fewer than forty words) are enclosed in quotation marks and integrated within the text. Longer quotations are indented five additional spaces from the left margin, typed on a new line, and double-spaced throughout. All other paragraphs of the same quotation are typed in blocked style. Quotation marks are not used. Closings such as "The End" or other similar phrases are not used. Sections such as "References" and "Notes" must start on a separate page following the text.

Headings. Headings should properly divide written material of any length, contribute to organization and the development of thoughts, and attract attention to the contents. Appropriate headings should be informative and descriptive about the content. Careful selection and wording of headings lends progression to the flow of ideas. Format of typing headings varies in capitalization, underlining, boldfacing, and spacing. It is important to follow a consistent format throughout the manuscript. The four commonly used heading levels sufficient for the preparation of most documents include: (1) main title heading, (2) second-degree main title heading, (3) third-degree flush or side subheading, and (4) indented paragraph subheading. The following explain and exemplify the formats of typing these four level headings:

Level (1) main title heading title centered and typed in upper and lower case letters.

Buyer Reaction to Centralized Marketing

Level (2) main heading title is also centered and typed in upper and lower case letters. Some may use underlining and boldfacing for this level to distinguish it from the main title headings.

Buyer Needs   <u>Buyer Needs</u>   **Buyer Needs**

Level (3) heading is underlined, typed at the margin in upper and lower case letters. The first indented line of the text is typed below this heading.

<u>Industrial Channels of Distribution</u>

Level (4), or paragraph heading, is indented and underlined, followed by a period, two spaces, and the text.

<u>Raw material purchases</u>. Raw materials include products that have been partially processed ....

References. The reference section is typed on a separate page following the text. The title "Reference" is centered and typed $1\frac{1}{2}$ inches from the top of the

Figure AP-3

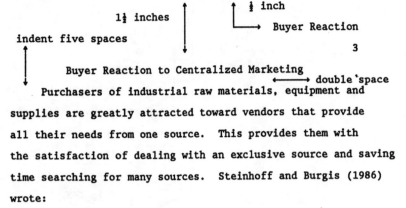

paper. The first entry is double-spaced from the "Reference" title. All lines between and among entries are double-spaced. Short papers written for courses in college may use single spacing within entries. This list is arranged alphabetically by the author's last name. In certain instances, an author's name may not be given. On these occasions the correct procedure is to list entries by the title of the article or book in alphabetical order by the first word of the title, excluding the words A, An, and The. Several works by the same author are listed in chronological order beginning with the earliest dates of publication. The first line of each entry is typed on the left margin with any additional lines of the same entry indented three spaces. Right and left margins of 1½ inches are maintained throughout.

Figure AP-4

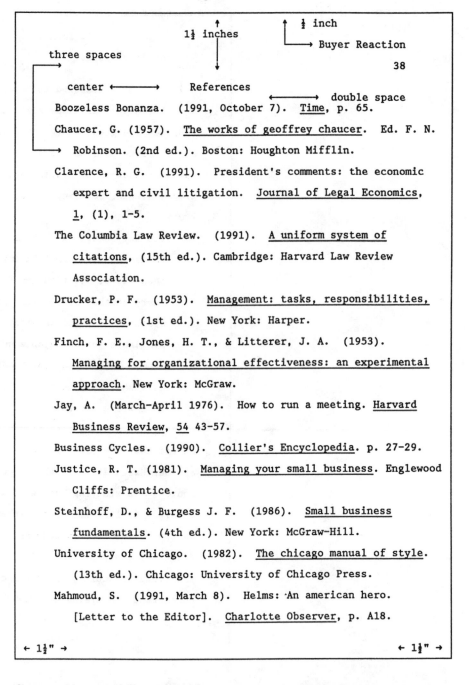

Content Notes and Footnotes. Content notes provide added information and clarifications on the subject in the text. This section may be placed at the end of the page or on a separate page after the references section. The title "Footnotes" is indicated for these sections, and is typed and centered 1¹/₂ inches from the top of the paper. Superscript numbers identifying the note with the corresponding entry in the text, starting with number one, are consecutively assigned for the footnotes. The first entry is double-spaced from this title. The first line of each entry is indented five spaces. All other lines within the same entry are typed flush with the left margin.

Whenever supplementary material is not suitable for inclusion in the text, it is placed at the end after the documentation section. This may include illustrations, examples of questionnaires used, computer printouts, and other documents. These materials are labelled "Appendix," and designated by alphabetical letters (A, B, etc.) and their title headings. Each separate appendix is typed on a new page. If there is only one appendix, only the title is used without any letter designation.

Figure AP-5

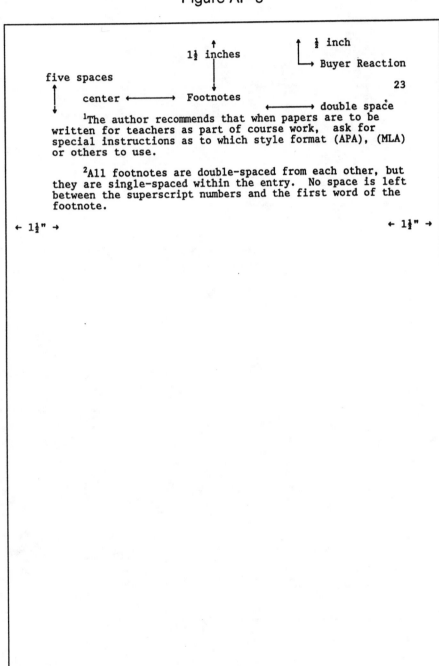

MLA Guidelines and Sample Pages

Divisions of the Manuscript. The Modern Language Association's (MLA) author/page format is the most popular style used for writing papers in the areas of humanities, fine arts, languages, and literature. This style is a parenthetical-reference format that uses brief information in parentheses in the text. This information guides the reader in locating the original source in a list that is placed at the end of the manuscript. This list eliminates the traditional bibliography and the typing of footnotes on pages. The guidelines for this format are presented in the publication *MLA Handbook for Writers of Research Papers*, 3rd ed. (New York: MLA, 1988). Detailed information on this style and its documentation techniques is discussed in Chapter 9. The following review exemplifies the methods for the composition of the title, outline, and abstract pages. The inclusion of these three sections is optional. Examples for the presentation of the text of the paper, endnotes, works cited, and footnotes are also included in this synopsis.

Margins, Spacing, and Page Numbering. One-inch margins should be kept throughout the paper, including the top and bottom margins. The first line of each paragraph is indented five spaces from the left margin. The typed lines are not justified, meaning that words that do not fit on the end of a line are not hyphenated; instead, the line is left short and the word is typed on the next line. Any included quoted material is indented ten spaces from the left margin. The entire manuscript is double-spaced. Pages are numbered in Arabic numerals without any punctuation marks, starting consecutively with the title pages through the "Works Cited" section. When preliminary pages are included, their page numbers are typed in small Roman numerals (i, ii). The title pages is counted as number (i), but this number is not typed. The author's last name is typed on every page at the top of the paper on the right margin, followed by a single space and the page number.

Title Pages. As a general rule, term papers and reports written for courses in college do not require a separate title page. However, a title page is required when an outline or other preliminary matter is included at the beginning of the paper. When a title page is not included, the heading, title, and other identifying information are written at the top of the first page. This includes typing the author's full name one inch below the top of the paper on the left margin; below this the instructor's title and name, the course number, and the date (day, month, year) are all typed. All entries in the heading are double-spaced, not boldfaced or underlined. The author's last name is typed $1/2$ inch below the top edge of the paper on the right margin, starting with the first page and continuing on all other pages throughout the manuscript. This is followed by a single space and the page number, which is typed in Arabic numerals and without punctuation marks.

The title of the manuscript is centered and typed one double space below the date. The initial letters of the first, last, and all other major words of the title are capitalized. No punctuation or other marks are included unless they are part of the title. Whenever a separate title page is prepared, only the title of the paper is typed on the first page. This is centered and typed one inch from the top of the paper. The indented first line of the text is typed four spaces below this title. Following are examples of a separate title page and the first page of the text, along with the first page format of a paper that has no title page.

Figure AP-6

```
                    Buyer Reaction to Centralized Marketing
                                      by
                          Creighton G. Frampton
```

← 1" →   ← 1" →

```
                        Professor B. Perry Woodside III
                               Marketing 3010
                              January 15, 199-
```

Figure AP-7

```
                                              ↑ ½ inch
                                       ┌────→
                 ↑              1 inch │              1
          1 inch │              └──────────→
                 ↓
(center)←──────→ Buyer Reaction to Centralized Marketing
                              ←────────────→ one double space
                 Purchasers of industrial raw material, equipment and

        supplies are greatly attracted toward vendors that provide

        all their needs from one source.  This provides them with

        the satisfaction of dealing with a single source and saving

        time searching for many sources.  Steinhoff and Burgis wrote:

            The key questions that small firm owners must ask themselves

            are: Am I buying through the established channels of

            distribution for this type of business?  Is there another

            source that would give me the same dependability and

            service?  Am I getting the best price available for

            comparable quality?  In what quantities should I be buying

            merchandise?  Most small retailers have wholesale houses

            available in their own locality that are eager and willing

            to serve them. (188-189)

            A great deal of attention and time should be devoted to

        ensure that the right raw materials, supplies and equipment

        are purchased at the right price and time from an appropriate

        source.




        ← 1" →                                        ← 1" →
```

Abstracts. The abstract details the purpose and content of the research paper. It is prepared when writing papers in the fields of both applied and social science. When typing the abstract, the title "Abstract" is centered and typed $1\frac{1}{2}$ inches below the top of the paper. The last name of the author and the page numbers are indicated on the left margin. Whenever the abstract is part of the preliminary matter, small Roman numerals are used for these pages. For example, if the abstract page is placed after the title page, it is assigned the small Roman numeral (ii). Abstracts are normally 200-300 words, typed as a single paragraph with no indentations.

Figure AP-8

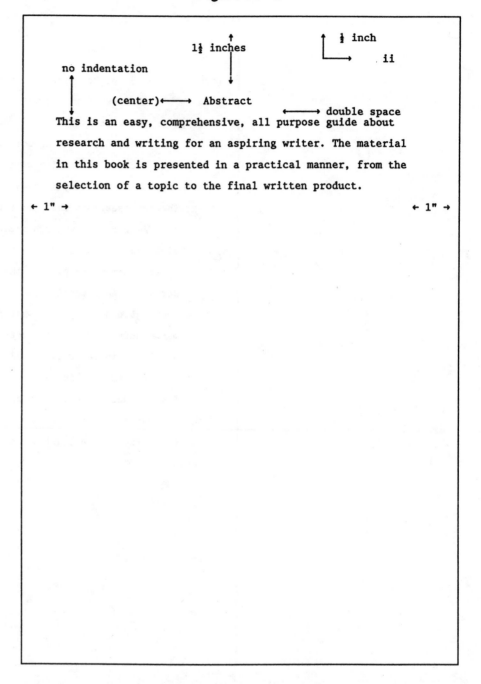

Text. Text is double-spaced below the title with the first lines of all paragraphs indented five spaces. Quoted material of fewer than four lines is enclosed in quotation marks and integrated into the text. Longer quotations are introduced with a colon and are typed on a new line. These should be indented ten spaces from the left margin, double-spaced, and not enclosed in quotation marks. The first paragraph of the quoted material is not indented.

Figure AP-9

```
                                              ↑ ¼ inch
          ↑                                   └──→              1
        1 inch
  ↓
      Creighton G. Frampton

      Professor B. Perry Woodside III

      Marketing  3010

      January 15, 199-

   (center)←────→ Buyer Reaction to Centralized Marketing


          Purchasers of industrial raw material, equipment and

      supplies are greatly attracted toward vendors that provide

      all their needs from one source.  This provides them with

      the satisfaction of dealing with a single source and saving

      time searching for many sources.  Steinhoff and Burgis wrote:

          The key questions that small firm owners must ask themselves

          are: Am I buying through the established channels of

          distribution for this type of business?  Is there another

          source that would give me the same dependability and

          service?  Am I getting the best price available for

          comparable quality?  In what quantities should I be buying

          merchandise?  Most small retailers have wholesale houses

          available in their own locality that are eager and willing

          to serve them. (188-189)

          Purchasing of raw materials, supplies and equipment are

      very important.  In studying business failures critically, "it

      is often possible to list improper purchasing and inventory

      management as two of the factors leading to the downfall of the

      business" (Justice 266).  Proper purchasing consists of

      individual functions which an entrepreneur or his agent must

      understand and evaluate seriously.


   ← 1" →                                              ← 1" →
```

Headings. Headings are important in the organization and development of thoughts in a manuscript. Headings should identify and divide sections in some appropriate and logical fashion. Titles and subtitles that are attractive and indicate the content heighten interest and enhance readability. Styles of typing headings in the *MLA Style* vary in capitalization, underlining, boldfacing, and spacing. Format usage should be consistent within a manuscript. The four regular heading levels are: (1) level A, for the main title heading; (2) level B, for secondary main heading; (3) level C, left margin or freestanding subheading; and (4) level D, paragraph indentation or run-in subheading. The following are examples for these heading formats:

Level A, main title headings are used for principal titles of chapters or major sections. The heading is centered and typed in upper and lower case letters.

`Buyer Reaction to Centralized Marketing`

Level B, major secondary headings are reserved for primary headings within chapters. These titles are centered and typed in upper and lower case letters. They may be underlined, boldfaced, and typed in all capital letters.

`BUYER NEEDS`   <u>`BUYER NEEDS`</u>   **`Buyer Needs`**

Level C headings are typed for subheadings of major segments within parts of the chapter. They are underlined and indented five spaces from the margin, typed in upper and lower case letters. They may also be typed in capital letters. The first indented line of the paragraph is typed below this heading.

<u>`Industrial Channels of Distribution`</u>

Level D headings are entered for subheadings within segments. These paragraph headings are indented and underlined, followed by a period, two spaces, and the first line of the paragraph.

<u>`Raw material purchases`</u>`. Raw materials include products that have been partially processed ....`

Footnotes. These are placed four lines below the text at the bottom of the page. The text is separated by a $1\frac{1}{2}$-inch bar or a solid line typed margin to margin. The first line of the footnote is indented five spaces. After one space, an Arabic number, identifying the footnote with its corresponding number in the text, is typed in superscript letters. Additional lines of the footnote are typed on the margin. Variations of the format are used; for example, the number may be typed on the margin, followed by a period and two spaces and then the footnote. Double spacing is used between and within individual entries. Some journals and instructors may require double spacing between and single spacing within the entries. It is important to be consistent in the usage of the footnote entry format throughout the document. Figure AP-10 illustrates an example of a footnote format.

Notes. The "Notes" and "Content Notes" sections are typed on a separate page following the text, preceding the "Works Cited" section. The heading "Notes" is typed and centered one inch from the top of the paper. The first entry is double-spaced below the title. The first line of each entry is indented five spaces, followed by a superscript number, a single space, and the note. All additional lines of the same entry are typed on the left margin. Entries are double-spaced throughout. Whenever the notes are too long and numerous, this section may be typed single-spaced. The notes are numbered consecutively and must correspond with the appropriate text items in order of presentation. The "Content Notes" are discussions or additional bibliographic information, the inclusion of which in the text may interrupt the thought process or the flow of the passages. The same format that is used for the "Notes" section is prepared for these, but they are titled "Content Notes" and placed separately at the end.

Works Cited. The works cited list corresponds to the traditional bibliography, listing every work cited in the paper. It is typed on a separate page following the "Notes" section, if included. Pages are numbered as a continuation of the manuscript with the same format. The heading "Works Cited" is centered and

Figure AP-10

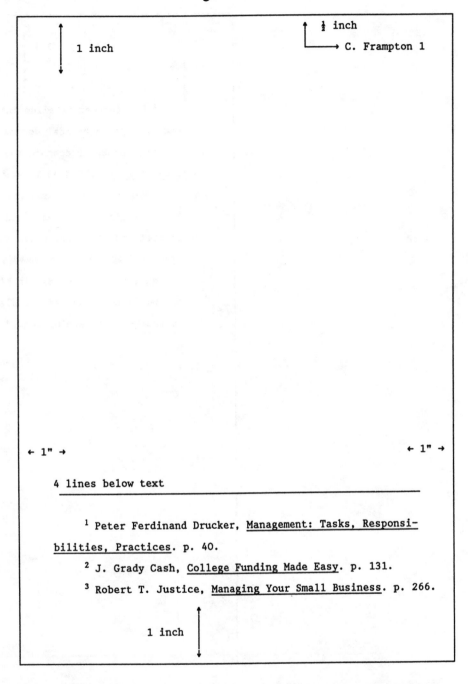

typed one inch from the top of the paper. The first line of each entry is typed on the left margin. Second and additional lines of each entry are indented five spaces. All lines within each entry and throughout this section are double-spaced. Works cited parenthetically in the manuscript are arranged alphabetically by the author's last name. Whenever the author is unknown, such as in the case of newspaper articles, pamphlets, or books, the first word of the title (excluding A, An, and The) is used in alphabetical order in listing the entry.

Whenever appropriate, if additional material such as illustrations, tables, or documents is included, it is titled "Appendix" and placed at the end of the paper after the "Notes" but before the "Works Cited" section. Additional sections

Figure AP-11

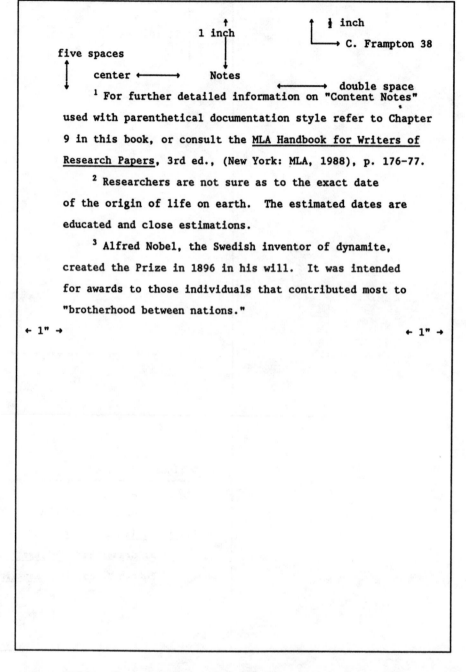

such as "Works Consulted," "Annotated Bibliography," "Annotated List of Works Cited," and "Literature Cited" precede the "Works Cited" section. Special information on the use and presentation of these sections is included in Chapter 9 of this book.

Figure AP-12

1 inch

½ inch

C. Frampton 38

five spaces

center ← → Works Cited

double space

"Boozeless Bonanza." Time 7 Oct. 1991: 65.

Chaucer, Geoffrey. The Works of Geoffrey Chaucer. Ed. F. N.
Robinson. 2nd ed. Boston: Houghton, 1957.

Clarence, Ray G. "President's Comments: The Economic Expert
and Civil Litigation." Journal of Legal Economics (1991):
1-5.

The Columbia Law Review. A Uniform System of Citations. 15th
ed. Cambridge: Harvard Law Review Association, 1991.

Drucker, Peter Ferdinand. Management: Tasks, Responsibilities,
Practices. 1st ed. New York: Harper, 1953.

Finch, Frederick E., Halsey T. Jones, and Joseph A. Litterer.
Managing for Organizational Effectiveness: An Experimental Approach. New York: McGraw, 1953.

Jay, Anthony. "How to Run a Meeting." Harvard Business
Review 54 (March-April 1976): 43-57.

"Business Cycles." Collier's Encyclopedia. 1944 ed. p. 27-29.

Justice, Robert T. Managing Your Small Business. Englewood
Cliffs: Prentice, 1981.

University of Chicago. The Chicago Manual of Style. 13th ed.
Chicago: U of Chicago P, 1982.

Mahmoud, Shah. "Helms: An American Hero." Charlotte Observer
8 Mar. 1991: A18.

← 1" →

← 1" →

CBE Guidelines and Sample Pages

Divisions of the Manuscript. Research papers prepared for college courses in natural sciences, or for publication in technical fields such as engineering, mathematics, biology, and chemistry, may require using the CBE style. When a reference is needed and the name of the author is mentioned in the text, a referral to this source is indicated through an assigned number in the sentence, such as (3). When the author's name is not given, then in parentheses the author's last name and the assigned number are typed, such as (Drucker 3). This number guides the reader to the original source in a prepared list at the end of the manuscript. Whenever a referral is made again in the text to the same source, the assigned number is repeated. If two or more works are cited, all assigned numbers are entered separated by a comma, such as (3,5). For quoted material, or when the information cannot be easily located in the original source, such as in long articles, the page number(s) is also included: (3, p. 12), (Drucker 3, p. 12), or (3, pp. 12, 18, 87). An alternative method uses colons to indicate the page number, such as (3:12), (Drucker 3:12). This assigning of numbers lessens distractions in the text and enhances readability. The method of linking Author-Number in this style makes it easier for the reader to turn to the "References" section at the end of the paper and locate the source from which the original information was obtained.

Citations are arranged in the order of their occurrence in the text. The first referral in the text is assigned the number (1). At the end of the manuscript in a prepared list titled "References," the entry under number one will contain the related documentation information. This style is recommended by many scientific organizations, including the American Association for the Advancement of Science. This format, referred to as the *numbers system*, is illustrated in the guidelines presented in the *CBE Style Manual*, 5th ed. (1983) by the Council of Biology Editors, and is recommended by most publishers of scholarly journals in sciences and instructors of technical courses in college. There are variations of this format; for additional information, the *CBE Manual* is available in the reference section of major libraries. One may also look at a specific journal to learn what style it uses, or ask the targeted journal for this information. At least once a year editors publish detailed guides in their journals that illustrate the mechanics and formats of documentation they require from prospective authors.

Margins, Spacing, and Page Numbering. Margins of one inch are maintained on all sides throughout the paper. The entire manuscript is typed double-spaced with a five space indentation for the first line of each paragraph. The Arabic page numbers are typed $\frac{1}{2}$ inch below the top of the paper on the right margin. This number is preceded by a single space and the running title that includes two or three key words from the title of the paper. The title is used when the manuscript is prepared for submission to journals, so that when evaluating the paper referees cannot identify the author. College papers may require using the last name of the author instead. This prevents the mixing or loss of pages of a student's paper by the instructor. When preliminary matter such as table of contents, list of illustrations, and abstract are included, all these pages precede the text and are separately numbered in small Roman numerals. The title page is counted page (i), but this number is not typed. Arabic numerals starting with the number (1) on the first page of the text are progressively assigned throughout.

Title Pages. A separate title page is prepared for most research papers using the CBE style. Four important items typed on this page include: title of the manuscript, identification of the author(s), the course or the journal for which the paper is prepared, and the date. The title of the research paper is centered and typed two to three inches from the top of the paper. One double space below this the word "by" is centered. Two spaces from this, the name of the author(s), principal investigator(s), and the compiler(s) are listed. Three to three and a half inches from the bottom margin of the paper the name of the professor or the organization to which the paper is submitted is entered. Two spaces below this the course and the section number for which the paper is written are indicated. The last item on this page is the date (day, month, year) the paper was submitted.

Abstract, Tables, and Illustrations. The abstract should be a brief summary of the research effort and findings in less than 250 words. It should state the objective of the research, the hypotheses tested, and the conclusions derived. For secondary or empirical research, the author may present the need for the research, the method, an overview of the existing body of knowledge, and significant conclusions. Other suitable information may include research methodology, specialized processes, conditions, and equipment used. The limitation and circumstances of the research may be stated.

The abstract is typed on a separate page preceding the first page of the text, and is page (ii). On the righthand margin, the running title and the page numbers are typed $1/2$ inch below the top of the paper. Two double spaces below this, the title "ABSTRACT" is centered and typed in capital letters. One double space below, the text of the abstract is typed in double-spaced format with the first line of each paragraph indented five spaces.

Technical papers may include tables with numerical information, diagrams, and illustrations; here a page is prepared and titled "List of Illustrations" and is placed between the abstract and the text. College papers may not contain many illustrations, in which case the list is not prepared. Tables, illustrations, and diagrams must be carefully presented in content and format. Each must be numbered individually and consecutively as it appears. All should have titles and any needed documentation typed at the bottom of the table or illustration.

Text. On the first page of the text, the running title and the page number are typed on the right margin. One double space below this, the heading of the section, such as INTRODUCTION, is typed. The text of manuscripts written for scientific and technical fields normally includes three parts: the introduction, the content of the research, and the conclusion. The introduction states the purpose and scope of the research paper. It may describe what is studied, why it is studied, and what is discovered. The introduction both informs readers

Figure AP-13

```
            CELL STRUCTURES, COMPONENTS AND CHEMICAL REACTIONS
                                   by
                         Creighton B. Frampton




















                       Professor B. Perry Woodside III
                          Chemistry Research 5010
                            December 14, 1991
```

← 1½"→   ← 1½"→

about the contents and gains their interest at the same time. The content, or body section, presents the researched facts and the analysis of existing or newly discovered information. The conclusion section is a summary of the researcher's recommendations based on the discovered facts in the content section. Following is an example of the first page of a text.

References and Notes. A list entitled "References" or "References and Notes" is prepared and placed at the end of the manuscript. This title is typed in capital letters and centered on the page, one double space below the running head title that is typed throughout the document. The first item of the list is typed one double space from the title. If there are any notes that include discussions or

Figure AP-14

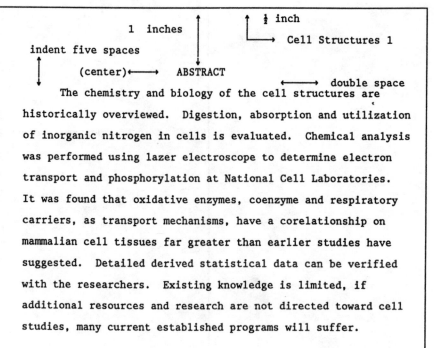

The chemistry and biology of the cell structures are historically overviewed. Digestion, absorption and utilization of inorganic nitrogen in cells is evaluated. Chemical analysis was performed using lazer electroscope to determine electron transport and phosphorylation at National Cell Laboratories. It was found that oxidative enzymes, coenzyme and respiratory carriers, as transport mechanisms, have a corelationship on mammalian cell tissues far greater than earlier studies have suggested. Detailed derived statistical data can be verified with the researchers. Existing knowledge is limited, if additional resources and research are not directed toward cell studies, many current established programs will suffer.

added information whose inclusion in the text is not desired, they are placed in the reference section, numbered, and treated as any entry. In this case the title of the reference section should be "References and Notes." All entries are double-spaced from each other and in between. The entries are typed in the following order: (1) in progressive numerical order of their appearance in the text, or (2) in alphabetical order, and then each assigned a number. When the latter classification is used, the citations in the text will not follow any numerical order.

In the reference section, each entry is preceded by an Arabic number typed on the margin followed by a period and two spaces. Any additional lines of the

Figure AP-15

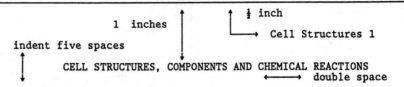

1 inches

indent five spaces

¼ inch

Cell Structures 1

CELL STRUCTURES, COMPONENTS AND CHEMICAL REACTIONS

←——→ double space

The genesis of modern chemistry progress is found in the works of early pioneers in chemistry. Ancient chemists sought answers to phenomenon created by general observations in such everyday common preparations as making dyes, wine, vinegar, pottery and glass (1, p. 1). Alchemists in the middle ages and other chemists during the renaissance and contemporary periods studied chemical properties and contributed to the knowledge of cell structures. Cells cannot function without the underlying chemical processes that creates them.

"It is this concept which has channeled teaching and research in biochemistry along two major lines of endeavor: (1) the quantitative and qualitative characterization of the chemical compounds of cells, and (2) the elucidation of the nature and mechanism of the reaction in which these components participate" (2, p. 1). Different kinds of cells exist, and each type has its own chemical components, both in quantity and quality, that gives it structure and behavioral characteristics. For example in observing mammalian tissue cells, it is found that one constituent water is contained in proportions of 60%, 78% and 20% in liver, brain, and skin tissue cells respectively (3, table 12, p. 56).

← 1"→   ← 1"→

entry are typed below the first letter of the citation and not on the margin. Another common practice is to use Arabic numbers in parentheses. The use of superscript numbers without brackets in the text and in the reference section is another practice. It is important to be consistent and use the method that the journal uses or the instructor recommends. For books, only the last name of the author and initials are given. Semicolons are used to separate multiple authors and after the publisher's name. The first word of the title of the book and any pronouns are capitalized. For journal articles, the first letter of the first word and all other important words are capitalized. The volume and page numbers followed by a semicolon, the year of publication, and a period are typed after the title.

Figure AP-16

```
                              ↑              ↑ ½ inch
                         1  inch         ┌─────→ Cell Structures 37
                              ↓           └──
      center ←──────→       REFERENCES
                                          ←──────→  double space
 1.  Norris, F. M.  A History of chemistry.  New York: McGraw-
     Book Company, Inc.; 1931.

 2.  White, A.; Smith L. E. Principles of chemistry. 3rd ed.
     New York: Houghton Mifflin; 1964.

 3.  West, E. S.; Todd, W. R. Textbook of biochemistry. New
     York: Macmillan company, New York; 1951.

 4.  Bergman, E. N.; Roe, W. E. Kon, K. Quantitative aspects of
     propionate metabolism and gluconeogensis in sheep. Am. J.
     Physiol. 211:793-799; 1966.

 5.  Curry, D. L.; Bennett, L. L.; Grodsky, G. M. Dynamics of
     insulin secretion by the perfused rat pancreas.
     Endocrinology 83:572-584; 1968.

 6.  Chamerliain B. Mawby R. J.; J. Chem. Soc. Dalton Trans.,
     1991, 2067.

 7.  Brock, D. W.  The Value of Prolonging Human Life.
     Philosophical Studies, 1986. 50, 401-26.

 8.  Gotlib. I, H.; Caine, D. B.  Self-report assessment of
     depression and anxiety.  In: Kendall P. C. and Watson,
     eds. Anxiety and depression, distinctive and overlapping
     features. San Diego, CA: Academic Press; 1989:131-169.

 9.  Anonymous. Neurochemical control of productive behavior
     Physiol. Behav. 21:873-875; 1978.

10.  Heston, L.; White, J. Dementia: A practical guide to
     alzheimer's disease and related illness. Baltimore: Johns
     Hopkins Univ. Press; 1985.

  ← 1"→                                              ← 1"→
```

Index